Tom Stoppard's work includes *Rosencrantz and Guildenstern Are Dead*, *The Real Inspector Hound*, *Jumpers*, *Travesties*, *Night and Day*, *Every Good Boy Deserves Favour*, *After Magritte*, *Dirty Linen*, *The Real Thing*, *Hapgood*, *Arcadia*, *Indian Ink*, *The Invention of Love*, the trilogy *The Coast of Utopia* and *Rock 'n' Roll*. His radio plays include *If You're Glad I'll Be Frank*, *Albert's Bridge*, *Where Are They Now?*, *Artist Descending a Staircase*, *The Dog It Was That Died* and *In the Native State*. Television work includes *Professional Foul*, *Squaring the Circle* and *Parade's End*. His film credits include *Empire of the Sun*, *Rosencrantz and Guildenstern Are Dead*, which he also directed, *Shakespeare in Love*, *Enigma* and *Anna Karenina*.

PARADE'S END

Tom Stoppard

based on the novel by
FORD MADOX FORD

faber and faber

First published in 2012
by Faber and Faber Limited
74–77 Great Russell Street, London WC1B 3DA

Typeset by Country Setting, Kingsdown, Kent CT14 8ES
Printed and bound by CPI Group (UK) Ltd, Croydon, CR0 4YY

Tom Stoppard is hereby identified as author
of this work in accordance with Section 77 of the
Copyright, Designs and Patents Act 1988

All rights whatsoever in this work, amateur or professional,
are strictly reserved. Applications for permission for any use
whatsoever including performance rights must be made in
advance, prior to any such proposed use, to United Agents,
12–26 Lexington Street, London W1F 0LE
(info@unitedagents.co.uk)

No performance may be given unless a licence
has first been obtained

A CIP record for this book
is available from the British Library

ISBN 978-0-571-29913-3

2 4 6 8 10 9 7 5 3 1

This dramatisation for television of *Parade's End* by Ford Madox Ford comprises a little more than was broadcast and less than was scripted. I have included some scenes and parts of scenes which were shot but squeezed out by the running time (five one-hour episodes); and some which were scheduled but not shot because there are never enough hours in the day, especially when you're waiting for the rain to stop; and some which were cut before we began because the budget wouldn't run to them. The pincer movement of time and money had the last word. In all this there is much to regret but nothing to complain about, given the imperatives under which broadcasters work.

A play I wrote for the BBC in 1977 – *Professional Foul*, directed by Michael Lindsay-Hogg – when shot and edited turned out (I'm relying on memory here) to last seventy minutes, so it went out as a seventy-minute play. As it happens, seventy minutes would have done nicely for the third episode of *Parade's End*; in other words, I had overwritten. Since I couldn't see any reason why Episode Three shouldn't be a bit longer than the others, and not wanting to cut it, I wrote to the BBC's Head of Drama suggesting as much. Considering that my letter must have struck the Head of Drama as one of the more bizarre proposals he had ever received, his reply was a model of courteous deflection. But, in retrospect, the most strange-seeming thing about the making of *Professional Foul* is that I can't remember Michael or I receiving any notes from above. We were pretty much left alone to deliver the piece; for a writer brought up in the theatre, the experience was really not very different. By contrast, in 2012 the cutting room was on the receiving end of notes from five directions – six counting mine, because by the editing stage I was as prolific as anyone in my comments on successive versions. But of course I had an author-centric view of things. Everyone else was 'giving notes'; I, on the other hand, was fulfilling my natural authorial function.

The underlying difference between 1977 and 2012 was that *Professional Foul* was made and paid for by the BBC, while *Parade's End* was a BBC production in a different sense. The BBC commissioned the script, and in due course commissioned an independent production company, Mammoth Screen, to make the piece. But *Parade's End* was always going to cost more than the BBC's ceiling for drama-per-hour, so a partnership with a foreign broadcaster, in effect an American broadcaster, was built in from the beginning as the way to go. In due course the home team went to Los Angeles to pitch *Parade's End* to HBO. It is a truth universally acknowledged that for a British TV drama in want of an American partner, HBO is Mr Darcy. It was a great day for *Parade's End* when HBO proved receptive. As was normal and expected, their actual commitment – the cheque – was conditional on approval of the director and the principal actors, but everything took a big step forward when Susanna White agreed to direct, with a fervour, luckily for us, which kept her with us against competing blandishments for a whole year before *Parade's End* went into pre-production. My greatest debt is to her.

Parade's End is a quartet of novels, or as Ford himself came to see it, a trilogy and a coda. It was Damien Timmer of Mammoth who conceived the idea that it would make a good TV drama and that I should be asked to write it. Like a lot of people, I knew Ford's *The Good Soldier* but had not read *Parade's End*. Subsequently I discovered that many of those who had read it cleaved to it as a favourite novel and a masterpiece. I read it at Damien's suggestion, and was converted. The story is of Christopher Tietjens, the self-proclaimed 'last Tory', his beautiful, disconcerting wife Sylvia, and Valentine Wannop, the virginal suffragette who completes the triangle of love among the English upper class before and during the Great War. Before I had read very far I knew I wanted the job.

When he came to write *Parade's End* Ford counted himself among the modernists, indeed an experimentalist. He often drops the reader into the middle of a situation, drawing up the past to give bearings to the present. A single remark or incident might have its moment in two or more places a hundred pages apart. The characters' thoughts seem to occur in an echo chamber. Getting the chronology clear is often the reader's reward for just staying in the moment and not fretting about it. Possibly I am making the book sound more difficult than it is. *Parade's End* is not a 'difficult book', it's a good read. But whatever else it is, it is not a linear book. It seemed to me that as an episodic drama, with a week between episodes, the storyline had to be unravelled. Unravelling it was an absorbing exercise and not straightforward: at one point I realised I was in the wrong *year*.

At my second or third meeting with Damien and Piers Wenger, the attached BBC producer (who was to leave us too soon when he moved to Channel 4), I produced a double-folio card on which I had broken the book into five episodes, and that remained the format. But would it be five sixties or five nineties or five seventy-fives, or what? Perhaps the best thing would be to write the first episode without worrying too much and see how it came out. And another thing: should I be keeping an eye on costs? Damien and Piers urged me to write freely; often, things which looked expensive could be done quite thriftily. I was not to think about it. So they were word-perfect producers, and I was glad to be ingenuous. In September 2008 I started writing, and by the following September delivered the fifth episode.

We hoped that *Parade's End* would start filming within a year, but it would take two. Months went by in finding actors who were available, willing and acceptable to both sides of the Atlantic. It would be wrong to think that star casting is an American cross which the British have to bear; nowadays the BBC takes a keen interest in marketing, too. In 1975, when Stephen Frears directed my adaptation of *Three Men in a Boat* for the BBC, I remember how the leading role was cast. Stephen mused one day that he thought Tim Curry was a good idea, so he phoned him up and asked him. There was to be none of that when it came to casting the leading role in *Parade's End*.

But delays can work in one's favour, too. Actors who had been unavailable become available again, and sometimes better known, and there came the day when with everyone's blessing I met Benedict Cumberbatch at the National Theatre, where he was alternating the starring roles of Frankenstein and the Monster, to talk to him about Christopher Tietjens. On that very day, HBO withdrew from *Parade's End*. We had been left at the altar! To its credit, the BBC didn't miss a beat. The global sales arm, BBC Worldwide, raised the tempo in selling the drama abroad sight unseen, and the valiant Mammoth set about reconciling the budget with the production.

The rural England of the first two episodes would be pre-eminently East Sussex. Susanna already had her eye on those green downs and flat marshlands. An important scene in the novel takes place on the golf links at Rye. We all made a recce and were delighted. One could take a camera around the golf links and see nothing which wasn't there in 1912. However, in the modern world of TV (and cinema), budgets can be reconciled by filming in the wrong place. In effect you can get, for example, Canadian money by taking the filming to Canada; and Canada beckoned. Susanna put her foot down. Then Northern Ireland beckoned. Susanna went to have a look, and reported that there was a golf links near Belfast which wasn't half bad, but pretty much everything else was wrong, the look of the countryside, the look of the houses, and she put her foot down again. We were saved by Belgium. France and Flanders figure importantly in the novel, and there was Belgian money available in return for taking the production – and some of the post-production – there for a few weeks, employing a Belgian crew and other elements including Belgian actors where possible (which is why 'Captain Thurston' became 'Capitaine Thurston' with good effect). It was a happy solution. The golf game of June 1912 was filmed on the Rye links, albeit in the intervals between the rain.

The mention of a scene which came whole from the novel brings to mind the absence of much that is in the book, and – even more – the presence of much that is not. Most of the audience would be none the wiser but the remainder would be wise indeed, so for them explanations are owed. The first problem is that structurally the novel does not fall into five equal parts. I used the first three episodes of the script to encompass the first book of the trilogy, and an episode for each of the two remaining books, while pillaging the 'fourth book' (the coda) for anything which threw light on the first three. The coda takes place some time later. It's impossible to say how much later because the internal evidence is conflicting, but that is when the all-important Groby Tree is cut down, and it is my vandalism which brings the tree down early.

The second problem is to keep several foreground characters in view and active in each episode, which accounts for whole scenes balanced on a passing reference, or not even as much.

The third problem is that the book is crammed with good stuff expressed through the inner lives of Christopher, Sylvia and Valentine, without, very often, a concrete dimension, let alone a dramatic momentum. This does the book no harm at all. It is equally compulsive reading whether it is staying still or moving forward, and compulsive, too, when the people are somewhere in particular or nowhere in particular. To keep the fiction going I turned to life. I put Valentine in the National Gallery at the moment, in 1914, when a feminist named Mary Richardson slashed 'The Rokeby Venus' by Velázquez. My Valentine, not Ford's, also profits, dramatically speaking, from the publication in 1918 of *Married Love* by Marie Stopes. My Eton versus Harrow cricket match at Lord's, published here as written, ended up on screen as a small affair played purportedly at Eton (with a computer-generated Windsor Castle in the background) and was none the worse for that, especially as there is no cricket match in the book.

A favourite source book for me was *The Perfect Summer* by Juliet Nicolson, packed with social detail of the period. It is thanks to her that at breakfast in Lowndes Street in the first episode we can note a small Union Jack ticket tied to the teapot for Darjeeling tea, and a yellow 'coolie hat' ticket for the China tea. But my favourite detail from *The Perfect Summer* never made the cut: I gave Sylvia a blue pencil with which to delineate the vein on one temple. We filmed the action but somehow it suggested that she had missed with an eyebrow pencil. The loss of Sylvia's blue pencil is a grief to me but of no significance to Ford fans. However, something which might be is that the dramatised *Parade's End* contains nothing substantial outside the upper classes. This is not wholly true of the novel. The golf game at Rye, for example, makes quite a lot of a couple of vulgarian golfers, 'City men'.

We had no room for them, but a little of their presence survives here. More seriously, a platoon of Cockney infantrymen in the trenches became a casualty of my over-extended script.

A painful omission, a scene we did film, had Rebecca Hall in superb form as Sylvia verbally laying in to a pair of young staff officers who'd had the temerity to try to pick her up. Alas, the picking-up part, which explained the officers' presence, was too expensive in time and money (street location, sports car, traffic, passers-by), and not much cheaper in the rewrite (interior lift in provision merchant's). A bare-bones version succumbed to scheduling problems. I have included the original scene here (in Episode Three). It becomes quite a game, finding ways to save scenes in danger of falling out of the schedule, and adds to the fun of the fair. There are four 'Victoria Station' scenes in the film, one written for Victoria Station, three not. Changing locations costs time which is money. But one of the conflations mothered by necessity was appealing: the hotel in France in which we find Sylvia and her lover in 1912 becomes in the screen version the very same hotel in which Sylvia and Christopher are reunited in the war in 1918: neatness, resonance and economy all in one.

On the economy front, things brightened in March 2011. Mr Darcy returned. His fortune was apparently diminished but the engagement was on again. America is naturally an important market for BBC Worldwide, and by that route HBO came back into the picture. To this day I never worked out the ranking between the BBC and HBO on *Parade's End*. As far as I knew, I was working for the BBC (they paid me) but there was an undeniable frisson that accompanied the distribution of 'the notes' from Los Angeles, and more than once in the cutting room momentum stalled until the latest notes arrived. But this was fair enough, since HBO ended up paying for refinements which were outside the post-production budget. From my point of view, a great thing about HBO's notes was that a BBC note I disagreed with would disappear off the radar if it happened to cut across the notes from Kary Antholis who was HBO's voice on *Parade's End*. Often enough, however, Kary's notes would be about something in the script, or something missing from the script, which either way might make for difficulty for an American audience.

My instinctive reaction was, 'Possibly so, but why are you telling me this? I sometimes have difficulty with *The Wire* but it wouldn't occur to me that David Simon should change *The Wire* on my account.' I was in the toils of an outmoded notion. The notion was that the 'creatives' (a useful new noun, meaning Susanna and me, mainly) deliver the piece as they think fit and the broadcasters broadcast it. Let it be said that it is a self-defeating notion. Most 'notes' from every direction are sensible correctives, or at the very least things to ponder, and quite often strokes of brilliance. Damien's notes were offered with a modesty ('Do you think perhaps . . . ?') which belied their acuity time and time again. Kary nagged at me for weeks to write some lines to spell out what Christopher stood for. He didn't know where the lines would go, or quite what they would say, but he was insistent that they were needed to let the audience in on the character. When I stopped bridling, I wrote the lines I would most miss if they weren't there.

Ought that to be the last word on authors' *amour propre*? I don't think so. It's a counter-example. There were many more instances where I stuck to my guns, usually from a horror of explicitness (over-explicitness, as I saw it), and some where I didn't stick to my guns but should have. In the novel, Christopher's father watching a ploughing team at work (in 1912) remarks, 'The motor plough didn't answer.' Kary and I seemed to spend days arguing over that one word. I loved 'answer' for being precise to the old-school ways of the character, but I got tired of fighting for it. There wasn't much wrong with my compromise offer ('The motor plough didn't serve') but it evades a principle that divides writers from broadcasters. Writers don't really care if half the audience doesn't understand 'answer'. They are writing for the other half. Otherwise, writing tends towards the mean.

That said and more unsaid, my residual sense is one of indebtedness, good fortune and a measure of awe when one considers the combination of resources, resourcefulness and sheer artistry that over the course of three years turned three hundred pages of script into five hours of television. Excluding one experience of directing a film, this was the first time I felt as involved in film as in working in theatre. My immersion in *Parade's End* from the writing to the finishing touches took up the time I might have given to writing my own play but, perhaps to an unwarranted degree, I think of this *Parade's End* as mine, such was the illusion of proprietorship over Ford's characters and story. I frequently couldn't remember whether a spoken sentence, or sometimes even a scene, came from the novel or from my head. While it was all going on, or failing to go on, I used to get cross from time to time and no doubt petulant. When it was over I knew that for a writer in television drama, *Parade's End* had been the best of times.

TOM STOPPARD
August 2012

PARADE'S END

A Mammoth Screen Production for the BBC
in association with HBO Miniseries and Trademark Films
and BBC Worldwide, ARTE France, Breakout Films
and Lookout Point.
Co-produced with BNP Paribas Fortis Film Fund
and Anchorage Entertainment.
Filmed with the support of the Belgian federal government's
Tax Shelter scheme.

The series was first transmitted on BBC2 in the autumn of 2012.

Executive Producers	Michele Buck
	Damien Timmer
	Ben Donald
	Simon Vaughan
	Judith Louis
Writer	Tom Stoppard
Producers	David Parfitt
	Selwyn Roberts
Director	Susanna White
Director of Photography	Mike Eley BSC
Production Designer	Martin Childs
Line Producer	Jennifer Wynne
Make-Up and Hair Designer	Jan Archibald
Costume Designer	Sheena Napier
Film Editors	Kristina Hetherington
	Tim Murrell
	Jason Krasucki
Composer	Dirk Brossé
Sound Mixer	Jim Greenhorn
Casting Director	Karen Lindsay-Stewart
Post Production Supervisor	Clare Maclean

Episode One

CAST OF EPISODE ONE

in order of appearance

HULLO CENTRAL (EVIE)	Lucinda Raikes
SYLVIA TIETJENS	Rebecca Hall
CHRISTOPHER TIETJENS	Benedict Cumberbatch
MACMASTER	Stephen Graham
PORTER	Jordan Long
GERALD DRAKE	Jack Huston
MARK TIETJENS	Rupert Everett
FATHER CONSETT	Ned Dennehy
MRS SATTERTHWAITE	Janet McTeer
MARCHANT	Sylvestra Le Touzel
MICHAEL (4 YEARS OLD)	Misha Handley
BRIDGET	Tessa Parr
BOBBIE PELHAM	Anna Skellern
POTTY PEROWNE	Tom Mison
SIR REGINALD	Denis Lawson
WATERHOUSE	Tim McMullan
LADY CLAUDINE	Clare Higgins
BERTRAM	Jonathan Coy
GLORVINA	Sasha Waddell
JOHNNY PELHAM	Garrett Moore
LORD BEICHEN	Leslie de Gruyter
SANDBACH	Malcolm Sinclair
GENERAL CAMPION	Roger Allam
EFFIE	Candida Benson
TIETJENS SENIOR	Alan Howard
MOTHER	Christine Cox
CAPITAINE THURSTON	Pierre Van Heddegem
VALENTINE WANNOP	Adelaide Clemens
GERTIE	Naomi Cooper-Davis
POLICEMAN	Howard Ward
REVEREND HORSLEY	Michael Mears
EDITH DUCHEMIN	Anne-Marie Duff
MISS FOX	Sheila Collings
MRS WANNOP	Miranda Richardson
REVEREND DUCHEMIN	Rufus Sewell
PARRY	Lee Whitlock

INT. HOTEL SUITE – NIGHT

Paris, 1908.

Lamplit luxury – the suite of a bride on her wedding eve, with everything laid out ready: the dress, underwear, the white satin shoes, coronet. There are orchids, wrapped gifts and honeymoon luggage. A lady's maid is completing the packing. Part of a bedroom is visible through the connecting door. The telephone shrills.

It is answered in the bedroom by Sylvia. Her voice has a low pitch. She is twenty-six, tall, slim, beautiful, with abundant reddish fair hair. Her manner is contained.

> SYLVIA
> (*on the phone*)
> Oui . . .? Qui . . .? Non. Ah, non – dites . . . dites à ce monsieur que c'est trop tard. (*She hangs up.*) Too bloody late.

She begins to take off her earrings. She wears – always – a small gold St Anthony medallion on a thin gold chain.

The phone call has upset her.

> (*Calls.*) Evie.

The maid has a distinctly 'telephone tinny' voice, which will later explain her cognomen: Hullo Central. She comes to the bedroom.

> HULLO CENTRAL
> Yes, mod'm?

> SYLVIA
> You can undress me now.

Hullo Central starts to help Sylvia out of her dress.

EXT. STATION PLATFORM (VICTORIA) – NIGHT

The Dover-for-France train is about to depart. A Railway Porter steps down from the open carriage door (first class), touching his cap and receiving a coin from Christopher Tietjens. The carriage is marked LONDON CHATHAM AND DOVER RAILWAY, *and the Porter has* LCDR *on his cap.*

PORTER

Thank you, sir.

Christopher is a tall, bulky young man, grim-faced now. He shakes hands with Vincent Macmaster, who is slightly older, shorter, dark, with a small jutting beard, a dapper Scotsman risen above his origins.

MACMASTER

. . . wish you every happiness, Chrissie.

Christopher nods, grim.

CHRISTOPHER

Paris is a backdoor way out of it. What do they say at the office?

MACMASTER

Sylvia's mother was married in Paris, I let it be known.

CHRISTOPHER

Thank you for that. But she's bitched me, Vinnie, old man. I don't even know if the child is mine.

He climbs aboard. A Guard closes the carriage door behind Christopher.

INT – HOTEL SUITE – PARIS (AS BEFORE)

Hullo Central hangs up Sylvia's dress. Sylvia is in a peignoir at the dressing table.

SYLVIA

Tea tray at 6.30.

Yes, mod'm. Goodnight, mod'm.

No answer expected. Hullo Central goes to the main door. The door buzzer sounds as she opens it, and a man, Gerald Drake, pushes past her: a good-looking, well-built English beast, half-drunk and raging. Sylvia has heard the buzzer.

DRAKE

Sylvia! – God damn you, I won't be –

Sylvia is at the bedroom door.

SYLVIA
(*coolly*)

Quite so.

Hullo Central leaves, closing the door.

Your wife must be wondering where you are.

DRAKE

I said, I won't be seen off like an errand boy!

SYLVIA

This is not fair.

Drake tries to grasp her.

SYLVIA

And you're drunk.

DRAKE
(*losing the rage*)

Sylvia, don't do this!

SYLVIA
(*flares angrily*)

Do what? – Save myself from ruin?

DRAKE

Whatever you want, it can't be that – that ox!

SYLVIA
(*coming apart*)

What I want is to die – death is what I –

Drake kisses her violently.

> SYLVIA
> No – don't – please, darling – Gerald – it's not fair – it's not . . .

His assault rips the silk off her shoulders. She kisses him back with equal violence.

INT. MOVING TRAIN – NIGHT

Christopher, on the train, reflects.

FLASHBACK – INT. TRAIN – DAY

The train is a 'local' pulling away from a tiny station in the English countryside. Christopher, in occupation, lifts Sylvia's suitcase up on the luggage rack. There is no corridor.

> SYLVIA
> Thank you. Are you going up to town?

> CHRISTOPHER
> Yes. My name is Tietjens.

> SYLVIA
> I'm Sylvia Satterthwaite.

> CHRISTOPHER
> I know.

She gives him a smile for that.

EXT. ROLLS-ROYCE (MOVING) – PARIS – DAY

The Rolls-Royce moves through Paris.

INT. ROLLS-ROYCE (MOVING) – PARIS – DAY

Close on Sylvia, composed, unblemished, the church-bound bride, using the mirror of a gold powder box to touch in, with a blue crayon, the vein on her temple.

INT. HORSE CAB (MOVING) – PARIS – DAY

Christopher, the bridegroom, is with Mark Tietjens, his half-brother, who is fifteen years older, dark, disapproving.

> CHRISTOPHER
> . . . a small house in Knightsbridge. Lowndes Street. Her mother will live with us. Mrs Satterthwaite has contributed handsomely.

Mark grunts, unbrotherly.

INT. ROLLS-ROYCE (AS BEFORE)

Sylvia snaps shut the powder box. With her in the back of the Rolls are her mother, Mrs Satterthwaite, rich, emaciated, overdressed; and a priest, Father Consett, big, brawny, unkempt, fiftyish, with the accent of a stage Irishman.

> MRS SATTERTHWAITE
> I haven't seen that pretty box . . .

> SYLVIA
> Gerald Drake gave it to me.

> FATHER CONSETT
> Ye have no shame! On your wedding day . . .!

> MRS SATTERTHWAITE
> When did he?

> SYLVIA
> Last night.

She takes pleasure in her mother's consternation.

> FATHER CONSETT
> You're a lying devil to say so! (*To Mrs Satterthwaite.*)
> I saw her with it on the Channel ferry.

> SYLVIA
> (*laughs*)
> So you're going to give me away twice in one morning!
> Will you give me a cigarette?

FATHER CONSETT

No, I will not. I'm glad your father's dead not to know this day's work, and I'm sorry for your mother.

MRS SATTERTHWAITE

Well, don't be. Christopher Tietjens is a godsend.

FATHER CONSETT
(*deeply offended*)

God-sent is one thing he is not!

INT. HORSE CAB (AS BEFORE)

CHRISTOPHER

Did Father send word?

MARK

He sent me.

Christopher nods.

CHRISTOPHER

And my mother?

MARK

Your mother's soft, and brought you up soft. Not your fault. Second wife, late child, and no Yorkshirewoman – a bad combination.

CHRISTOPHER

My mother's Yorkshire.

MARK
(*dismissively*)

South Riding by a whisker. So you get yourself trapped by a papist bitch carrying a seven-month baby.

His face is a thundercloud.

Yes! – I won't marry now. You're next, after me, and after you it's that whore's child who will be the fourteenth Tietjens of Groby.

14

CHRISTOPHER
(to the Coachman)
Ici – c'est bien – merci!

The horse cab arrives (at a church). Mark prepares to alight.

MARK
One heard things about you . . . that you were a
wrong'un, but better a wrong'un than a mug.

CHRISTOPHER
Yes, I suppose I was a mug . . .

FLASHBACK – INT. MOVING TRAIN (ENGLAND) – DAY

*In the rocking, racketing 'local', Sylvia, in disarray, her skirts
hoisted, bucks astride seated Christopher, kissing him deeply.*

INT./EXT. – HORSE CAB (AS BEFORE)

CHRISTOPHER
(following Mark)
And yet there's something glorious about her.

FLASHBACK – INT. TRAIN (AS BEFORE)

*The train's steam-whistle blasts a long, human shriek as Sylvia
rears up and throws back her head in unsimulated satisfaction.*

EXT. LOWNDES STREET (1911) – NIGHT

An elegant address, dark windows, street lamps.

INT. MARITAL BEDROOM (LOWNDES STREET, 1911) – NIGHT

*Sylvia sleeps. Next to her, Christopher is woken by Michael
crying in the room above.*

INT. CHILD'S BEDROOM (LOWNDES STREET, 1911) — NIGHT

Marchant, brought from sleep, comforts Michael. She is middle-aged, formerly Christopher's nursemaid. Christopher, with a dressing gown over his pyjamas, joins them. There is almost no light. Michael is barely three years old.

CHRISTOPHER
What is it, old fellow?

MARCHANT
We had a nasty dream, didn't we? (*Firmly.*) Lie back now . . .

CHRISTOPHER
No, no . . .

He turns on a shady lamp.

I know what to do. A little warm milk, Marchie. Best thing for bad dreams.

Marchant clucks but goes obediently. Christopher gently lifts the boy on to his lap.

A bit of conversation till we're sleepy, that's what I do, hmm?

Michael nods, snuggles, comforted, thumb in mouth. On the wall the largest picture is a print of Groby, a very old, very large country house overshadowed by an immense cedar.

CHRISTOPHER
I had bad dreams sometimes when I was little at my papa's house . . . see there? I could nearly touch Groby Tree from the night-nursery window.

FLASHBACK: INT. NIGHT NURSERY. GROBY — NIGHT

Flash of lightning.

All we see is a very small boy in the shock moment of a thunderclap and a tree branch slapping the rain-slashed windowpane by his head. It's barely more than a beat. This is Christopher in pyjamas on the window seat at Groby.

INT. CHILD'S BEDROOM {AS BEFORE} – NIGHT

> CHRISTOPHER
> There's a wishing well in the stableyard. They say it's twice as deep as the Groby Tree is high, and you can drop in a penny and make a wish . . . Should I tell you how long it falls?

Michael nods.

> CHRISTOPHER
> I used to count, as long as this: one . . . two . . . three . . .

Christopher keeps counting and lays Michael back on the pillow and covers him. Michael falls asleep while Christopher counts. Marchant arrives with the milk, watches a moment until Christopher notices her. There is an intimacy, and things which cannot be spoken.

> CHRISTOPHER
> (*wry about himself*)

Soft.

> MARCHANT
> (*on the brink of tears*)
> Oh, Mr Christopher!

> CHRISTOPHER
> Now, now, Marchie.

He turns off the lamp.

EXT. LOWNDES STREET – DAY

At the open front door, a parlourmaid, Bridget, is accepting a telegram from a Telegram Boy, while Marchant and Michael are leaving the house, both dressed for their routine morning outing. Michael carries a simple sailing boat.

INT. BREAKFAST ROOM, LOWNDES STREET – DAY

Modernity in 1911: Post Toasties on the sideboard, with an array of electrical gadgets for toasting, warming, kettle-boiling.

*An excess of hothouse flowers. Three at breakfast: Mrs
Satterthwaite, wearing an immense hat with her negligee, is
rattling and reading* The Times; *Christopher, dressed formally
for the office, is tucking into haddock and poached eggs while
skim-reading a volume of the new edition of the* Encyclopaedia
Britannica; *Sylvia has an 'illustrated paper', a celebrity mag of
its time, devoted to high society.*

*Bridget enters with the telegram for Christopher, who thanks
her. He reads the telegram, which seems to be unimportant,
and he puts it in his pocket.*

SYLVIA

While you're there, please, Bridget, teapot.

BRIDGET

Yes 'm.

*Bridget goes to the sideboard for a teapot which has a Union
Jack ticket tied to it. Bridget's inscrutable listening face is the
fourth corner of the conversation.*

SYLVIA

'Maisie Mulgrew wishes it to be known that she is
enjoying sexual connection with Captain W. M.
O'Donnell . . .'

MRS SATTERTHWAITE
(*startled*)

What?

SYLVIA
(*to Bridget*)

No! China!

*Bridget goes back to the sideboard for the other teapot, which
has a yellow 'coolie hat' ticket.*

MRS SATTERTHWAITE
Oh, you! Pulling the strings of the shower bath.

Mrs Satterthwaite returns to her Times. *Sylvia reads out the
real version of the gossip item, a photo caption.*

SYLVIA

'The Hon. Mrs Frederick Mulgrew, whose husband, we
hear, is spoken of for the Vienna Embassy, enjoys the
polo with Captain W. M. O'Donnell . . .' That's Maisie
getting even with Freddie Mulgrew for his fling with
Lady Egret.

MRS SATTERTHWAITE

You have no reason to say so.

*She holds her cup and saucer high in the air, her eyes on her
paper.*

Thank you, Bridget – Darjeeling. And Mr Tietjens needs
more coffee, I expect.

Bridget makes the necessary journeys. Meanwhile . . .

SYLVIA

Oh, I don't think Maisie's got the gumption to go
through with it. But the readers like a whiff of sex
coming off our crowd . . . like a vapour, like the bit of
steam on the water in the crocodile house at the zoo.

*Sylvia flings her paper aside and stands up, stalking up and
down nervily with a plate and a piece of toast.*

I'm bored!

MRS SATTERTHWAITE

Only you could be bored with the end of the world
upon us.

SYLVIA

Who says?

MRS SATTERTHWAITE

I says. A hundred degrees in the shade recorded yesterday
at Greenwich, and the Prime Minister has asked the King
to create four hundred Liberal peers so the working
classes can have free medicines. (*Still reading.*) Oh, but
I see the Association of Domestic Servants is against the
Insurance Bill. Why would that be, I wonder.

Christopher writes in pencil in the margin of the encyclopedia.

CHRISTOPHER

Now is your chance to ask. (*To Bridget for the coffee.*)
Thank you.

MRS SATTERTHWAITE
(*missing his meaning*)

Go on, then.

CHRISTOPHER
(*in a kindly tone*)

Well, Bridget?

BRIDGET

I'm sure I don't know, sir.

CHRISTOPHER

I'm sure I do. It's because the National Insurance Bill
would violate the beautiful intimacy that exists between
servant and mistress.

*Bridget is free to go now (the sideboard is for self-help), and
she leaves.*

CHRISTOPHER

The Association of Domestic Servants are Tories through
and through! It is the duty of employers to look after the
welfare of their employees, and those who don't should
go to prison.

MRS SATTERTHWAITE

Who thinks that?

CHRISTOPHER

I am the last, except for a few dukes like your cousin
Westershire.

Christopher's calm superior manner infuriates Sylvia.

SYLVIA

Do you wonder I can't bear him?

MRS SATTERTHWAITE

No. You married above your intellect and don't take kindly to disadvantage.

CHRISTOPHER
(*to Mrs Satterthwaite*)
However, the new Liberal peers won't be necessary. The Upper House will cave in and vote to make itself irrelevant.

SYLVIA
(*caustic*)
And is that the end of the world?

CHRISTOPHER
No. The world ended long ago, in the eighteenth century.

Sylvia flings her plate at him. It misses and smashes.

SYLVIA
(*almost screaming*)
Do you know what he's doing? He's making corrections in the *Encyclopaedia Britannica*! If I'd killed him no jury would convict!

INT. KITCHEN LOWNDES STREET (SAME TIME) – DAY

Bridget, Hullo Central and also Mrs Satterthwaite's Maid and Cook, at their own breakfast, can hear Sylvia's continuing outburst and the smash of another plate. Their only reactions are expressive sighs, eye-cockings, lip-pursings. Bridget is reading a 'society page' over her cup of tea. A bell jangles. She gets up to go, passing the paper meaningfully to Hullo Central . . . who looks to see: a photograph of Sylvia 'sharing a joke' with a handsome man, Perowne, at a garden party.

HULLO CENTRAL
(*sniffs*)

Him again.

EXT. WHITEHALL – DAY

*In hot sunshine Christopher alights from a hansom cab.
Horse-drawn cabs are outnumbered by motor taxis and motor
buses in the heavy traffic, but many goods vehicles are horse-
drawn.*

> CHRISTOPHER
> (*paying the cabman*)
> You've been giving the mare less liquorice in her mash.
> I told you she'd go better.

> CABMAN
> Trust you to remember, sir!

*Christopher, top-hatted, enters the portals, which announce
'Imperial Department of Statistics'.*

INT. DEPARTMENT LOBBY (SAME TIME) – DAY

*A Porter salutes Christopher, who ascends the staircase,
nodding to two or three formally dressed men coming and
going.*

INT. WHITEHALL STAIRCASE (SAME TIME) – DAY

The staircase is quite grand.

*Macmaster, arriving for work in formal dress like Christopher,
hurries up the stairs.*

> MACMASTER
> Tietjens! – you received my telegram?

> CHRISTOPHER
> (*walking on*)
> And a very good morning to you, too, Macmaster. So you
> looked over my figures.

> MACMASTER
> The Chief will have my head if I give them to him.

CHRISTOPHER

Well, don't then. You asked for my help.

MACMASTER

But you've weighted the calculations as though people
become ill according to what they have to pay for
medical treatment!

CHRISTOPHER
(calm)
They do – and they'll ruin the Exchequer. I intend Sir
Reginald to know it.

INT. MARITAL BEDROOM, LOWNDES STREET – DAY

*Sylvia's pal Bobbie, a young married woman, is watching
Sylvia trying on hats, and trying on one herself.*

BOBBIE

Suppose you could bolt with a new man every week
and no questions asked. Ripping! (*With hat.*) Can I have
this?

SYLVIA

No.

BOBBIE

But the question is, how long would it stay ripping before
you're simply yawning to get back to your husband?

SYLVIA

How long?

BOBBIE

It's not a riddle, Sylvia. I'm asking.

SYLVIA

It would have to be weekends only. One would still need
a home – a husband for show midweek, and a place to
store one's maid. I couldn't do without Hullo Central.

*Alerted by the noise of an arriving car, Sylvia looks down from
the window.*

EXT. LOWNDES STREET (SAME TIME) – DAY

Perowne, the man in the society page photograph, is the driver of the enormous gleaming car. He gets out and approaches the front door. He wears smart 'country clothes'.

Bridget answers the door, and gives him the bad news. Perowne returns to the car, angry, and drives away.

INT. MARITAL BEDROOM (SAME TIME) – DAY

Sylvia is settling on a hat.

> SYLVIA
> I'm not dressed for a picnic. Anyway I've realised there's no point in a fling if one's husband doesn't notice.

> BOBBIE
> I'll go!

> SYLVIA
> No use. Potty loves *me*. He wants me to leave Christopher and go abroad with him. Oh, I'd like to shake him!

> BOBBIE
> Who?

> SYLVIA
> My husband, of course. Shake some reaction out of that great lump!

INT. SIR REGINALD'S OFFICE – DAY

The same hot day shows through Sir Reginald's window. A grand office. Sir Reginald is somewhat in awe of Christopher and bewildered by him. Macmaster is present, anxious, and furious with Christopher.

> SIR REGINALD
> . . . Don't be obtuse, Tietjens – dammit man, it is the Department's duty to support the Minister in making his case to the House. Do you understand that? The

Minister has to show that the figures for the Insurance
Bill will balance.

CHRISTOPHER

Well, they won't, and I should have thought it was the
Department's duty to tell him so.

Macmaster is agitated into interruption.

MACMASTER

Forgive me, Sir Reginald, may I – ?

SIR REGINALD

Yes. Tietjens, you're the cleverest young man in London,
Macmaster says, and I'm inclined to believe him, but he
and I with our blunt instruments have managed to grasp
something that you cannot –

MACMASTER
(*murmurs*)

You're very good, Sir Reginald.

SIR REGINALD

Which is that if they don't get what they require from
you, they'll put some competition-wallah Head Clerk on
it and take our credit from us.

CHRISTOPHER

I simply wished you to be aware of the facts. There's no
difficulty in adjusting the calculations to produce a more
congenial result, and I can let Macmaster have that in the
hour and ten minutes remaining. But I insist on his taking
the credit for it.

Macmaster would like to demur but –

SIR REGINALD

Good man!

EXT. GLORVINA HOUSE, LONDON – DECEMBER – NIGHT

*The wheels of a car move through snow as the chauffeur-
driven vehicle draws up outside the brightly lit door of a house*

in, perhaps, Eaton Square. The Chauffeur lets out a formally dressed man. Suddenly the man is under siege, not quite under attack, from a group of shouting Suffragettes, some with placards. Their target is called Waterhouse, a Liberal Cabinet Minister.

SUFFRAGETTES
It's him! . . . Votes for women! . . . Shame! Shame on you! . . . (*Etc.*)

The Chauffeur defends Waterhouse, who hurries into the house as a police whistle is heard and two Policemen run up and struggle with the women who break away and run off, pursued. It's all over in seconds.

INT. GLORVINA HOUSE (SAME TIME) – NIGHT

A Christmas party and dance at the London home of a senior Tory and his wife: Bertram and Lady Glorvina. In society, Glorvina is a famous and imperious hostess.

Waterhouse, the hero-martyr of the hour, is telling his story to a group including Paul Sandbach MP, his wife Lady Claudine, and General Campion, Lady Claudine's brother, who is tall, thin, pink-cheeked, white-haired, moustached.

WATERHOUSE
(*accepting a drink*)
. . . came through without a scratch! Thanks, Bertram.

BERTRAM
My fault for inviting a Liberal – Christmas spirit, you know.

This is overheard by Johnnie Pelham, passing by. Johnnie is Bobbie's husband, later described by her as a 'good old sausage' . . . which is to say that he is a comfortable, good-natured dimwit.

JOHNNIE
I see you also invited Beichen – I don't think they go in for the Christmas spirit, Bertram.

LADY CLAUDINE

Lord Beichen? Where?

Johnnie indicates a portly press baron, who happens to be bending over Bobbie's outstretched hand. Bobbie is smiling, having a good time.

JOHNNIE

Kissing my wife's fingers. What's his charm for *you*, Bertram?

BERTRAM

A million readers, half of them with the vote.

The women are in long dresses, the men in white ties. It is not a ball – the music is from a gramophone – but there is dancing. The party is loud and crowded.

Sylvia is dancing animatedly with Perowne. Her eyes search out Christopher. Christopher, elsewhere, is for once slightly agitated . . . but it' s Macmaster he finally spots and moves towards.

Sylvia sees him, abandons Perowne without ceremony and intercepts Christopher.

SYLVIA

You're here at last.

CHRISTOPHER

Yes – I'm sorry. You look lovely.

SYLVIA

You look like thunder. You didn't mind that I let Potty bring me ahead?

CHRISTOPHER

Of course not.

SYLVIA

Will you dance?

CHRISTOPHER

I would if this were dancing. Will you save me one when there's a tune?

Sylvia, feeling snubbed, turns on her heel.

Macmaster has a Lady on his hands.

> LADY
> (*trills*)

You're a writer!

> MACMASTER

No, no . . . at odd moments. A critic, perhaps, yes a
little of the critic. My little book on Rossetti will be
appearing –

Christopher grips his arm.

> CHRISTOPHER

Macmaster.

The Lady is fortuitously squired away by another Guest.

> MACMASTER
> (*annoyed*)

That was rude.

> CHRISTOPHER
> (*indicating*)

That fellow there with Sandbach is the Right Honourable
Stephen Waterhouse – he's the swine who made us fake
that schedule at the office. I'm going to have a word with
him.

> MACMASTER
> (*in agony*)

For God's sake, Chrissie!

*Christopher makes his way over. Bertram has departed on host
duty.*

> LADY CLAUDINE

I would have them whipped till they bled!

> SANDBACH

Spank them, that's what I say.

GLORVINA

What have we come to, when a Government Minister can't go anywhere without a policeman . . . ?

WATERHOUSE

I ought to have invited them to talk things over in my office.

CHRISTOPHER

Perhaps if the Prime Minister had kept his promise to address the women's concerns after the summer recess . . .

CAMPION

Chrissie, dear fellow –

CHRISTOPHER

The women kept their promise to stop demonstrating while the police had their hands full with the Coronation –

CAMPION

Give the PM a chit – he had the dockers holding the country to ransom, and the railwaymen – troops under canvas in Hyde Park –

SANDBACH

Quite right! Tietjens, hark to my brother-in-law the General!

WATERHOUSE

Tietjens?! – You must be the genius. Allow me to thank you.

CHRISTOPHER

Good God, what for?

WATERHOUSE

We couldn't have got the Insurance Bill before the House till next session without your figures.

CHRISTOPHER
(*taut with fury*)
You're taking the credit from Macmaster.

WATERHOUSE

Oh no, we know whom to thank – Sir Reginald let it out.

LADY CLAUDINE

Macmaster? That fellow you brought with you? Who are his people?

CHRISTOPHER

His father was a shipping clerk in Edinburgh.

Christopher walks away rudely.

LADY CLAUDINE

Well!

WATERHOUSE

Was he angry with me?

SANDBACH
(*indicating*)

Angry with his wife, I expect – we got the brunt.

Sylvia is still dancing with Perowne where the party is louder. They can shout in confidence.

SYLVIA

No.

PEROWNE

Yes.

SYLVIA

No, Potty.

PEROWNE

Don't call me Potty.

SYLVIA
(*laughs*)

But it suits you!

PEROWNE

Will you?

SYLVIA

Well, I might. One day.

The party noise and jollity come to a peak.

INT. MARITAL BEDROOM, LOWNDES STREET, FEBRUARY —
DAY

*Heavy frost on the window. Christopher sits on the bed.
Drawers are pulled out, wardrobe doors are open, the dressing
table mostly bare. He sits expressionless, thinking, holding a
very short letter.*

INT. WHITEHALL STAIRCASE — DAY

*Christopher and Macmaster come down the stairs, leaving
from work.*

> CHRISTOPHER
> Sylvia has gone off with that fellow Perowne.

> MACMASTER
> Ah!

> CHRISTOPHER
> I'm letting Lowndes Street and warehousing the
> furniture. I'm taking Michael to my sister Effie. She's
> married to a vicar who has one of our livings. Marchant
> will go with him.

> MACMASTER
> Then you'll be wanting your old rooms.

EXT. GROBY — DAY

*The drive to the great house has rose bushes on either side.
The Head Gardener, mysteriously, is placing a clay pipe
(smoker's) in a rose bush. He has several more filled pipes in
an open shoebox. He takes another pipe and places it in
another rose bush further on. He pauses to salute a dog cart
(pony and carriage) coming towards the house. Effie,
Christopher's older sister, is driving.*

EXT. GROBY STABLEYARD – DAY

Christopher stands by the well, watching Michael, who drops a penny into the well, looking down after it. Michael starts counting, almost to himself.

INT. GROBY WELL

The penny falling.

EXT. GROBY FRONT (SAME TIME) – DAY

A Footman puts luggage into the dog cart. Marchant is there with more luggage.

INSERT – INT. GROBY WELL

The penny falling.

EXT. GROBY STABLEYARD (AS BEFORE)

Effie is approaching on foot. Christopher waves to her. Michael is still counting . . . 'Four . . . five . . .'

INSERT – INT. GROBY WELL

The penny falls into a circle of reflected light, breaking it.

EXT. GROBY FRONT – DAY

The loaded dog cart, Michael and Marchant sitting by Effie, trundles away, the pony breaking into a trot. Watching them go are Christopher and his father and mother, who is dying in her late fifties. She is in a wheelchair, attended by a Nurse. Christopher takes her hand. Tietjens Senior is elderly, old school.

FLASHBACK – THE SAME POV AND REVERSE

– of a pony trap taking seven-year-old Christopher away to

school with his school trunk, looking back unhappily at his young Mother waving goodbye.

EXT. GROBY FRONT (AS BEFORE) — DAY

CHRISTOPHER
Bear up, old girl. You'll be nearer at hand now for Michael.

MOTHER
Your wife has shamed you both. All of us.

Michael, unhappy, looks back at them. Mother waves. Christopher waves, stone-faced. The Nurse takes Mother indoors.

TIETJENS
I thought your mother would see me out with time to spare.

Tietjens retrieves a clay pipe from a rose bush, and lights it.

You will divorce?

CHRISTOPHER
No! Only a blackguard would submit his wife to that. Mrs Satterthwaite has established herself at a German spa so that Sylvia may be said to have gone abroad to nurse her. The mother's a bitch but a sensible one.

TIETJENS
(*pause*)
Dutch William took Groby for us from the papists. God chose sides then.

He watches a ploughing team at work in the field.

The motor plough didn't answer.

CHRISTOPHER
(*bitterly*)
It will, though. It's all coming.

33

EXT. ROUEN HOTEL — DAY

The front of the Hôtel de la Poste.

INT. ROUEN HOTEL (LOBBY) — DAY

There is a young married couple in a lounge/conservatory adjoining the lobby. The man, Thurston, sees Sylvia and Perowne enter the lobby.

Sylvia glances at Thurston, who smiles and inclines his head.

INT. ROUEN HOTEL BEDROOM — DAY

Sylvia and Perowne enter the room.

> SYLVIA
> He's someone called Thurston, I met him somewhere. He won't gossip.

> PEROWNE
> Don't care if he does.

> SYLVIA
> Well, thank you very much.

> PEROWNE
> Well, what does it matter? Now or later. We're not going to hide for ever.

> SYLVIA
> Well, that's the thing, Potty.

> PEROWNE
> What thing?

> SYLVIA
> It's not for ever.

> PEROWNE
> Yes, it is!

> SYLVIA
> I hope you're not going to behave badly.

PEROWNE

About what?

SYLVIA

About my going back before it's too late.

Perowne is devastated, shocked, furious.

PEROWNE

Oh no, you're not. What are you talking about?

SYLVIA

I miss my husband.

PEROWNE

No, you don't! You call him a great – a great – lump of
wood –

SYLVIA

Oh, he is. I often want to kill him just to see if there's any
blood in him. I'm permanently angry with him. But he's
spoiled me for any other decently groomed man in
London. He knows everything about everything, it's the
difference between being with a grown man and trying to
entertain a schoolboy –

PEROWNE

But you love me! Don't you?

SYLVIA

I overlooked you, your dullness and, oh, I don't know,
everything really, from being all over me as soon as we
were on the train, and sulking if I'm not all over you –

*In a rush of rage and despair, Perowne starts opening and
slamming drawers until he finds what he's looking for: a
revolver.*

SYLVIA

(*meanwhile*)

– especially that side of things, which became like reading
a book you've read before – oh! why can't one get a man
to go away with one and be just . . . oh, light comedy? I
say, you're not going to kill yourself, I hope, Potty.

Perowne goes to the door, locks it and puts the key in his pocket. He points the gun at her.

PEROWNE

I want you to swear on your St Anthony that you won't leave me.

Sylvia touches the St Anthony she wears on a gold chain round her neck.

SYLVIA

I'll do no such thing.

PEROWNE

Then I'll kill you if you try. The French understand these things!

Sylvia goes to the bureau and sits down to write a letter.

SYLVIA

And these hotels one's been hiding in . . . the notepaper is simply shaming . . .

She starts to write. Perowne starts to weep.

EXT. GRAY'S INN – DAY

A Postman delivers to Macmaster's tall brick building with tall elegant eighteenth-century windows.

INT – GRAY'S INN, BREAKFAST – DAY

Ferens, Macmaster's servant, enters with a tray, to place a water-heated silver dish of haddock and poached eggs on the table and to deliver the post, including a letter from Sylvia.

MACMASTER

I'll change into my golfing togs when we get to our digs. One never knows who might be on the train – Mr Sandbach MP going down to his constituency . . . and General Campion is doubtless of the weekend party at Mountby. Is he a golfer? (*Opening his post.*) Ah – the proofs of my monograph!

Christopher freezes at the sight of his letter. Macmaster notices. Ferens leaves with the bacon plates. Macmaster watches Christopher open his letter and read it. Christopher stares at the very short letter like a man gone mad.

CHRISTOPHER

Sylvia asks me to take her back.

Macmaster springs up, and at the sideboard pours a brandy for Christopher.

CHRISTOPHER

She's gone to join her mother in Germany.

MACMASTER

Shall you take her back?

CHRISTOPHER

I imagine so. There's the boy to be considered. Marchant says he's already beginning to talk broad Yorkshire. (*Pause.*) But I won't have a house again. A certain discredit attaches to cuckolds, quite properly. Anything beyond a flat would look like impudence in a man who can't keep his wife.

MACMASTER
(*passionately*)

I wish you'd divorce her, drag her through the mud!

CHRISTOPHER

For a gentleman, there is such a thing as . . . call it 'parade' . . .

MACMASTER

And if you met someone you wanted to marry?

CHRISTOPHER

It would change nothing. I stand for monogamy.

MACMASTER

You!

CHRISTOPHER

I! Monogamy and chastity. And for not talking about it.

Christopher starts writing rapidly on the back of Sylvia's letter.

MACMASTER
(*reading from his proofs*)
'Better far tho' hearts may break
  Bid farewell for aye!
Lest thy sad eyes, meeting mine,
  Tempt my soul away!'

Ah, but that's great poetry!

CHRISTOPHER
(*contemptuously*)
That . . . is your obese poet-painter talking about it – in
language like congealed bacon fat, rhapsodising a five-
shilling model in his grease-stained dressing gown and
underclothes he's slept in.

Christopher resumes writing.

MACMASTER
(*frigid with anger*)
You've a way of putting things.

CHRISTOPHER
I haven't. If I had, it would be better for me.

Christopher finishes writing.

CHRISTOPHER
Here. (*He reads out.*) 'ACCEPT RESUMPTION YOKE ON
CONDITION CHILD REMAIN SISTER EFFIE AND
ANGLICAN WIRE IF ACCEPTABLE.'

MACMASTER
Well, I for one am sorry. She must have a way of putting
things!

CHRISTOPHER
She has! (*Reads.*) 'I am now ready to return to you if
I can keep Hullo Central, there being *no one else*' –
underlined – 'no one else I can bear to have near me
when I retire for the night.' That's all. She should be the
consort of – I don't know – the Viceroy of India!

EXT. KENT COUNTRYSIDE – DAY

A steam train moves through the Kent countryside, passing the White Horse.

INT. TRAIN – DAY

In an otherwise empty first class compartment, Christopher and Macmaster sit opposite each other, en route to Rye. Macmaster is looking through the proofs of his book.

> MACMASTER
> Tomorrow we're breakfasting with a parson who helped me with my book. I accepted for you.

> CHRISTOPHER
> Did your poet know parsons? But of course he did! – You mean 'Breakfast' Duchemin of Magdalene?

> MACMASTER
> He's no longer at Cambridge. He has a rectory near Rye.

EXT. GOLF CLUBHOUSE, RYE – DAY

A motor car arrives speedily at the clubhouse, General Campion at the wheel, Sandbach beside him. Christopher and Macmaster are arriving on foot, carrying their golf clubs. Christopher has to skip out of the car's way as it pulls up. Campion and Sandbach, both dressed for golf, get down. Campion limps now.

> CHRISTOPHER
> (*indignantly*)
> You're a menace, General! You've already lamed yourself once for thinking you can drive your motor!

Club Servants come to relieve the men of their golf bags.

> CAMPION
> (*genially*)
> Lady Claude says come and pick a bone tonight at Mountby; you too, Macmaster.

CHRISTOPHER

Thank you, but I won't. Macmaster would be delighted.

Sandbach notes that there is another distinguished arrival, the Rt. Hon. Stephen Waterhouse MP, accompanied by his male secretary, Sanderson, both clothed and equipped for golf. They have driven from London. Sanderson takes two golf bags from the back of the car. A middle-aged Policeman is waiting for them. He salutes Waterhouse. They exchange a few words.

SANDBACH
(*indicating Waterhouse*)

We're honoured.

WATERHOUSE
(*to Sanderson*)

Get my policeman a drink, would you?

CAMPION
(*calls*)

Hullo, Waterhouse. I'm president here. Enjoy our links.

There is a movement into the clubhouse, with exchanges of greetings and courtesies. Campion hangs back to have a word with Macmaster.

CAMPION

Get him back to Sylvia as quick as you can. Had a little tiff, haven't they? Nothing serious?

MACMASTER

Well . . . I . . .

CAMPION

Believe me, Sylvia is a splendid girl, straight as a die, takes her fences clean.

Macmaster continues to flounder.

CAMPION

Chrissie must have been running after the skirts. No? I dare say a little. No?

MACMASTER
(*strangled*)

No! –

CAMPION

It would be resented . . . half the houses in London would be closed to him . . . so . . . do what you can!

Campion pats Macmaster on the shoulder and follows the others indoors.

EXT. GOLF COURSE – RYE

The golf course is by the sea. The natural terrain is sandhills and dune grass. Ultimately we will see that there is a leeward boundary road with a wide, deep ditch alongside.

We are concerned with eight golfers: Two City Men; Waterhouse and Sanderson; Campion, Macmaster, Sandbach and Christopher, who will tee off in pairs. Christopher and Macmaster carry their own (unbulky) golf bags. The rest are shadowed by their caddies.

A. *Waterhouse and Sanderson are playing against each other somewhere down the course. Waterhouse lifts a shot towards a green. Sanderson waits by his ball.*

B. *Waterhouse's Policeman uses binoculars to scan the terrain from a vantage.*

C. *Sanderson plays his shot.*

D. *The two City Men occupy the first tee. They are loud, vulgar, happy and tight. The First City Man drives off.*

SECOND CITY MAN

Gawd's truth, I can piss further than that. So can my old woman!

FIRST CITY MAN

I know, she showed me!

More raucous laughter. They are being watched by our quartet waiting their turn.

CAMPION

Sorry about the riff-raff.

Christopher, uninterested in golf, follows the flight of a bird over the dunes – and sees something white appear and disappear behind a dune. He watches. Nothing shows.

The Second City Man makes his shot. More loud laughter.

E. *The Policeman, already suffering from helmet to boots, moves to keep up with Waterhouse.*

F. *Our quartet move to occupy the first tee.*

SANDBACH

You're the great Macmaster.

MACMASTER
(*deeply gratified*)

You're very good to say so, sir.

SANDBACH

Oh, my caddy has heard tell.

Macmaster is deeply disappointed.

CHRISTOPHER

He's plus one at North Berwick.

CAMPION
(*to Macmaster*)

You're with me, then. Chrissie's no good, he can take on Paul.

Christopher, still intrigued, looks into the distance and is rewarded: two female hats, white and dark, appear and disappear on the move.

MACMASTER

I think you can go now, General.

Campion hits a decent drive. Macmaster places his ball on the grass, pinching up the ground.

CAMPION

Don't you use a tee?

MACMASTER

Never have, and I've managed without since I was four.

Macmaster hits a prodigious drive.

G. *The Policeman climbs to look over a dune.*

H. *Waterhouse holes a putt watched by Sanderson. He writes on a card.*

WATERHOUSE

. . . puts you seventeen bob and a tanner up.

I. *The City Men swig from flasks, joshing, and prepare loudly to drive off again.*

J. *Christopher and Sandbach (who is slightly lame) walk down the fairway. Distant laughter reaches them from the City Men.*

SANDBACH

It's swine like those two that turn decent girls into suffragette whores.

INSERT: SOMEWHERE

Sandbach in his underwear, holding a golf club by the wrong end, brings it down on a bare female bottom.

BACK TO SCENE

CHRISTOPHER

I loathe this game.

SANDBACH

So do I, but it gets one away from the memsahib. What's your excuse?

CHRISTOPHER

Macmaster has no one else.

K. *Waterhouse has got himself into the rough. Suddenly 'from nowhere' he is ambushed by two young women, Valentine (white cap) and Gertie (black brimmed hat pinned to her hair). Valentine shouts suffragette slogans into his face. Gertie attacks Waterhouse physically, throwing a rotten cabbage at*

43

*him and then splattering him with 'blood' – red ink – from a
bottle.*

GERTIE
(*cockney*)
Is it our blood you want before you give in!

VALENTINE
Run, Gertie!

The elderly Caddy stares open-mouthed.

L. *Sanderson wakes up to the situation and runs towards the
action.*

M. *Gertie runs one way, to safety for now.*

N. *Valentine runs towards Sanderson, deliberately, drawing
Waterhouse after her. She 'dances' around and between them,
shouting 'Votes for women' etc., eluding the men effortlessly
and trotting away.*

O. *The Policeman is running down a small hill when he sees
Gertie running. He changes course to run after Gertie,
shouting for her to stop.*

P. *Elsewhere, Valentine runs between Macmaster and Campion,
who see and hear Waterhouse and Sanderson chasing.*

Campion reacts to Valentine. He knows her.

CAMPION
By Jove!

Macmaster also gives chase. Campion walks, following.

Valentine changes course sharply.

Q. *Elsewhere, Gertie runs slap into the City Men. Way behind
her, the Policeman is hollering.*

FIRST CITY MAN
Suffragettes!

*The Second City Man makes a grab for Gertie and is left with
a piece of her blouse.*

SECOND CITY MAN
Skirt hunt!

They stagger after her.

Valentine runs into the scene, circles around the City Men, calling them 'beasts'.

POLICEMAN
Stop! You're under arrest!

Valentine skips round him and runs. Gertie is getting away. The City Men stagger after Gertie, delighted and vindictive.

R. *Far from the action, Christopher is near the boundary road. He is glad to be alone, with his mis-hit ball. He chooses a club. He considers the ball.*

VALENTINE
I say . . .

Christopher ignores the voice.

VALENTINE
Sorry to spoil your shot, but . . .

Christopher drops his club and straightens. He sees: a fair young woman scowling at him from under a white canvas cap. She's wearing a striped cotton blouse, a 'short' tweed skirt and boy's white sandals. She's a little out of breath. Her name is Valentine Wannop.

VALENTINE
I say, go and see that they don't hurt Gertie. I've lost her . . .

She points beyond the sand dunes, further along the course.

S. *A hundred yards away, Sandbach plays his shot, and then notices that a young woman is with Christopher. Perked up, he walks towards them.*

T. *With Christopher and Valentine.*

VALENTINE
There looked to be some beasts among them.

45

Noises are heard – yip-yip-yip of hunt followers, and 'Hi-hi-hi!' from Sanderson waving his club.

CHRISTOPHER

You've been demonstrating.

VALENTINE

Of course we have, but you won't let a girl be manhandled.

The Policeman is on top of the nearest sand dune, windmilling and shouting. From behind him, Macmaster breasts the slope. Waterhouse, waving a club, enters the view on the flat with Sanderson. They're all shouting.

v. *With Christopher and Valentine.*

VALENTINE

A regular rat-hunt. I led them off except for two drunk beasts who couldn't run. But neither can Gertie.

CHRISTOPHER

Cut away, then. I'll look after Gertie.

He picks up his bag.

VALENTINE

No, I'll come with you.

CHRISTOPHER

Clear out! Unless you want to go to gaol.

There are screams heard and Gertie comes round the corner, her black skirt sanded from rolling down a sand dune, her blouse partly torn away, showing her white camisole. The two City Men now appear on the shoulder of the slope. One of them waves a piece of Gertie's blouse.

FIRST CITY MAN

Strip the bitch naked! Strip the bitch stark naked!

The City Men jump down the little hill, cannoning into Christopher.

CHRISTOPHER

Stand still, you swine! – I'll knock your head off if you
move!

VALENTINE

Come along, Gertie – it's not far!

*The City Men stare at Christopher, their jaws dropped.
Christopher hears Gertie give a scream behind him. He
turns round to see the Policeman lumbering downhill
unenthusiastically towards the girls, who are staggering
towards the road.*

w. *Sandbach from a little distance sees and reacts to what
happens next.*

x. *The Policeman is only a yard or two from Christopher . . .
who slips his golf bag off his shoulder and throws it between
the Policeman's legs. The Policeman pitches forward, his
helmet over his eyes. He gives up. He mops his brow with a
handkerchief.*

Christopher offers his silver flask to the Policeman.

CHRISTOPHER

You couldn't have done more. I expect you're a bit
shaken.

POLICEMAN

Anyone would be! Thank you, sir.

*The girls cross the road to the dyke's steep bank, Valentine
holding up Gertie's hat as it flaps from a hairpin. Waterhouse,
Sanderson, Macmaster and Sandbach have arrived.*

SANDBACH

We've got them!

*But as the four men approach, they see Gertie crossing the
dyke on a plank, and Valentine – amazingly, neatly – leap the
dyke, and help Gertie 'ashore'. Valentine then pulls the plank
towards her and drags it up on the grass.*

VALENTINE
(*crows*)
You'll have to go round by Camber railway bridge.

The two girls run away across the vast marshy field. The pursuers, standing in a line on the road, consider the nine-foot wide jump and the ten-foot drop to deep mud.

SANDBACH
Come on! We have to do something!

WATERHOUSE
Oh, chuck it, Sandy. Who's for finishing the round? Come on, Sanderson.

Bloody but unbowed, Waterhouse walks off. The Policeman gets smartly to his feet and makes to follow him. Sanderson gives the Policeman an ironic put-down look, and follows Waterhouse. The Policeman trails unhappily after them.

Sandbach comes to Christopher, snorting.

SANDBACH
I refuse to play with you. In fact I've a good mind to issue a warrant for your arrest for obstructing justice.

CHRISTOPHER
You can't. You're not a borough magistrate. Look it up.

Campion arrives at a walk.

SANDBACH
(*to Campion*)
Tietjens scuppered the bobby, I saw him do it. I bet he put them up to it.

Sandbach stalks off. The City Men, who have been mesmerised, fascinated, turn on Campion.

FIRST CITY MAN
That man called us a swine!

CAMPION
Well, you are ruddy swine, and you'll never get another ticket at this club.

The City Men stare at him. Campion turns to Christopher and walks him firmly away. Macmaster, ignored, remains, out of everything.

Y. *A little later . . .*

CAMPION

Chrissie, you are the bloody limit!

CHRISTOPHER

The bobby didn't want to catch the girls, he was yearning not to.

CAMPION

Was that skirt your . . . a friend of yours? Had you arranged it with her? If it was the Wannop girl – if the woman that's come between you and Sylvia – dammit – is our little suffragette . . .

CHRISTOPHER

Good God!

CAMPION

Put her back, Chrissie!

CHRISTOPHER

I give you my word –

CAMPION

They say they're all whores . . . I beg your pardon if you like the Wannop girl . . . Her father was a great friend of your father's.

Christopher has a moment of realisation.

CHRISTOPHER

Of course, I remember Professor Wannop the classicist.

CAMPION

He didn't leave a farthing, and there's a son at Eton. The widow and daughter have a deuced hard row to hoe. I know Claudine takes them all the peaches she can cadge out of Paul's gardener. Perhaps you feel sorry for her, is that it?

49

CHRISTOPHER

I think that's enough confusion to go on with. But you should know that Mrs Satterthwaite is much recovered at her German spa, and I'm expecting to go over there in a day or two to bring Sylvia and her mother home.

CAMPION

Good boy! Kiss her fingertips for me. She's the real thing, you lucky beggar.

They have been walking, and now suddenly the view opens hugely to sea and sky. Christopher stops to breathe it in.

CHRISTOPHER
(*voice-over*)

The littleness of it, our drawing-room comedy of sex-obsession! When the war comes . . .

INT. 'DIGS', RYE – NIGHT

Christopher and Macmaster, in evening dress, in Christopher's room in their digs – beams, sloping floors, old furniture. Christopher is drinking whisky, the bottle to hand.

CHRISTOPHER

. . . it'll blow right through it, thank God!

MACMASTER

How old-fashioned you are, Chrissie. War is impossible, at any rate with this country in it.

CHRISTOPHER

Is that what they said at your dinner with the Tories? In two years, round about the time of the grouse-shooting, there'll be a European war with Britain plumb in the middle of it.

MACMASTER

Ah, the Tietjens exactitude! Where's your evidence?

CHRISTOPHER

At the office.

MACMASTER

It's late. We're expected at Duchemin's breakfast – if you haven't been arrested.

CHRISTOPHER
(*laughs*)

I gave the policeman a five-pound note from the swine of a Government Minister, though I shouldn't call him that, he gave me dinner; besides which he's a decent fellow. So it's hands off the Wannop girl. The fair one is Miss Valentine Wannop, holder of the quarter-mile, half-mile, high-jump and long-jump records for East Sussex, and housemaid-typewriter for her mother, the novelist. The other girl was not local, probably from London. Never underestimate the Sussex constabulary. Oh, and it is generally believed that Miss Wannop and I are in cahoots, if not worse.

MACMASTER

Why do you look like that?

CHRISTOPHER

I'm waiting for my wife to wire me to fetch her home, and this is what I look like.

EXT. HOTEL (GERMANY) – NIGHT

Establish the exterior of the German hotel.

INT. HOTEL SUITE (GERMANY) – NIGHT

The hotel is a gloomy spa in a remote place, formerly a hunting lodge, shabbily furnished. Mrs Satterthwaite is playing cards with Father Consett, by oil lamp. A painting or two of dead and bleeding game.

MRS SATTERTHWAITE

There are times when a woman hates a man, even a good man, as my husband was . . . I've walked behind a man's back and nearly screamed because of the desire to put my nails into the veins of his neck. And Sylvia's got it worse than I.

FATHER CONSETT

If the woman, as the Church directs, would have children and live decent . . .

MRS SATTERTHWAITE

But Sylvia's had a child.

FATHER CONSETT

Whose?! It was Drake's, wasn't it?

MRS SATTERTHWAITE

But Sylvia's had a child. It was probably Drake's.

SYLVIA

I am here, you know!

Sylvia speaks from a writing desk, where she is busy. The room is the sitting room of a suite.

I am done with men. Think of all the ruin that child has meant for me . . . and Christopher's perfectly soppy about him.

MRS SATTERTHWAITE

You don't deserve your husband, anyway. I can't imagine why he sent that telegram. 'Resume yoke', indeed!

SYLVIA

He sent it out of lordly, dull, full-dress consideration that drives me distracted. He couldn't write a letter because he'd have to write 'Dear Sylvia' and I'm not. He's that precise sort of imbecile. I'll settle down by his side and I'll be chaste. I've made up my mind to it. I'll be bored stiff for the rest of my life. Except for one thing. I can torment that man, and I'll do it, for all the times he's tormented me.

Sylvia appears to be deranged, mad-eyed and gasping for breath. She calms.

I've come from Normandy without sleep, you see.

52

I wish you'd remember that you were once the pure
young girl I knew.

SYLVIA

(*laughs*)

I don't believe I ever was. If the nuns had known me
I would have been expelled.

Sylvia tears up the paper she has written on.

Oh! . . . I'm going to tell them downstairs to telegraph
simply: 'Righto'.

Sylvia leaves the room.

FATHER CONSETT

Her hell will come when her husband goes running blind
and mad after another woman. Then she'll tear the house
down.

EXT. MARSHES NEAR RYE – DAY

*A sunny morning. Christopher and Macmaster are on their
way on foot to the Duchemin rectory for breakfast.*

INT. DUCHEMIN RECTORY – DAY

*The room is large and high and panelled, with tall windows
looking over a lawn and garden. The furniture is the best of
the eighteenth century. The pictures are mostly Turners. The
silverware on the sideboard and on the breakfast table, laid for
eight, is opulent. The table holds chafing dishes, chinaware
supporting peaches, great silver rose bowls, two large silver
urns, a silver kettle on a tripod and a tall vase of delphiniums.
The arrangement seems designed to blockade one end of the
table, an effect confirmed by Mrs Duchemin adding yet
another vase.*

*Mrs Duchemin is thirty, in dark blue silk and heavy amber
necklace, with a rose in her black hair – a Pre-Raphaelite
beauty, almost. Looking on is Valentine Wannop: well-groomed,
neat in a silk blouse and woollen skirt, blonde, bright and shiny.*

VALENTINE

That's perfect. Nobody will even see him.

MRS DUCHEMIN
(*hopefully*)

Well, he may say nothing, or only in Latin. I'm not sure it's playing the game, asking you to be here, Valentine. If your mother knew what . . .

VALENTINE

Women must back each other up, these days. Mother wanted to come with me when I told her it was to meet a critic.

MRS DUCHEMIN

Oh! – I hope . . .

VALENTINE

And don't worry about shocking me, either! Latin makes no difference because Father used to talk Latin to me and Edward as soon as we talked at all. And when he died, I worked as a backstairs slavey in a house with a drunken cook, which completed all the education I need to ensure that nothing your husband might say will be news to me.

MRS DUCHEMIN

Oh, you darling. You were seventeen!

VALENTINE

Oh, but don't misunderstand me – I'm entirely virtuous – quite pure!

Mrs Duchemin takes Valentine's hands and kisses them.

MRS DUCHEMIN

You're a heroine, Valentine!

VALENTINE

I'm not a heroine. Gertie has been to prison, and force-fed, and it was she who went for the Minister yesterday, while I just hopped about stuttering at him, 'V-v-votes f-f-for w-w-women!' I did get a big golfing idiot to save Gertie, though. Now I'm terrified every moment that the police are coming for me.

EXT. RECTORY (SAME TIME) — DAY

Christopher and Macmaster turn into the gateway. The Wannop carriage, with its driver, Joel, on the box, is waiting. A big bruiser in clerical clothes, insecure on a bone-shaking bicycle, overtakes them in the short drive, ringing his bell and roaring. He is the curate, Horsley.

> HORSLEY
> Welcome, welcome! I'm the curate here!

Horsley, raising his hat, loses control of the bicycle, which falls over, sliding almost into the carriage mare, which dances dangerously. The mare is too large for the carriage. Macmaster is alarmed. Christopher goes straight to the mare, enraged.

> CHRISTOPHER
> *(to Joel)*
> Here, get down, you!

He goes to the mare's head, calming the animal.

> There, there! Yes . . .

The mare rubs its forehead against his chest. Joel comes awkwardly down from his high seat.

Macmaster comes to assist Horsley, who continues booming and roaring. He has a nervous vocal tic: he makes a giggling sound like 'tee-hee!' every few words.

> HORSLEY
> Thank you, thank you! – tee-hee! – ups-a-daisy – Horsley's my name.

> CHRISTOPHER
> Where did you get this job lot? Blast you, don't you see you've got a thirteen-hands pony's harness for a sixteen-and-a-half-hands horse? Let the bit out three holes, it's cutting the animal's tongue in half. Put her in the shade and don't go anywhere till I tell you.

INT. DUCHEMIN RECTORY, DINING ROOM (SAME TIME)

Mrs Duchemin is at a peak of nervous apprehension.

MRS DUCHEMIN

I made a place for your Gertie but never mind – we have the old curate's sister staying, Miss Fox, and she's stone deaf so an empty chair next to her makes no difference. She can pour out.

The huge voice of Horsley is heard in the hall.

HORSLEY

This way! This way! The ladies will be in here!

Horsley flings open the door and enters.

We arrived together! Tee-hee!

INT. HALL AND DINING ROOM (SAME TIME)

Christopher and Macmaster pause to give precedence to the elderly Miss Fox, who is descending the last few steps of the staircase, smiling vacantly.

MACMASTER

Good morning. I'm Mac—

Too late. Miss Fox hears nothing, and so does not acknowledge him. She enters the room, past Mrs Duchemin who has come to the door, smiling welcome.

MRS DUCHEMIN

Oh, how good of you to come . . .

But her welcome has already been obliterated by Mr Horsley's roar.

HORSLEY

We're living in a state of siege, ladies – tee-hee! Did you hear about it?

Mrs Duchemin's naming of Macmaster and Christopher to Valentine is lost in the storm.

Macmaster does not recognise Valentine. Christopher and Valentine look straightly at each other without embarrassment.

MRS DUCHEMIN
(*introducing, shouts*)
. . . Miss Wannop!

MACMASTER
(*catching up*)
Wannop!

*Horsley's speech is simultaneous and continuous. Miss Fox,
placed to the left of the empty chair at the head of the table, is
in charge of the silver urn. She placidly offers tea to Horsley
(whose place is next to the empty chair on Miss Fox's left) and
assumes his assent. She continues in this mode through
everything which ensues, until tea has been dispensed. Horsley,
while speaking, goes to help himself to a liberal selection from
the sideboard.*

*Valentine is to be next to Horsley. Mrs Duchemin nominates
the next chair for Christopher, and, leaving the place to his left
free for herself, shows Macmaster to the place on her own left,
opposite Miss Fox. All this is achieved with suitable remarks,
unheard owing to Horsley's speech . . .*

HORSLEY
(*meanwhile*)
Yes – a veritable state of siege! Mr Sandbach MP and
half-a-dozen young bloods who'd been dining at
Mountby, tee-hee! – went out last night mounted on
motor bicycles and armed with loaded canes, hunting
suffragettes – scouring the country lanes, tee-hee! –
stopped every woman they came across and abused her
with foul language – drink had been taken, tee-hee! – The
countryside's up in arms!

MRS DUCHEMIN
(*shouts to Macmaster*)
And I next to you!

*Having established the placements, she leads her two guests to
the feast on the sideboard. Horsley returns to his place with a
plate of food, still talking.*

General Lord Edward Campion is said to have egged
them on. He's putting up at Lady Claudine's for royal
duties at Dover.

VALENTINE
(*to Christopher*)
I must thank you for yesterday . . .

*She considers him. He silently inclines his head. She goes to the
sideboard.*

*Christopher, after giving Valentine precedence at the sideboard,
follows her with his own loaded plate to the table.*

*A woman enters the room at speed. The newcomer, Mrs
Wannop, middle-aged, apple-cheeked, still in notional
mourning, pats Horsley on the arm. Ignored, she takes his
hand and shakes it.*

HORSLEY
(*to Mrs Wannop*)
The General – tee hee! – is taking the escort for the
King, laying the Buffs' colours on the altar of St Peter's
tomorrow morning.

MRS WANNOP
Which is Mr Macmaster the critic?

In the lull, she turns to Christopher.

Are you Mr Macmaster the critic?

MACMASTER
I am Macmaster.

*Mrs Duchemin is shepherding Macmaster to his chair with his
plate. Mrs Wannop scampers round to his side of the table,
and pulls him to the windows.*

MRS WANNOP
Oh, Mr Macmaster, my new book is coming out on
Tuesday . . .

Mother! What have you done with Gertie?

MRS WANNOP

What? Oh, Gertie! Lying low in the attic – high, rather.
(*To Macmaster.*) It will be of use to you to hear about my
novel.

*Mrs Duchemin affects a rescue of Macmaster, leading him
back to his place.*

MRS WANNOP

To you journalists, a bit of inside information is always –

MACMASTER
(*horrified*)

I'm not a journalist!

MRS WANNOP

Well, a critic.

She pulls him back towards the windows.

MACMASTER

I don't review books, I'm not a critic in the sense of –

MRS WANNOP

Of course you are.

Mrs Duchemin follows them in pursuit.

MACMASTER

I write for the critical quarterlies.

*On her second attempt Mrs Duchemin gets Macmaster seated.
Mrs Wannop tries to sit down in Mrs Duchemin's place but
is thwarted by Mrs Duchemin firmly seating herself. Mrs
Wannop scoots around Macmaster's chair.*

MRS WANNOP

The critical quarterlies!

She establishes herself on his other side, at the head of the table.

MRS DUCHEMIN

Mr Horsley! Put Mrs Wannop next to you and feed her!

MRS WANNOP

But that's just what my book needs – a good, long, deep –

Horsley lifts Mrs Wannop out of the chair and propels her to his side of the table. She tries to sit opposite Macmaster, not noticing that Miss Fox is already in occupation.

Christopher, amused, smiles at Valentine.

MRS WANNOP

The quarterlies show a deplorable lack of serious interest in –

Horsley puts Mrs Wannop firmly into the chair next to Miss Fox, who smilingly offers tea.

Horsley goes to get food for Mrs Wannop. Christopher notes that Mrs Duchemin has yet to help herself.

CHRISTOPHER

Would you allow me to help you to . . . ?

MRS DUCHEMIN

Oh . . . A little caviar . . . A peach!

Mrs Wannop peers through and around the rampart of silverware, and sees that Mrs Duchemin has captured all of Macmaster's attention. Christopher goes on his errand to the sideboard. Valentine butters some toast and watches him with new interest.

MRS DUCHEMIN
(*to Macmaster*)

I'm afraid I . . . I'm afraid you must . . . you see, my husband . . .

She darts nervous glances at a discreet door in the panelling behind the empty chair at the head of the table.

MACMASTER

I beg you, dear lady . . . don't concern yourself . . . I ask it for my own sake. You look troubled and I would not have it so.

MRS DUCHEMIN

Oh . . .! Oh, how good you are!

MRS WANNOP

I think this party's very badly arranged. Very bad management.

She periodically repeats variations of this remark to no one in particular. Horsley returns to put a plate of food in front of her.

MRS DUCHEMIN
(meanwhile to Macmaster)

You'll find my husband will . . . or might . . . or perhaps not . . . sometimes you'd never know he was . . .

MACMASTER

Oh, one understands. One is surely brought up to understand that these great scholars . . . these abstracted cognoscenti . . .!

MRS DUCHEMIN

Oh, yes, yes! You do understand!

Christopher places before her an exquisite plate with a mound of caviar and a slice of lemon, and a pretty bowl containing a perfect peach. She ignores him.

MACMASTER

Merely to spend a fleeting hour in these perfect surroundings . . . You know the lines . . . 'As when the swallow gliding from lofty portal to lofty portal . . .'

MRS DUCHEMIN

Oh yes! Yes! It takes a poet!

They have eyes only for each other. Christopher sits down.

CHRISTOPHER
(to Valentine)

I have a message for you from Mr Waterhouse. I told him I did not know you and did not expect to see you. He didn't believe me.

VALENTINE

If it's to invite me for a chat, I don't intend to place myself in the way of his condescension.

CHRISTOPHER

No, not that. He wants you to know that there are no charges against you.

VALENTINE

What about Gertie?

CHRISTOPHER

Gertie, too, as far as yesterday is concerned, but you should get her out of your attic if she's on the run from the Metropolitan Police . . . which she is.

Christopher turns to Mrs Duchemin, who is not pleased to be diverted.

CHRISTOPHER

How do you manage fresh caviar for breakfast?

MRS DUCHEMIN

My husband has trained Simkins of New Bond Street . . . a telegram overnight, messengers to Billingsgate at dawn . . . the car goes to Ashford Junction before seven . . . If it were my doing, I'd find it a bit ostentatious.

CHRISTOPHER

No! It's the Great Tradition! Your husband was 'Breakfast' Duchemin of Magdalene!

The door in the panelling opens silently to admit the Reverend Mr Duchemin. He is very tall, handsome, grey-haired, stooped. He surveys the table for a moment. A second man follows him, moves quickly to hold back the chair for Duchemin. Duchemin sits. The second man stands behind the chair.

Christopher has seen this. He knows the second man, who is a prizefighter, Parry, in tight leggings, tight whipcord breeches, and short tight jacket buttoned up to his chin. Mrs Duchemin catches up a moment later. Her face makes Macmaster turn to see the same. Macmaster recognises Parry, too. Parry notes

Macmaster and Christopher, to whom he rolls his eyes and slips away to the sideboard to bring his charge some breakfast.

CHRISTOPHER
(*to Valentine*)
Good God, it's Parry! The Bermondsey light-middleweight!

Macmaster exchanges a look with Christopher.

VALENTINE
Mr Macmaster seems to know him, too. Do you go to the prize fights together?

CHRISTOPHER
Parry taught me to box at Cambridge.

Duchemin looks slyly at Macmaster.

DUCHEMIN
Good morning, Doctor.

MACMASTER
I'm not –

DUCHEMIN
Yes! Yes! The stethoscope packed into the hat left in the hall!

Duchemin raises himself to look beyond the vases and silverware.

DUCHEMIN
And your friend? Another medical man? It takes two doctors, of course, to certify a lunatic . . .

Parry slides a plate of soles in front of him.

DUCHEMIN
(*loudly*)
Take away these conducements to the filthy lusts of –

He checks himself. Valentine, Mrs Wannop and Horsley keep their heads down.

DUCHEMIN
Ah – yes. Parry! Sole fillets – good! Kidneys to follow.

MACMASTER

I am Macmaster. We corresponded and you invited me to breakfast.

Duchemin stares at Macmaster, then relaxes.

DUCHEMIN

Of course I did! Macmaster, the budding critic! And your friend! Macmaster and friend to breakfast! Not medical men. But you look tired. Worn! Worn out! I detect the pallor of self-abuse.

CHRISTOPHER
(*to Mrs Duchemin*)

Don't look round. Vincent Macmaster is quite capable.

DUCHEMIN
(*to Macmaster*)

Post coitum tristia. Ah, the sorrows of spent semen! Boys or girls in your case?

PARRY
(*shouts to him*)

Your fish is getting cold! I'll bring you the kidneys!

MACMASTER
(*to Mrs Duchemin*)

If he'll eat a little . . . It calls the blood down from the head.

MRS DUCHEMIN

Oh, forgive! It's dreadful for you.

MACMASTER

No! No! . . . Why, it's what I'm for.

MRS DUCHEMIN

Oh . . . you good man.

They gaze at each other.

Mr Duchemin is meanwhile declaiming Latin, a filthy epigram of Martial.

DUCHEMIN

'*Deprensum in puero tetricis me vocibus, uxor,*
corripis et culum te quoque habere refers.'

Christopher hears Valentine give a small gasp.

CHRISTOPHER

Of course! The daughter of Professor Wannop would
know her Latin!

MACMASTER

Schoolboy smut! Fifth form! Have some of the galantine.
I'm going to. (*To Mrs Duchemin.*) I can stop this. Shall I?

MRS DUCHEMIN

Yes! Yes! Anything!

*Macmaster goes to join Parry at the sideboard. Duchemin tries
to look round the table. Only Miss Fox is wholly visible because
of the barricade of vases, etc. She meets his gaze, smiling.*

DUCHEMIN

Marcus Valerius Martialis, Book Eleven, Epigram Forty-
three, the lament of the wife of a boy-buggerer – 'My
dear, I have an arsehole too!'

Miss Fox smiles and nods.

MACMASTER
(*tersely to Parry*)
Get him out – the way you beat Kid Cantor at Hackney
Baths!

DUCHEMIN

I have often had to refer my wife to Martial Eleven Forty-
three!

*Mrs Duchemin gives a small scream of premonition, and closes
her eyes. Parry is on his way to Duchemin, who has now stood
up.*

DUCHEMIN

'Alas, my love, with women, it's more a case of having
two cu— ugh –'

Parry, bending over him, has driven his fist into Duchemin's kidney. Duchemin falls back into his chair.

Mrs Duchemin gives a sob. Macmaster sits down.

MACMASTER
Dearest lady, it's all over. I assure you.

MRS DUCHEMIN
Forgive! You can never respect me . . .

MACMASTER
You're the bravest woman I know.

She gives a gasp, and closes her eyes in bliss. This is because Macmaster has taken her hand in his beneath the table.

MACMASTER
You're from Edinburgh, I think. You'll know the Fifeshire coast, then.

MRS DUCHEMIN
Do I not?

PARRY
. . . time to write your sermon, sir . . .

Parry helps Mr Duchemin to his door and they leave.

CHRISTOPHER
(*to Valentine*)
I remember meeting your father. He came to stay at Groby.

VALENTINE
Groby? Is your name Tietjens?

Mrs Wannop has overheard. She jumps up with a small scream.

MRS WANNOP
Are you a Tietjens of Groby?

INT. DUCHEMIN RECTORY – DAY

Half an hour later the room is empty except for Mrs Duchemin and Macmaster, who are locked together in a kiss.

Horsley is cycling away down the drive.

Joel has taken the mare out of the shafts and stays holding her by the bridle. Christopher is using part of the carriage as a workbench.

He is using a punch on a clasp knife to punch a hole in each broken end of the girth-strap. Mrs Wannop is doing the talking meanwhile. Valentine is watching Christopher with interest and irony.

>   MRS WANNOP
>   (*meanwhile*)
> . . . your father was abroad when my husband died. I was thinking of letting go, killing myself somehow . . .

>   CHRISTOPHER
>   (*to Joel*)
> You'll have a rabbit-snare about you or you're not a handyman.

Joel produces a rabbit-snare from his hat and gives it to Christopher.

>   MRS WANNOP
>   (*meanwhile*)
> He came and said, 'Now, Mrs Wannop, what's all this?' He brought champagne and watched me drink half the bottle out of my tooth mug, and took me to lunch . . . and lectured me . . . and got me a job writing on a paper he had shares in . . . He saved my life body and soul.

>   CHRISTOPHER
> So have I. The cart would have gone over backwards.

Christopher starts joining the ends of the girth-strap.

>   MRS WANNOP
> And, one day, your father said, 'Why don't you write a novel on that story you told me?'

Joel is entranced by Christopher.

CHRISTOPHER

Women's work. But it'll take you home.

VALENTINE

It's irritating to have to stand like a stuffed rabbit while a man is acting like . . . a man – setting poor, weak women in their places . . . being good with horses. I suppose you soothe women the same way. I pity your wife.

CHRISTOPHER

This rig isn't for you, Mrs Wannop, a pony and basket-work chaise is the rig for ladies. But she'll do well for tonight's work.

MRS WANNOP

Tonight . . . ?

VALENTINE

Mr Tietjens means Gertie. Don't you?

CHRISTOPHER

Yes. Do you know somewhere Gertie can wait it out? They'll be watching the trains at Ashford Junction.

MRS WANNOP

Oh, you'll help?

CHRISTOPHER

I won't have you incommoded. You've written the only novel since the eighteenth century I haven't had to correct in the margins.

He tests the repaired girth.

There.

MRS WANNOP

Well! But what shall we do with Gertie?

CHRISTOPHER

(*to Joel*)

Bring her over, only don't pull at her mouth, she'll come easy.

Oh, he is a beast – you can't tell when he's not talking about Gertie.

EXT. RIVER-BOAT / RIVER – NIGHT

Moonlight. A moored river-boat, ancient but serviceable, oil-lamplight showing at the windows, smoke drifting from the tin chimney, deck space in the stern, outside the cabin door. Here, Valentine and Gertie hug farewell . . . watched by Christopher atop the Wannop cart. The carriage lamps glow dimly. He sees an Older Woman in shapeless clothes come out of the cabin and take charge of Gertie, her kindly, country voice carrying to him: 'Make you comfy, never fear . . .'

The cart stands in a moonlit wilderness of marshland. A few boats on the water, no houses. Christopher removes one of the two carriage lamps from its socket, feeling the weight. He puts it back. He looks up at the stars through wisps of clouds. The cart moves slightly as Valentine clambers up beside him. She gives him a hunk of bread, a sandwich. She has another for herself, bites into it.

CHRISTOPHER

VALENTINE
She'll be all right. Do you know the stars, Mr Tietjens?

CHRISTOPHER
I despise astronomy.

He gets the mare going.

VALENTINE
I'll remember our way, I know all the lanes and turnings backwards.

CHRISTOPHER
Ah. I wish you'd known them forwards. We must be an hour or two adrift, the lamps won't last us. (*Pause.*) You should know, Miss Wannop, we're being talked about. That will teach you not to speak to strange men on golf courses.

VALENTINE

It doesn't matter. It really doesn't matter. You'll live it down. The only thing that matters is to do good work.

CHRISTOPHER

It's true. I oughtn't to care what those swines say about me, but I do, and I care about what they say about you.

They glance at each other.

EXT. COUNTRY LANE – NIGHT

Moonlight. The mare draws the cart at a steady walk, between high hedges now.

VALENTINE

. . . Oh, say it, why don't you? – with that approved pompous country-gentleman air I'm sure you know . . .

CHRISTOPHER

I'm told I do.

VALENTINE

Your wife tells you? Sorry! Well, say it anyway: you sympathise with our aims, of course, but you disapprove – oh, how you disapprove – of our methods.

CHRISTOPHER

I don't. I approve entirely of your methods, but your aims are idiotic.

VALENTINE

Oh. You're one of those who say the vote won't do women any good. But you couldn't stand it if you knew what I know.

CHRISTOPHER

But I don't, so I can!

VALENTINE

Then you're an ignoble, heartless beast and I shall never beg your pardon for saying so.

70

A silence separates them. Birdsound from the hedge. A nightingale.

VALENTINE
Listen! . . .

A lark somewhere.

CHRISTOPHER
A lark.

VALENTINE
Not that. Listen. It was a nightingale.

A lark somewhere.

CHRISTOPHER
'It was the lark, the herald of the morn,
No nightingale . . . '

VALENTINE
'Believe me, love, it was the nightingale!'

The nightingale again.

VALENTINE
(*triumphant*)
There! He sounds hoarse now – their song changes in June.

They are put into better humour by the sharing of the quotations, which are from Romeo and Juliet in bed.

VALENTINE
I'm not sleepy, and I can't be cross with you, although you were unpardonable just now. I'm loving it all.

CHRISTOPHER
I'm rather loving it, too. (*Pause.*) I don't know if you know, but for some minutes we have been running nearly due west. We ought to be going south-east by a bit south. I suppose you do know this road, Miss Wannop . . .?

VALENTINE
Not a bit! I never drove it in my life.

CHRISTOPHER

We shall probably be out all night, then. Do you mind?

VALENTINE

You mind, but I don't. I *meant* us to be out all night.
(*Pause.*) The road turns back because of the old iron pits.
I haven't the least notion where we are and I don't care.
Here's a signpost, though. Pull up to it.

*Christopher stops level with the signpost, which is a little
below him. He takes a carriage lamp to it, leaning down.*

CHRISTOPHER

We're thirteen miles from Brede, six and a half from . . .
something like Uddlemere. The lamp went out . . . and
there's fog coming in, ground fog. We are on the road to
Uddlemere. Do you mind telling me if you know this
road at all?

VALENTINE

It's Udimore, not Uddlemere.

*Christopher restores the dead lamp in its socket and moves the
mare on a little way.*

CHRISTOPHER

So it is the right road.

VALENTINE

Is it?

CHRISTOPHER

You wouldn't let the mare go another five steps if it
wasn't. You're soft on her.

VALENTINE

Not as soft as you . . . You're not so dreadfully ugly,
really. (*Laughs.*) Don't mind me. I'm so happy! . . . I'm so
happy. The next crossroad is Grandfather's Wantways.
An old gentleman used to sit there called Gran'fer Finn.
Every Tenterden market day, he sold fleed cakes from a
basket to the carts going by. Tenterden market was
abolished in 1845, done in by the repeal of the Corn Laws.

CHRISTOPHER

Why do you suppose I make a collection of obsolescent facts?

VALENTINE

Because you do, you make Toryism out of them. I thought your type was all in museums. You want to be an English country gentleman, spinning principles out of quaintness, and letting the country go to hell – you'll never stir a finger except to say: I told you so.

Ground fog wreathes them.

EXT. GROUND FOG – NIGHT

The cart is stationary. Christopher appears to be sitting chest-deep and alone in a silver ocean. The snuffle of the mare comes from below the surface of the ocean, the reins disappearing into it.

On his right, an immense brilliant horn of moon. Opposite the moon, a few shreds of cloud, pink on the underside, pallid blue sky below the dark purple vault.

VALENTINE
(*out of shot, muffled from a distance*)
I wish you'd make some noise.

Christopher starts singing, flat but loud.

CHRISTOPHER
'D'ye ken John Peel with his coat so grey,
D'ye ken John Peel at the break of day . . .'

He continues to sing, then breaks off.

What are you doing?

Her voice comes muffled by fog.

VALENTINE
Trying the other side.

He stays silent.

VALENTINE
(*further away*)

Where are you?

Christopher starts the song again, lustily, feeling foolish. Looking for her, he leans over where she had descended, putting an arm out to steady himself on the cart's edge.

Suddenly she comes up almost into his arms – face and hair shining with moisture, beads of moisture sparkling all over her as she rises from the ocean like a seal in one movement that for a moment puts their faces close enough to kiss: for both of them, too close for comfort.

Each recovers. Valentine regains her seat.

VALENTINE
We're nearly home – I found a milestone – we're just above Mountby. You can go on now – the Mountby drive is a hundred yards, pull to the left there or the horse will walk right up to the house. And look! The sun!

The sun is just breaking through the silver ocean.

It's the beginning of the longest day, the summer solstice. *Sistere* and *sol*, because the sun seems to stand still. We got through the night . . .

CHRISTOPHER
Miss Wannop . . . Oh – damn Mountby!

She looks into his face for a moment.

VALENTINE
My dear, it couldn't have lasted for ever. But you're a good man. And very clever. You will get through.

A motor noise makes Christopher look. The walking mare is half visible now, her upper half. Ten yards ahead the radiator of a car glides towards them. Christopher shouts and swings the mare to the left. The side of the car hits the mare near the top of her right leg. The mare screams and rears. The car – it is General Campion's car – scrapes along the side of the cart, and then the horse goes hell for leather . . . uphill.

The cart bursts into bright sunlight, up the steep lane between green banks of short grass. The hill tells on their speed. Valentine jumps from the cart, reaching for the bridle, hits the ground running and grasps the bridle, the horse's head nearly lifting her off her feet. Christopher using all his strength brings the animal to a standstill.

VALENTINE
She's cut – blood! – come quick!

CHRISTOPHER
I must hold her a minute. Badly cut?

VALENTINE
Red stocking up to the shoulder nearly.

Christopher gets down and takes over the bridle, covers the mare's eyes with his arm.

CHRISTOPHER
Need your petticoat, half of it for strips . . . You can jump that hedge, I saw you jump.

Valentine scrambles over the hedge. Blood pools at the mare's hoofs.

The car, with crumpled mudguards, returns backwards and stops ten yards behind the cart. General Campion, dressed up like a cockatoo, scarlet and white, plumes and all, scrambles out of the car, walks back, his gold-hilted sword swinging.

CHRISTOPHER
God damn you, go away!

CAMPION
I went past to get you out of Claudine's sight.

CHRISTOPHER
You'll have to pay for the horse.

CAMPION
Why should I?

CHRISTOPHER
For not sounding your horn.

CAMPION

You drove right into my drive. Besides, I did.

CHRISTOPHER

No, you didn't.

A ball of white linen sails over the hedge. Campion picks it up and hands it to Christopher.

CAMPION

What am I to tell my sister? I believe she saw the girl.

CHRISTOPHER

Go away. Say what you like. But you'll pay for her horse –

CAMPION

I'm damned if I will!

CHRISTOPHER

– and send out the horse-ambulance when you go through Rye. There's your sister getting out . . .

Lady Claudine, a black-velvet bolster topped by black feathers, is half out of the closed car. Campion scurries back to her. Christopher unwinds the bundle. Half the petticoat is in strips. Campion bundles Lady Claudine back into the car, and drives it forward and away.

EXT. GRASSY SLOPE – LATER

Valentine sits on the grassy slope, the sun on her. Christopher sits next to her. The mare's injured leg is bandaged up, with some blood showing through the petticoat dressing.

VALENTINE

Why did you try to quarrel with the General?

CHRISTOPHER

You need a quarrel with him, it'll account for Lady Claudine spreading slander.

VALENTINE

You think of everything when most men wouldn't be able to think at all. Tell me about Groby.

CHRISTOPHER

It's older than Protestantism, and Groby Great Tree is the symbol of the Yorkshire Tietjens. It's a big cedar. The crown darkens our topmost windows, and the roots undermine our foundations. So one of them will have to go – house or tree, one day. If I ever take you there . . .

She puts her arm round his.

VALENTINE

My dear, you won't ever take me to Groby.

The moment between them holds.

There's a fly coming.

She removes her arm.

Oh . . . it's the postmaster's boy. It's been perhaps, oh, short acquaintance, but I think you're the splendidest . . .

Christopher stands up and goes to the fly which stops below them. Valentine waits, watching him talk to the Postmaster's Boy, who gives Christopher a telegram. She goes down to join them.

Good morning, Jimmy.

JIMMY

Miss.

CHRISTOPHER

A telegram re-directed to care of Wannop. (*To Jimmy.*) You'll take Miss Wannop home, she's got her mother's breakfast to see to.

Jimmy puts a coin into his pocket. Christopher hands Valentine up to sit by Jimmy, and the little gig moves off.

Christopher watches for a moment. Valentine doesn't look back. He opens the telegram, reads it.

CHRISTOPHER

'Righto'.

He goes to the mare, strokes her jaw.

> . . . damn near forty miles in a night. You've lost a lot
> of blood. I let you down, didn't I, old girl?

*He crumples the telegram and puts his face against the mare's
neck, and everything catches up with him, his large body
racked with dry sobs.*

End of Episode One.

Episode Two

CAST OF EPISODE TWO

in order of appearance

SYLVIA TIETJENS	Rebecca Hall
CHRISTOPHER TIETJENS	Benedict Cumberbatch
MRS SATTERTHWAITE	Janet McTeer
FATHER CONSETT	Ned Dennehy
MARK TIETJENS	Rupert Everett
TIETJENS SENIOR	Alan Howard
EFFIE	Candida Benson
REVEREND (EFFIE'S HUSBAND)	Christopher Bowen
MICHAEL (4 YEARS OLD)	Misha Handley
MARCHANT	Sylvestra Le Touzel
LADY CLAUDINE	Clare Higgins
GENERAL CAMPION	Roger Allam
HULLO CENTRAL (EVIE)	Lucinda Raikes
BOBBIE PELHAM	Anna Skellern
EDWARD WANNOP	Freddie Fox
MRS WANNOP	Miranda Richardson
VALENTINE WANNOP	Adelaide Clemens
SANDBACH	Malcolm Sinclair
WATERHOUSE	Tim McMullan
EDITH DUCHEMIN	Anne-Marie Duff
BISHOP	Geoffrey Palmer
REVEREND DUCHEMIN	Rufus Sewell
CHAPLAIN	Richard Freeman
POTTY PEROWNE	Tom Mison
BROWNLIE	Jamie Parker
COMMISSIONAIRE	Michael Fitzgerald
MARY RICHARDSON	Letty Butler
MACMASTER	Stephen Graham
HOTEL HUSBAND	Gilly Gilchrist
HOTEL WIFE	Kathryn Howden
WESTERSHIRE	Timothy Carlton
GLORVINA	Sasha Waddell
SIR REGINALD	Denis Lawson
MICHELANGELO WOMAN	Siobhan Hewlett
CRITIC AT MACMASTER'S FLAT	Jurgen Delnaet
RUGGLES	Sebastian Armesto

EXT. FORESTS – DAY

Germany, 1912.

A motor bus is arriving at a remote bus stop among pine forests.

EXT. REMOTE BUS STOP – SAME TIME (DAY)

When Christopher gets down with his valise, he sees that Sylvia is waiting for him, standing by Mrs Satterthwaite's Rolls-Royce, a chauffeur at the wheel. Christopher walks up to her.

> CHRISTOPHER
> Sylvia. It was good of you to come yourself.

Her face and her tone are soft with sympathetic concern.

> SYLVIA
> Then you don't know. I'm so sorry, Christopher. There was a telegram from the office, from Macmaster. Your mother died yesterday.

> CHRISTOPHER
> *(pause, he masters himself)*
> I did not expect it quite yet.

INT. ROLLS-ROYCE (MOVING) – DAY

Christopher and Sylvia are being chauffeured away. A glass partition gives them privacy.

> SYLVIA
> I killed your mother. She died of a broken heart because I left you.

CHRISTOPHER

No, she didn't.

SYLVIA

Then, it was because I asked you to take me back.

CHRISTOPHER

My mother died of a medical condition, not a literary convention.

SYLVIA

I suppose it's all over town that I went off with Potty Perowne.

CHRISTOPHER

I told Vincent Macmaster, no one else.

SYLVIA

That was nearish, though. Oh, Christopher, was it awful for you?

CHRISTOPHER

It is thought that you went abroad to look after your mother.

SYLVIA

Oh, but you'll get your own back! – Only, I wish you wouldn't do it by punishing me with your . . . your mealsack Anglican sainthood. Give me Father Consett any day – he called me a harlot and refused to shake my hand till he confessed me.

CHRISTOPHER

Father Consett is here?

SYLVIA

I showed him your telegram. I want him to know that your condition for taking me back is to have your son damned for all eternity.

Sylvia checks her face in the powder box given to her by Gerald Drake. Christopher glances at the box: a ghost of a wince. Sylvia catches the wince.

She sighs as to a child and winds down the window. She tosses the gold box out of the window.

SYLVIA

If it bothers you so much . . .

But Christopher has already rapped on the partition.

EXT. THE ROAD — SAME TIME

The car slows to a halt. Christopher gets out and walks back.

INT. ROLLS-ROYCE (STATIONARY) — DAY

Christopher gets back into the car, closes the door. The car moves. Christopher gives Sylvia the box.

SYLVIA

Thank you. I saw Gerald somewhere and I thought,
'What a brute!' . . . How could I possibly have . . .
Pretty box, though.

EXT. GERMAN SPA HOTEL — DAY

The Rolls-Royce arrives at a secluded former hunting lodge. There are a few patients about, including some perambulated by nurses.

INT. HOTEL SUITE (GERMANY) — DAY

We already know this room, the sitting room of Mrs Satterthwaite's suite. Sylvia tours the paintings of bleeding corpses of hares, pheasants, boar, etc. Tea for four: Father Consett, Sylvia, Christopher and Mrs Satterthwaite, who is examining a thick book of railway timetables.

FATHER CONSETT

The pictures no doubt belong to the hotel's former existence.

SYLVIA

Was it an abattoir?

MRS SATTERTHWAITE

So very sad. In the midst of life . . . Here we are . . . !

Mrs Satterthwaite means the train times.

You're right, there's a night express . . . *wagons lits*,
dining car . . . you'll be at Groby with a day to spare
before the funeral. A public appearance together couldn't
be more timely. My cousin Westershire got wind of
something and I was forced to lie to him. As head of the
family the Duke takes it personally when lives become
untidy.

SYLVIA

I'm not going back to Christopher if I have to be in bed
by nine o'clock, my own bed, I mean, of course.

FATHER CONSETT

This was the last place Christianised in Europe. The old
pagan demons are still at their work and the sooner you
are away from here the sooner you'll not have such
wicked thoughts.

SYLVIA

They are yours, not mine: I meant my own bed as distinct
from my husband's.

*Mrs Satterthwaite puts the timetable aside. She has learned to
ignore their bickering.*

MRS SATTERTHWAITE

Father Consett and I will return at leisure by road. He
has business in Berlin.

That lands on Christopher . . .

CHRISTOPHER

Irish business?

FATHER CONSETT

Now, why would you think that?

CHRISTOPHER
(to Sylvia)

I will not interfere with your social life. (To Mrs
Satterthwaite.) But our old life, with a town house to
keep up and entertain in . . . I could not accept your
generosity as before.

SYLVIA

I'm not going to live in Yorkshire.

CHRISTOPHER

Macmaster knows of a suitable flat across the way from
his rooms in Gray's Inn.

SYLVIA

A flat in Holborn! I couldn't I have imagined anything so
humiliating.

FATHER CONSETT

It's supposed to be a penance, not a reward.

SYLVIA

And you mind your own business!

FATHER CONSETT

Your soul is my business!

MRS SATTERTHWAITE

But, dear boy, the whole world would understand exactly
what we have managed to keep from it.

CHRISTOPHER
(shakes his head)

You would not be the first landowner to give up a house
in town in protest against the new tax. The Duke would
applaud you. I shouldn't wonder if he lends you the
Westershire box at the opera.

SYLVIA

I never heard such bosh! I will be in my room praying for
death, or at least packing for it. Would you send me your
maid?

Sylvia leaves.

I'd better go myself – Sylvia hit my maid with her hairbrush and I've only borrowed her, I don't want to return her damaged.

She leaves. Father Consett fills his empty tea cup with whisky from his flask. He offers the flask to Christopher. Christopher accepts.

FATHER CONSETT

Now then, Christopher . . .

CHRISTOPHER

Yes. But never mind that now.

FATHER CONSETT

Your son is Roman Catholic born, and that's the fact of the matter.

CHRISTOPHER

But Michael will be brought up with my sister's children in an Anglican parsonage, and the facts must jostle as they may.

He toasts in Gaelic.

Slainte. By the way, Father, your Republican friends should know, Germany is looking for a European war and will find a reason for one, probably in the next two years . . . so don't fill your dance card in Berlin.

INT. BEDROOM (GERMANY) – DAY

Sylvia, still smouldering, opens her powder box to examine her face in its mirror. The mirror is cracked across the reflection of her face.

EXT. GROBY – DAY

The full complement of Groby staff – from butler to skivvy, from estate manager to gardener's boy – and the tenantry from miles around, all in their Sunday best, several dozen in all,

*flank the path to the little church where generations of Tietjens
are buried. Mrs Tietjens's coffin is borne along the path in
procession: Tietjens Senior followed by Mark, then Effie and
her husband and two sons; then by Christopher, Sylvia and
Michael, who is five, with his nurse, Marchant, a pace behind;
then by family and friends unknown to us, including a few
gentry.*

*It becomes apparent that Sylvia is the story here. Her Paul
Poiret dress has the latest hobble skirt. Among the honest
cloth coats, sturdy shoes and country complexions, Sylvia's
black silks and feathers and veil are a magnet for fascinated
and disapproving glances from either side.*

*Among the local gentry, a Lady in the procession shares a
moment with her husband.*

> LADY
> It doesn't do . . . stealing the show from her mother-in-
> law . . .

EXT. CHURCHYARD DAY

*The coffin is lowered. Tietjens Senior has precedence of place.
Christopher stands with Michael and Sylvia. Effie, temporarily
separated from Michael's life, directs her censure through her
parson-husband. Mark stares across the grave at Sylvia,
thunderous. Christopher looks down at Michael, squeezes his
shoulder reassuringly.*

Later:

*In broken order, the family mourners depart the churchyard,
Mark in close attendance on his father.*

> TIETJENS
> By God, she looks like a . . .

> MARK
> Yes, sir. But the tyke will be brought up Yorkshire.
> A Tietjens right enough.

EXT. GROBY – DAY

Now the family and the more favoured mourners are retracing their steps towards the great house. Tietjens Senior walks ahead with Mark. Michael has joined his older cousins, Effie's children, friends together. There is a burst of furtive horseplay among them – cap-snatching – and Effie sharply brings them to order. Christopher walks with Sylvia.

Sylvia looks up at the cedar which is the Groby Great Tree.

> SYLVIA
> The cedar will have to come down before it knocks over the house.

> CHRISTOPHER
> Father would sooner take down the house. Young men and maidens have made their marriage vows by the Groby Tree for longer than memory.

> SYLVIA
> (*laughs*)
> 'Maidens'. And their 'swains', do you mean?

Tietjens Senior darts a scowl back at the sound of her quiet laughter.

> CHRISTOPHER
> The old words, yes.

> SYLVIA
> Well, it will have to be your brother . . . or Michael.

Christopher almost imperceptibly flinches at that.

> CHRISTOPHER
> I didn't know how much I miss the boy.

EXT. STABLE, GROBY– DAY

Christopher is introducing a pony to Michael, who is nervous at first but is persuaded to let the pony smell his hand. A Groom, meanwhile, is tightening the saddle girth.

EXT. STABLE, GROBY — DAY

Christopher and Marchant watch Michael aboard the pony, walked by the Groom.

> CHRISTOPHER
> Has he stopped wetting the bed?

> MARCHANT
> Oh yes, sir. It only needed a little firmness.

> CHRISTOPHER
> (*smiles*)
> I remember, Marchie.

EXT. GROBY ENTRANCE FRONT — DAY

Mark comes out of the house. Tietjens Senior stands staring at the landscape. Mark approaches.

> TIETJENS
> Damnable business. Do you want a pipe?

> MARK
> Thanks, no, but I'll join you.

Mark takes out a cigar and lights it. He walks with his father a little way until they come to a rose bush where a clay pipe has been placed by the gardener. Tietjens lights the pipe.

> TIETJENS
> There's a boy I'm putting through Eton. Gilbert Wannop's boy, for old times' sake . . . Eton, then his father's old college. Nothing in writing. But you'll see to it if it comes to that.

> MARK
> Of course, Father.

> TIETJENS
> Will you stay over?

MARK

No. There's a horse I'd like to see in the third race at
York . . . since I'm up here.

Tietjens nods, finding it reasonable.

INT. BACK STAIRS, GROBY — DAY

*Two 'Watermen', giants in leather aprons and gaiters, are
bringing a large cauldron of steaming water up the stairs,
using a pole from which the cauldron is suspended; a tricky
business but they are practised.*

INT. SYLVIA'S DRESSING ROOM, GROBY — DAY

*Hullo Central, Sylvia's maid, holds the door for the cauldron
to enter. There is a freestanding iron tub, positioned beneath
a spout, which delivers cold water, and an attendant pump
handle. The Watermen empty the cauldron into the tub. Hullo
Central thanks them and lets them out. She tests the water, and
pumps some cold water. She takes a thermometer from her
pocket and tests the water's temperature, which is satisfactory.
She knocks at an internal door.*

HULLO CENTRAL

Your bath, mod'm.

Sylvia comes out of her bedroom, smoking, wearing a peignoir.

SYLVIA

Do you know, Evie, there isn't a water closet in the whole
damn house. I got a flea in my ear . . . No ashtrays either
– master's orders!

*She hands her lit cigarette to Hullo Central, takes off the robe,
steps into the tub, takes back the cigarette and lies back in the
water. Hullo Central stands by with a towel. Soap and sponge
are on a stool by the tub.*

SYLVIA

Are they looking after you?

HULLO CENTRAL
(*pleased*)

Yes'm. Mr Jenkins the butler chose me to sit next to him at lunch on account of your turnout! Best in show, Mr Jenkins said, first hobble skirt at Groby! – they've only seen them in the picture papers . . . That's somebody knocking at the bedroom.

SYLVIA

I rang down for a housemaid. I won't have you emptying chamber pots. Here.

She gives Hullo Central the cigarette to dispose of. Hullo Central goes into the bedroom. Sylvia sponges. She hears Christopher's voice.

SYLVIA
(*calls*)

Oh . . . ! It's all right – come in here!

Hullo Central shows Christopher into the dressing room, and disappears, closing the door behind him.

CHRISTOPHER

I'm so sorry . . . I didn't . . .

He turns his back.

Effie and her family are waiting to go home – you'll want to say goodbye to Michael.

SYLVIA

Yes – yes, of course.

She stands and steps out of the bath.

She took the towel.

Christopher looks around helplessly, keeping his eyes averted.

Oh, go away if you can't bear to look! Higher than the beasts, lower than the angels. Stuck between the two in our idiots' Eden. God, I'm so bored with it all, guarding or granting admission to a temple which no decent butcher would give room to on his offal tray – I'd rather be a cow in a field.

She puts on the peignoir without drying herself. Christopher goes to leave.

SYLVIA

Ask someone to bring Michael to me, will you, please?

CHRISTOPHER

I'll bring him.

SYLVIA

You're hurting yourself for no reason, keeping the boy in Yorkshire. I'm going to live chaste, just because I want to. It will be Swedish exercises and retreats – Father Consett knows a convent where you can bring your own maid!

Christopher leaves by the corridor door.

INT. CONVENT ROOM – DAY

Sylvia's fashionable pal, Bobbie, smoking a cigarette in a holder, is looking critically around the barely furnished room, while Sylvia unpacks toiletries from her vanity case and places them on a table, although there is no mirror. Bobbie discovers a cell adjoining, containing only a simple narrow bed. Hullo Central has stripped the bed and is remaking it with voluminous sheets and soft pillows, beneath a small crucifix on the wall.

BOBBIE

A suite!

She returns to the larger room. Two Nuns walk past outside the open door.

But, darling, what does one do here?

She flicks her ash into a holy-water scoop in the wall. Sylvia arranges two or three devotional books on a small shelf. Her mood and tone are quiet, unexpressive.

SYLVIA

I don't think that's an ashtray.

BOBBIE

No, I don't think Johnnie would wear it . . . He'd just
look at me as if I'd gone off to Maidenhead with
someone and we both knew it. (*Pause: overtaken by
melancholy.*) I've had some rotten times at Maidenhead.

*Sylvia regards her steadily. Bobbie looks around for
somewhere to put her cigarette.*

SYLVIA

Evie!

Hullo Central comes in from the adjoining cell.

Would you take Mrs Pelham's cigarette outside and put it
somewhere . . . in the street . . .

HULLO CENTRAL

Yes, mod'm.

Hullo Central goes out with Bobbie's cigarette.

BOBBIE

So she does have a name.

SYLVIA

It was decent of you to come with me, but – I don't know
why – I don't feel my retreat can begin until you go.

BOBBIE

I bet you'll be on the up train tomorrow – not enough
men here.

SYLVIA

If there's one thing that drove me out of London it's the
way I can't enter a room without all the little women
instantly cleaving to their men as though to say, 'Hands
off!' . . . And then hating me all the more when they
realise I have no use for their treasured rubbish. No more
he-and-she for me! I owe it to myself to be fair to
Christopher. The move to Gray's Inn has been a success.

He knows his stuff with furniture and pictures, he'll walk into a saleroom and sniff out what everybody else has missed . . . He just knows everything! Of course, he wants to make me suffer. What man wouldn't? I will make him know his failure by living with him in perfect good humour . . . Then one day, after a whisky or two . . . He must want to sometimes.

BOBBIE

Why, you're soppy about him!

Sylvia receives that like a blow, only for an instant. She turns away.

EXT. LORD'S CRICKET GROUND, 1913 – DAY

A Young Cricketer makes a shot. He is wearing whites and the appropriate cap for an Etonian in the First XI but in some respects – socks, footwear, the tie round his waist – cricket wear is not yet standardised . . . as becomes more apparent as we take in more of the field of play, the two batsmen crossing over for a single, the ball fielded and returned to the bowler via the wicket-keeper. It's the annual Eton versus Harrow match, a fixture of the London Season, played at Lord's in July. There are spectators in the public stand, but also grassy room for spectators on the boundary, and a picnic atmosphere: hampers, champagne, folding chairs. The women are dressed as for a garden party. The men, with few exceptions, display their allegiance in their choice of necktie or blazer. Some of the old men wear 'colours' which are no longer current, including cricket caps in which they look somewhat ridiculous. A tea tent has numerous customers.

There is a pavilion for the players, but some of the batting side visit family parties and friends among the spectators, who include young Etonians and Harrovians interested in each other's sisters. And so on.

Edward Wannop, aged eighteen, is sitting with his sister Valentine, aged twenty-three, and Mrs Wannop. He is not a cricketer. In fact, he believes he is a Communist.

Cricketing action and reaction cut in as and when.

EDWARD

Can somebody tell me why I'm here, watching the ruling
class in its death throes?

MRS WANNOP

Where else would you be?

EDWARD

I would be at a lecture on 'Imperialism, the Last Stage of
Capitalism' at the Working Men's College in Camberwell.

MRS WANNOP

Well, since you're here, why don't you introduce us to
your friends?

EDWARD

Because both my friends are at the lecture.

VALENTINE

Perhaps you should go up to the Working Men's College
in Camberwell in September instead of Oxford.

EDWARD

Some of us are working to destroy the citadels of
privilege from within.

MRS WANNOP

Well, that's lucky for some of us.

*On the field, the ball is struck hard over the boundary – a six –
in the Wannops' direction. Valentine scrambles to her feet,
runs a few yards and takes the catch neatly, then – even more
astonishingly – throws the ball smartly straight into the distant
wicket-keeper's gloves, first bounce. The applause for the six
includes a general amusement for her catch and throw.
Valentine goes back to her place and sits down.*

EDWARD

You beastly little show-off!

*A little way off among the spectators, General Campion spots
Valentine and comes to her.*

CAMPION

Of course it had to be Miss Wannop!

MRS WANNOP

General! Are we on speaking terms? You still owe me fifty pounds for driving your motor into my mare last year.

CAMPION

Tietjens had the rig on the wrong side of the road in the fog, that's what!

Campion's sister, Lady Claudine, and her husband, Paul Sandbach MP, are in Campion's train. Sandbach is not an Etonian, nor a Harrovian.

LADY CLAUDINE

Tietjens?!

FLASHBACK: EXT. ROAD IN FOG — DAWN

The mare rears and screams as the car hits her.

EXT. LORD'S — BACK TO SCENE

LADY CLAUDINE

So it was him! Driving your rig! At daybreak!

She gives Valentine a level look. Sandbach thinks he's seen Valentine before.

VALENTINE

Good morning, Lady Claudine. Actually it was partly the fog and partly that your brother didn't sound his horn. I was a witness.

LADY CLAUDINE

A witness indeed! So was I!

FLASHBACK: EXT. ROAD IN FOG — DAWN

Just before the accident, Valentine looks for a long moment into Christopher's face. The car hits the horse, which rears and screams.

EXT. LORD'S – BACK TO SCENE

> LADY CLAUDINE
> A witness to what, I wouldn't know.

> SANDBACH
> Tell you what, General, you should pay the fifty quid to see the lady take that catch.

> CAMPION
> (*angrily*)
> I'd like to know what you're doing here, anyway!

> SANDBACH
> I'm an honorary Harrovian by marriage. I'll go halves with you – how's that?

> MRS WANNOP
> Oh, please do, Mr Sandbach! I'm quite poor. This is my daughter Valentine, and my son Edward, the Communist.

> EDWARD
> How d'you do? A Marxist Communist, yes.

> SANDBACH
> Quite right – at your age I was a Liberal. What about it, General?

> CAMPION
> Make it twenty pounds each and let bygones.

> MRS WANNOP
> Done.

> LADY CLAUDINE
> (*angrily to Sandbach*)
> Paul, people will think you're betting on the Eton and Harrow match!

Sandbach laughs and hands Mrs Wannop white banknotes from his wallet.

SANDBACH

Pay up, Campion!

INT. TEA TENT (LORD'S) — DAY

In the crowded tent, Mrs Satterthwaite in one of her hats has encountered Mr Waterhouse MP.

MRS SATTERTHWAITE

. . . I've just been complaining about you to Westershire.

WATERHOUSE

Good lord, what have I done?

MRS SATTERTHWAITE

Your lot, I mean. Perhaps you didn't notice, I had to rusticate myself this year to the West Country and miss the Season.

WATERHOUSE

The Season missed you the more.

Waterhouse sees Valentine, with a cup of tea, squeezing her way near him.

MRS SATTERTHWAITE

Soft words butter no parsnips here. My milliner has let go three of her girls, and serve you right if you lose the footman vote, too.

WATERHOUSE

Miss Wannop! Are you Eton or Harrow?

VALENTINE

Eton.

WATERHOUSE

Do you know Mrs Satterthwaite? She is our friend Tietjens's mother-in-law.

MRS SATTERTHWAITE

Oh, is that my fame? (*To Valentine.*) But you know Christopher?

VALENTINE

Hardly, but I did meet Mr Tietjens last year at Rye. I haven't seen him since then. Actually, this tea is for my mother, and I mustn't inflict myself on Mr Waterhouse with my inferior mind and general incapacity for anything much except motherhood, so if you'll excuse me . . .

Valentine smiles and moves on. Mrs Satterthwaite stares. Mr Waterhouse attempts to reply . . .

WATERHOUSE

That's not at all what I . . .

MRS SATTERTHWAITE

My first suffragette!

EXT. OUTSIDE TEA TENT (LORD'S) – DAY

Valentine emerges with her cup of tea. Suddenly she finds Sandbach's face an inch from her own.

SANDBACH

Got it! – You're Tietjens's feminist!

Valentine is shocked by the attack, a combination of loathing and lechery.

SANDBACH

If you're thinking of starting something . . . I've a good mind to smack your bare bottom.

VALENTINE

I'm sure you think of little else.

Valentine moves to get away. Sandbach grasps her elbow and walks her away, speaking into her ear.

SANDBACH

You have a nerve showing your face here. I know you're Tietjens's whore, you're all gasping for it, you militant bitches –

Valentine stops to face him, almost tearful in her fury.

VALENTINE

How dare you say such a thing about a man you're not
fit to serve as a boot-boy?

Sandbach is taken by surprise, in wonder.

SANDBACH

About *him*? Good God, the girl's in love.

FLASHBACK: EXT. FOG – NIGHT

*Slow motion: Valentine surfaces shining through an ocean of
mist almost into Christopher's arms, their faces close enough
to kiss.*

EXT. LORD'S CRICKET GROUND – DAY

The scene is silent.

*Valentine is lost in herself, staring sightlessly at the unseen
cricketers, everybody around her animated by social intercourse
and reactions to the field of play.*

EXT. WANNOP COTTAGE – DAY

Autumn.

*The Wannops, mother and daughter, live very modestly in
a small, unpretentious country cottage in very pretty
surroundings, not especially isolated; in fact, as we know,
walkable from the hamlet containing the Duchemin rectory.*

Nearer, out of shot: the sound of a busy typewriter.

INT. WANNOP COTTAGE – DAY

*Valentine is typing on onion paper from handwritten pages at
a good dining table. The furnishings reflect good taste on
a small budget, with some good pieces long in the family.*

Mrs Wannop's writing desk is in speaking distance. There are books around her, some in use on the desk. She is addressing an envelope.

MRS WANNOP

I wanted to write about the Women's Bill . . . but the editor said, 'My dear Mrs Wannop, our readers already know that the Lords will chuck it back – what they don't have a grasp of is the Balkan crisis.'

VALENTINE

Where did you get all this from?

MRS WANNOP

Christopher Tietjens.

VALENTINE

Oh . . . you spoke to Mr Tietjens.

Valentine is unsettled by that. She types. Mrs Wannop stamps the envelope. Valentine finishes and removes the typed sheet, the fourth.

Is he an expert on the Balkan situation? Oh, I suppose he is . . .

MRS WANNOP

I mean: since his father boodled me into this job because he had shares in the paper, it would reflect badly on him if I made a bish of my article . . .

Mrs Wannop, pen in hand, goes through the typed sheets.

. . . quite apart from losing five guineas a week . . . Do you think it's all right?

VALENTINE

The last sentence is unintentionally comic.

MRS WANNOP

'*The Weekly Intelligencer* has its eye on the Tsar' . . . ? Do you think so? I'll change it, there's time.

VALENTINE
There isn't – I'm expected by Mrs Duchemin . . .

Valentine takes the sheets, puts them in the envelope, seals it.

. . . so it's going in the box! She has need of me today.

Valentine is hurrying to leave, finding hat and coat.

MRS WANNOP
Go, go! We should all do something to help that poor
woman! – Oh, bother it! – I forgot to put in that Serbia
has no more right to demand access to the sea than
Berkshire. Christopher, of course!

VALENTINE
Oh – men waving their spears! As if war were only about
maps! A plague on the Tsar, and the Emperor of Austria
too!

EXT. KENT MARSHES – DAY

Valentine cycles across Kent marshes.

INT. DUCHEMIN RECTORY (STUDY) – DAY

*The Reverend Mr Duchemin has a distinguished visitor, the
Bishop, who has a Chaplain in support to bear witness in case
things get tricky. This is an investigation in the form of a social
call, with an opulent tea tray to help things along.*

BISHOP
. . . I don't wish to come between a country parson –
albeit a gentleman of means, to say the least; and one,
moreover, with a distinguished association with a great
university –

CHAPLAIN
'Breakfast' Duchemin of Cambridge!

BISHOP
– between even such a man! – and the organ of the
parish –

                    DUCHEMIN
Organ!

                    BISHOP
What . . . ?

                    DUCHEMIN
You refer to my organ?

                    BISHOP
No. Yes. I refer to the parish magazine.

                    DUCHEMIN
Of course!

INT. DUCHEMIN DINING ROOM – SAME TIME

Mrs Duchemin has her ear pressed to the door.

EXT. DUCHEMIN RECTORY – DAY

A motor car is waiting outside. Valentine, hurrying, arrives by bicycle and lets herself in by the front door.

INT. DUCHEMIN DINING ROOM – AS BEFORE

Valentine hurries in, removing her hat and coat and throwing them down. Seeing her, Mrs Duchemin removes her ear from the door, agitated by nervous anxiety.

                    MRS DUCHEMIN
I think it's going to be all right . . . He had a cooked breakfast, thank God. It's the fasting that brings it on . . .

INT. DUCHEMIN RECTORY (STUDY) – SAME TIME

                    BISHOP
. . . but the parish magazine is not self-evidently the appropriate platform from which to condemn restrictive female undergarments as being a danger to the sexual health of our women . . .

DUCHEMIN
(*thoughtfully*)

Ah . . . you think so . . .

INT. DUCHEMIN RECTORY (DRAWING ROOM)

MRS DUCHEMIN

You are sweet to come and hold my hand.

VALENTINE

Are you sure you're safe here, Edith?

MRS DUCHEMIN

There's nothing to be done . . . I run a bath and think of
Browning.

VALENTINE

Drowning?

MRS DUCHEMIN

The poet Browning, and the Rossettis . . . Mr Macmaster
has taken to coming down at weekends to talk to my
husband about the poets he knew in his young days. I
would like you to know Mr Macmaster better. He has
opened worlds to me. I have the honour of receiving for
him on what are becoming known as Macmaster's
Fridays! We might find a little role for you, behind the tea
table, what do you think?

VALENTINE

Oh . . . I don't think . . .

MRS DUCHEMIN

Vincent – Mr Macmaster – has rooms in Gray's Inn . . .
across the way from people you know, I think – Mr and
Mrs Tietjens.

VALENTINE
(*shifting*)

Does he . . .?

*The door to the study admits Mr Duchemin, followed by the
Bishop and the Chaplain.*

DUCHEMIN

Ah, my dear, His Grace was most complimentary about
the Lapsang Soochong – he enjoys the aroma of smoke!

BISHOP

Thank you . . . delightful . . .

*Mrs Duchemin accompanies the group into the hall. Valentine
is ignored.*

INT. DUCHEMIN RECTORY, HALL – DAY

MRS DUCHEMIN

I hope your little convocation, should I call it? – was . . .

BISHOP

Oh, indeed, yes . . .

DUCHEMIN

Sweetness and light!

The Chaplain adds his smile and handshake.

CHAPLAIN
(*murmurs*)

All well.

*Duchemin opens the front door. Exchanges of fellowship and
farewell are continued.*

INT. DUCHEMIN DINING ROOM – DAY

*The Bishop's car is heard driving away. Mrs Duchemin almost
swoons with relief as she re-enters.*

MRS DUCHEMIN

Oh . . .! I hadn't dared hope . . .

*Duchemin re-enters, rubbing his hands gleefully. He stops
suddenly and sniffs the air several times.*

MRS DUCHEMIN

What is it, dear?

DUCHEMIN

Sulphur! Can't you smell it? Brimstone!

He cackles. Mrs Duchemin fears the worst.

DUCHEMIN

I smelled him out the minute he walked in!

MRS DUCHEMIN

Who, dear?

DUCHEMIN

Beelzebub! He thought I was taken in!

MRS DUCHEMIN
(*alarmed*)

My dear, you remember Miss Wannop . . . ?

Duchemin ignores that. His eyes glitter.

DUCHEMIN
(*shouts*)

Beelzebub and his minion! Tails tucked up! He takes a
pleasing shape!

*He approaches his wife. Mrs Duchemin becomes an
automaton, frozen, speaking as though nothing untoward is
occurring.*

MRS DUCHEMIN

I have just been telling Miss Wannop about Mr
Macmaster's circle of beautiful intellects . . . devoted
to the higher things, the poetical . . .

*But something is already occurring. Mr Duchemin is
rummaging in her blouse. Mrs Duchemin starts babbling,
otherwise paying no attention. Valentine is paralysed by terror.*

DUCHEMIN

But I was ready for him!

MRS DUCHEMIN

. . . beauty . . . truth . . . the shepherd's pipe, the gem-like
flame, the wine-dark sea . . .

Mr Duchemin's voice rises.

DUCHEMIN

Lord, your servant slept when your handmaiden was taken into bondage by the corset! – but he wakes now!

MRS DUCHEMIN
(*overlapping*)

. . . and, and the soul, the beautiful soul, souls, in harmony at our little gathering of the finer minds, quite the finest really, all the best young writers, artists . . .

As Mr Duchemin continues busy in her bosom, his voice obliterates hers.

DUCHEMIN

I will sound tlhe trumpet, ha ha! – and cast out the Devil's new contraption, the brassiere! – and all the swaddling and strapping that constricts the freely flowing, God-glorifying bounty of belly and breast, of airy buttock and –

But Valentine has recovered her presence of mind. As Duchemin casts out, literally, the ripped chassis of his wife's newfangled French innovation, the 'soutien gorge', Valentine clasps his hand, with a show of eagerness.

VALENTINE

Why, Mr Duchemin, you are one of us!

Duchemin pauses.

VALENTINE

All we new women are united against the corset – it's the very Devil!

She leads Duchemin by the hand towards his study. He is disarmed, restored, docile.

VALENTINE

You must write an article for our paper . . .

Mrs Duchemin collapses to the floor.

EXT. SMALL VILLAGE CHURCH, YORKSHIRE – NIGHT

Midnight on Christmas Eve, and very pretty, the church standing by itself. The windows glow, and a small village choir within is singing.

INT. CHURCH – SAME TIME

Effie, her two sons, Marchant, and Tietjens, with six-year-old Michael asleep on his lap, occupy one of the pews, the choir singing. The Reverend, Effie's husband, is (perhaps) seen officiating.

The singing overlaps the following scene.

EXT. HYDE PARK – DAY

On Rotten Row on a clear crisp December day, Sylvia is out riding, side-saddle. Horse and rider are perfectly turned out. Two riders come towards her: Campion and Perowne. As officers in mufti, their riding clothes are as correct as uniforms. Seeing Sylvia, Campion pulls up, and Perowne, somewhat uneasily, does likewise.

> CAMPION
> Sylvia! Good morning! A merry Christmas!

> SYLVIA
> *(pulling up)*
> Merry Christmas, General.

> CAMPION
> You don't know my ADC, Major Perowne . . .

> SYLVIA
> Of course I do – Merry Christmas, Potty!

> CAMPION
> Potty? You've been keeping that one under your hat, Peter!

Perowne does his best to smile. He mutters his Christmas greeting.

CAMPION
(*barks*)
Look here, I want to talk to that husband of yours –
where is he?

SYLVIA
What has he done?

CAMPION
Never you mind. Just tell him that the War Office wants
to have the entire Department of Statistics lined up and
shot.

Sylvia laughs and spurs her horse.

SYLVIA
He's in Yorkshire over the New Year.

EXT. WANNOP COTTAGE – DAY

Christmas time. Snow. Heavy hoar frost on the window.

INT. WANNOP COTTAGE – DAY

*Valentine examines an ungaudy Christmas card. She reads the
handwritten message: 'With my warm regards for Christmas
and the New Year. Christopher Tietjens'. And below that:
'Kindly remember me to Miss Wannop, too.'*

Valentine is made thoughtful by it.

EXT. BIG BEN – NIGHT

Exactly midnight. Big Ben strikes. It's 1914.

*Fireworks. Boats and barges on the Thames sound their horns
and hooters (sound only). Church bells.*

INT. LOUCHE CLUB – NIGHT

*Posh people rowdily see the New Year in, exchanging kisses,
wearing paper hats, garlanded in coloured streamers. Close on*

Sylvia sitting in low spirits. An unscrupulous young toff, Brownlie, pulls at her arm, wanting her to dance. She shrugs him off. Brownlie in turn is pulled by a female hand out of frame. Brownlie dances. Sylvia sits alone.

INT. VICARAGE – NIGHT

It is still 'midnight'. A long-case clock is striking the hour. There is a modest amount of Christmas decoration. There is a coal fire, and a couple of oil lamps. On the table there is a large, just-started many-pieces jigsaw puzzle. Effie and the Reverend are sitting by the fire. Marchant is sitting on a settle. The clock ceases to strike. There is a bold, formal knocking at the front door. Effie goes to open it. Christopher is there, holding a lump of coal and a loaf.

>   EFFIE
> Enter, sir, and welcome!

>   CHRISTOPHER
> A warm hearth and food on the table!

Effie takes the coal and the loaf, and receives a cheek-kiss. Christopher comes in, closes the door.

>   MARCHANT
> You went outside without your coat, Mr Christopher! What will I do with you?

Effie puts the coal in the scuttle. Christopher shakes hands with the Reverend, and kisses Marchant, 'Happy New Year!' Effie kisses her husband and they each shake hands with Marchant, who bobs fractionally, confused by all this egalitarianism. 'Happy New Year!' is wished inter omnia. Christopher reclaims a glass of whisky.

>   MARCHANT
> It's up the stairs to Bedfordshire for me! Good night, sir . . . Goodnight . . .

Christopher broods over the jigsaw for a moment, picks up a piece.

CHRISTOPHER

I'll go back to town tomorrow . . . to face the
warmongers.

EFFIE

Are they after your blood?

CHRISTOPHER
(*laughs*)
Oh, I have no fears about that. I only did the sums.
Nearly half our export trade is with the Continent; its
disruption would cost us more than the military expense
of fighting a war, yet no one was counting it in.

REVEREND

All the sabre-rattling over the Balkans . . . it seems rather
remote. Do you think there will be war?

CHRISTOPHER

If Germany puts if off much longer, Russia will have
enough railway to put her army on the frontier in twenty
days . . . so the Germans are in a panic, because they
need twice that long to beat the French and they don't
want to be fighting on two fronts.

REVEREND

Goodness, the things you chaps in London know . . .

CHRISTOPHER

France would have to declare war on Germany – that's
what the French-Russian pact is for. Then we'll have
twenty-four hours to decide whether to go in or stay out.
At school they'll tell our sons how the bugles sounded
across the counties to save the best of everything there is .
. . They won't tell them we're a nation of robbers, reivers,
pirates and swindlers. No country in the world trusts us
now.

*Christopher places a piece of the jigsaw, which is developing
into a colourful picture of Trafalgar Square and the National
Gallery.*

EXT. GRAY'S INN – DAY/DAWN

*Brownlie motors Sylvia to her door. He would like to be
invited in. Before he manages to say anything, Sylvia leaves the
car with the briefest of thanks and enters the building, using
her latchkey.*

INT. GRAY'S INN FLAT, DRAWING ROOM – DAWN

*Our first sight of this room . . . Her spirits lowered, Sylvia
enters the grey light of the drawing room. This drawing room
is very large, with eighteenth-century pieces, mirrors, sconces,
paintings, bookcase, etc. . . . The effect is uncrowded,
unpretentious and beautiful.*

*The old windows of the Inns of Court are large with thin
divisions between old glass panes. The walls are white. Sylvia
leaves the room.*

INT. GRAY'S INN FLAT, SYLVIA'S BEDROOM – DAWN

*Entering, Sylvia sees at once that there is a light in the adjoining
dressing room. Her heart lifts.*

> SYLVIA
> Christopher . . . ?

Hullo Central, asleep in a chair, wakes up, stands up.

> HULLO CENTRAL
> I hope you had a lovely evening, mod'm. Happy New
> Year.

> SYLVIA
> (*crossly*)
> What are you doing, waiting up? Go to bed. (*Contrite.*)
> Oh . . . well, now you're here . . .

*She turns her back for Hullo Central to undo the clasp of her
necklace, at the same time kicking off her shoes and letting her
dress fall to her feet. Hullo Central picks up the shoes
and dress.*

EXT. NATIONAL GALLERY – DAY

A small group of Suffragette Leafleteers, caught in the rain, mostly without umbrellas, run into the shelter of the portico, laughing, in good humour. A couple of them carry placards: SHAME ON THE LORDS!

Valentine is among them. She hands a leaflet to a couple of bystanders.

> VALENTINE
> Thank you – stand up for democracy!

A Commissionaire puts in an appearance.

> COMMISSIONAIRE
> You can't do that here, ladies. Be off with you now.

> VALENTINE
> It's open to the public and we're the public!

She nips around him and enters the Gallery. Her friends make to follow, along with the 'public'.

> COMMISSIONAIRE
> No, you don't!

INT. NATIONAL GALLERY – DAY

Valentine, alone, at unobtrusive speed, enters one of the rooms deep inside the building. She has eluded interception.

One painting seems to draw and hold attention. Several men have paused in front of it. Valentine makes an angle to get a view. In between the backs of male visitors she sees naked flesh. She approaches and makes a view for herself. The painting is the Venus by Velázquez, the 'Rokeby Venus'. The painting is nearly six feet wide, showing Venus reclining full-length and naked, from the back.

Valentine notices a Woman approaching the painting. The Woman wears a long jacket, buttoned up to its collar, a matching long skirt, a wide-brimmed straw hat, a long scarf. Her lips are set grimly. Her name is known to history: Mary

Richardson. She suddenly rounds on two or three men in front of the painting.

WOMAN

What are you gawping at?!

The Woman takes a meat cleaver from her handbag and violently attacks the canvas, slashing at it, cutting it several times, making cuts on the bare back and shoulders of the image. Valentine cries out. Before she can move, others have rushed to overpower the Woman.

INT. MAYFAIR ART GALLERY – DAY

A post-Impressionist nude, artfully disintegrated. A number of well-dressed society types populate the fashionable gallery.

One of them is Brownlie. He is waiting for someone, meanwhile wrinkling his nose at the pictures. He looks at his pocket watch and takes a leaflet-catalogue from a table, giving a bored glance at its title: 'Post-Impressionists, 1914'.

Sylvia enters the gallery and pauses, looking for Brownlie. A Mayfair Wife takes one look at her and moves to establish ownership of her Mayfair Husband. The man knows Sylvia and prepares a smile. Sylvia spots Brownlie and moves forward past the couple as though they were invisible. The Mayfair Wife stares after Sylvia resentfully.

SYLVIA

There you are at last, Brownie.

She calls him 'Brownie' as a familiarity.

BROWNLIE

Dash it, Sylvia, I don't know what you mean – I've been waiting ages. I said let's meet at the Ritz.

SYLVIA

Well, it's near the Ritz. Don't sulk or I'll be sorry I came at all. What should I look at?

BROWNLIE

I don't much care for any of them . . . *Well* past, if you ask me!

Sylvia ignores him, moving along the nearest pictures. He is determined to save his witticism.

BROWNLIE

Past Impressionism, you see. They're called Past-Impressionists.

SYLVIA

You stay with the banking, Brownie, that's what I advise.

BROWNLIE
(*checking his catalogue*)
Aren't they?

SYLVIA

I might buy one to annoy Christopher.

BROWNLIE

I'm all for that. I'll buy it for you if you stop being so cruel to me.

Sylvia considers a small Gauguin nude.

INT. GRAY'S INN FLAT – NIGHT

Christopher, holding a whisky, is looking carefully at a small painting propped up on a chair in front of his own armchair.

CHRISTOPHER

Yes. Yes. Where did you find it?

SYLVIA

In Dover Street.

Sylvia is dressed for bed. She looks like a bride, her hair down. She comes to look at the picture, her skin glowing, her silk-satin gown shimmering and alive. We see the picture now, an eighteenth-century watercolour landscape.

CHRISTOPHER

I've no doubt it's young Tom Girtin on one of his
topographical tours in the 1790s. You must have it in
your bedroom.

SYLVIA
(*laughs*)

Now I'm hurt.

CHRISTOPHER

Oh . . .! No! I like it very much! The breakfast room,
then . . .

SYLVIA

Yes, perhaps. I'll leave it for you. Goodnight.

She moves away. He could stop her.

CHRISTOPHER

Goodnight.

He drinks his whisky.

EXT. GRAY'S INN – DAY

*It's early summer 1914, evening light. Christopher and
Macmaster are in office uniform, with top hats and furled
umbrellas. Walking home.*

CHRISTOPHER

You would marry Mrs Duchemin, of course, if she were
free.

MACMASTER

Yes.

CHRISTOPHER

Why doesn't she have her husband certified?

MACMASTER

Well . . . she's loyal. Do you find that contradictory?

CHRISTOPHER

No. I don't. But – no disrespect – a better reason is that
the Lunacy Commissioners would hold the purse-strings.

MACMASTER

Yes.

CHRISTOPHER

Whereas, as things are . . .

MACMASTER

(*becoming agitated*)

I'm asking your advice. Suppose she *lent* me the money.
It's only a thousand or two! I want to live in a manner . . .
worthy of Edith. Naturally. (*Pause.*) Chrissie, it's only
timing – the money will all come to her in the end!
What's the difference?

CHRISTOPHER

None, except as to how you are perceived as a gentleman.
Don't touch Duchemin's money. I'll give you what you
need.

MACMASTER

Chrissie . . .

CHRISTOPHER

It's of no consequence. Some funds came to me from my
mother, rather a lot by my standard.

MACMASTER

Chrissie . . . it would be a loan!

CHRISTOPHER

I'm afraid I never lend money.

MACMASTER

I won't take it otherwise!

CHRISTOPHER

Think of it as you wish. Come in, I'll write you a cheque.

*They walk towards Christopher's doorway. A gleaming car,
empty, is parked outside.*

Sylvia is going to the opera and supper with some great
nobs . . .

INT. GRAY'S INN STAIRCASE – DAY

Sylvia, dressed magnificently, is coming down the stairs with Brownlie, who is in formal evening wear.

> BROWNLIE
> Let's cut out early and go dancing.

> SYLVIA
> Can't, I have a rendezvous.

> BROWNLIE
> Dash it, Sylvia – who with?

Christopher and Macmaster enter from outside.

> SYLVIA
> (*pleased*)
> Christopher! You'll come and take me home from the Duke's?

> CHRISTOPHER
> Of course.

He nods at Brownlie, who greets him civilly: 'Tietjens . . .'

> CHRISTOPHER
> You know Macmaster?

Macmaster goggles at Sylvia's glamour. With bare acknowledge-ment, Sylvia and Brownlie hurry out to the car. Christopher and Macmaster mount the stairs.

INT. GRAY'S INN FLAT – DAY

Christopher is at a desk, blotting a cheque. Macmaster is sitting with a whisky. Christopher gives Macmaster the cheque and returns to his own whisky.

> MACMASTER
> Thank you, Chrissie. I'm about to be handing out
> sums of money, too, small sums from the Royal Literary
> Fund – it seems some poor beggar has to supervise

the disbursements . . . and the King's Goldstick-of-the-Bedchamber or somesuch liked my little book on Browning.

CHRISTOPHER

Congratulations. You'll be in the honours list soon enough.

MACMASTER
(anxiously)

Do you think so? I wish you'd come to one of my Fridays, Chrissie.

CHRISTOPHER

I wouldn't want to be rude to your aesthetes.

Macmaster finishes his whisky and stands up.

MACMASTER

You know I'm taking August in Scotland this year . . . ?

He's not quite himself about it. Christopher intuits the reason but only nods equably, for the moment.

What about you?

CHRISTOPHER

Sylvia accepted to join the Duke's house party at his place in Northumbria . . .

MACMASTER

Do you remember telling me once – two years ago at Rye – we' d be at war about the time the grouse-shooting began in 1914? (Laughs.) Time's nearly up!

CHRISTOPHER
(drily)

Yes, I'm afraid so. Make the most of Scotland. And do be circumspect. I know what it is that makes a man want to get away with a woman he likes, but that desire, which is to be allowed to finish his conversations with her, must be resisted.

MACMASTER
(*laughs*)
Oh, Chrissie . . . What you know!

EXT. COUNTRY HOTEL (SCOTLAND) – DAY

A 'small' car drives up to the hotel . . . which is a small hotel on a loch, with a lawn sloping down to the water, where there is a jetty. Macmaster parks, gets out, and opens the passenger door for Mrs Duchemin.

INT. HOTEL, HALL – DAY

The hotel is run by a husband and wife. The Wife is behind 'the desk'. The Husband has watched the arrival from the window.

HUSBAND
. . . opened the car door for the lady-wife, I don't think!

Macmaster enters with two heavy suitcases. The Husband goes to his aid.

WIFE
Oh . . . Mr and Mrs Macmaster, is it? Welcome!

EXT. HOTEL – DAY

Mrs Duchemin has elected to keep out of the way during the business of registering. She is very nervous. She acts out an interest in her surroundings.

INT. HOTEL, HALL – DAY

Macmaster signs the book.

WIFE
Will you be wanting early morning tea?

MACMASTER
N'yes . . . yes . . . thank you.

Mrs Duchemin enters looking everywhere and nowhere.

MACMASTER

Here we are, my dear!

WIFE

And a newspaper? There's an Edinburgh paper on the table . . .

Mrs Duchemin picks up the paper.

INT. BEDROOM, HOTEL – DAY

The Husband leads the way into a front room.

Very pleasing. Macmaster and Mrs Duchemin are pleased.

HUSBAND

View of the loch . . .

Mrs Duchemin views the loch with enthusiasm.

HUSBAND

Are you a fishing man, Mr Macmaster?

MACMASTER

No! – golf is my game!

HUSBAND

Ah! Where's your clubs?

Macmaster's mind goes blank.

MRS DUCHEMIN

In the car!

HUSBAND
(*leaving*)

You'll let Mrs Mackenzie know if you need anything.

He shuts the door.

Mrs Duchemin is in a panic, keeping her voice low.

MRS DUCHEMIN

They know! They know!

She flings away the newspaper, which has suffered considerable damage in her clutches.

MACMASTER

Of course they don't. Darling, darling, it's all right.

Macmaster hushes her lovingly. Mrs Duchemin suddenly changes tack.

MRS DUCHEMIN

I don't care! I simply don't care. Who are they? They aren't anybody! This is what we've dreamed of – to be away together . . .

She kisses him with passion.

Lock the door!

Macmaster doesn't need a second invitation. With the door locked, he is all over her.

No, no, don't mess up the bed!

She drags him to the floor. Within a few moments her features are distorting in the heat of passion . . . Her outstretched hand grips and tears and crumples the discarded 'Edinburgh paper', which, shredding in her fingers, reports RUSSIA MOBILISES HER ARMY.

EXT. MOORS (NORTHUMBRIA) – DAY

A 'house party' of gentry are making an expedition in the form of a walking party: tweeds, cavalry twill, flannels, country boots and shoes, walking sticks, field glasses, a parasol or two, and a couple of happy dogs. A fine August day. The destination is a posh picnic; but at the moment the party are making their way alongside a stream bed among rocks and tussocky grass bounded by bracken and endless heather. One or two or more of the older ladies are not actually walking; they are on fat little ponies.

The people are: Westershire, a heavyweight widower in his sixties, Mrs Satterthwaite, General Campion, Lady Claudine,

Sandbach, Sylvia, Christopher, Glorvina, and a few others we don't need to know.

The dogs come and go, on forays. One of the dogs freezes and points. The Duke lets the dog put up the birds: a brace of grouse whirr away at speed. Campion gives them a right-and-left with his stick.

CAMPION

Won't be long now!

EXT. CLIFF EDGE

The North Sea slaps up against Northumbria. Gulls are wheeling and squealing.

EXT. MOORS – DAY

The house party is comfortably deployed mid-picnic around a natural table of rock, served by a couple of Footmen. The picnic is an affair of considerable administration: hampers, panniers, wine-coolers, ice, rugs, cushions, Thermos flasks, crockery, cutlery, glasses, and a feast of fowls, delicacies in aspic, jellies in moulds, etc., like a picture from Mrs Beeton . . . The estate staff all wear suits of identical tweed unique to the Westershire estates. They have beer and sandwiches by the cart, at a discreet distance.

GLORVINA

. . . no good asking *me*. Bertram says Asquith and Lord Grey never talk about war in Cabinet. Not in front of the children. The Cabinet talks about women . . .

MRS SATTERTHWAITE

Women? Oh . . . women . . .

GLORVINA

Women and Ireland. If there's war the Government will shelve the Home Rule Bill, Bertram did tell me that.

SYLVIA

Mother's priest has turned her Republican.

MRS SATTERTHWAITE

It's only Sylvia pulling the strings of the shower bath.

LADY CLAUDINE

What war, Glorvina? It's not going to be our war.

CAMPION

If it had been us and a tinpot country like Serbia we'd have declared war three weeks ago.

SANDBACH

Exactly. What are the Austrians waiting for?

CHRISTOPHER

For an assurance that Russia won't come in on the Serbian side. Russia is waiting for an assurance that Germany won't come in on the Austrian side.

WESTERSHIRE

There you are – no stomach for a fight. There's not going to be any war. (*To a servant.*) This isn't our own chutney. Get rid of it.

The offending jar of branded chutney is taken away.

Christopher notices that Sylvia has got up and strolled towards the sea.

WESTERSHIRE

Chutney from a shop! What next?

EXT. CLIFF EDGE

Herring gulls are swooping and calling below Sylvia's feet. The gulls are in a panic, some dropping their catches back into the sea. Sylvia sees Christopher coming up to her.

SYLVIA

Why are they all . . . ? What's frightening them? They're all in a panic . . .

CHRISTOPHER

Up there, look.

Sylvia looks up. High above, a bird is circling lazily.

CHRISTOPHER
A fish eagle . . . and not even on duty!

Sylvia stares up, fascinated, pleased.

Listen, Sylvia, they're all in cloud-cuckoo-land. I want to
see Michael before we find ourselves on a train south.

SYLVIA
A fish eagle . . . !

CHRISTOPHER
Germany will attack France through Belgium. Britain is
committed to defend Belgian neutrality . . .

SYLVIA
(*threatens*)
I'm going to jump. (*Staring upward.*) That's what I'd
want to come back as . . . a fish eagle . . .

Christopher looks at her, gives up. He turns back.

She stares upward. The eagle circles.

EXT. LAKE (SCOTLAND) – DAY

*Macmaster is rowing Mrs Duchemin, in holiday spirits,
towards the hotel jetty. She has a parasol. She is proud of him.*

EXT. LAKESIDE (SCOTLAND) – DAY

*Macmaster ships the oars, jumps ashore, secures the boat, and
helps Mrs Duchemin ashore.*

EXT. ON LAND (SCOTLAND) – DAY

*A middle-aged couple are at a tea table on the lawn, the man
under a panama hat, and as yet unknown. Panama Hat's
attention is caught by the lovers' laughter. Macmaster and
Mrs Duchemin advance hand in hand.*

PANAMA HAT

I say . . . isn't that . . .?

Mrs Duchemin notices that Panama Hat wears purple under his coat and a clerical collar . . . Duchemin's Bishop. She lets go of Macmaster's hand like a hot coal. The Bishop stands and raises his hat to her.

BISHOP

Mrs Duchemin . . .

Mrs Duchemin's face betrays the full horror of her ruin and disgrace. She loses her nerve completely and almost runs into the hotel. Macmaster nods to the table and follows her.

INT. HOTEL BEDROOM – DAY

Mrs Duchemin moans, sobs, and screams discreetly. Macmaster has his head in his hands.

MRS DUCHEMIN

We're not leaving here together! You oaf!

MACMASTER

But . . . what . . . how . . . how will you . . .?

MRS DUCHEMIN

You've ruined me!

EXT. HOTEL (SCOTLAND) – EVENING

A local taxi brings Christopher. By the time he has alighted and told the driver to wait, Macmaster has hurried out of the hotel.

MACMASTER

Chrissie! Thank God!

CHRISTOPHER

Your telegram bounced, I was in Yorkshire, seeing Michael. What's happened?

MACMASTER

Edith will tell you on the train. I won't forget today in a
hurry.

CHRISTOPHER

None of us will. Haven't you heard? We're at war with
Germany.

INT. TRAIN COMPARTMENT, SCOTLAND – EVENING

*Christopher helps Mrs Duchemin into her seat in a train
compartment. She is almost in a faint with distress.*

INT. CINEMA

*Edward, now an Oxford undergraduate, is watching a silent
newsreel.*

*Patriotic and jingoistic title cards are interpolated into the
newsreel of the chief actors (Asquith, Grey, Lloyd George,
Sir John French, General Joffre) and of celebrating crowds
outside Buckingham Palace, troops departing with smiles
and waves at the camera . . . 'Home by Christmas!'*

Edward jumps to his feet, shouting.

EDWARD

This is a capitalist war! The German workers have no
quarrel with British workers! We're on the same side
against capital! We can stop this war by refusing to fight!
The imperialist-capitalist ruling class is setting us to kill
our comrades . . .

*He doesn't get far with this before he is drowned out by
catcalls, jeers, insults . . . and finally small missiles. Then he
is attacked physically.*

INT. RAILWAY STATION (LONDON)

*Wounded and blinded soldiers are arriving home, ministered
to by Red Cross nurses, stretcher-bearers, etc.*

INT. WANNOP HOUSE – DAY

An unhappy meal for three has turned into a shouting match between Mrs Wannop and Edward, with Valentine a silent, suffering witness.

MRS WANNOP
. . . Oh God, give me the strength to strangle the Kaiser with my bare hands – I'd flay him alive – I'd torture him to death –!

EDWARD
You innocent! – it's the soldiers who betrayed the cause –

Edward starts to cry with rage.

Class traitors! – and the German socialists too! – Voting for war like lickspittle lackeys . . .

VALENTINE
Stop it – stop it –

EDWARD
I hope they die with blood spouting out of their lungs.

Valentine puts her hands over her ears. The phone starts ringing.

VALENTINE
I thought you were a pacifist!

EDWARD
Yes – I refuse to fight, but let the guilty get what they deserve.

Valentine answers the phone.

MRS WANNOP
You're simply a coward – a lily-livered –

EDWARD
As for you, I hope both sides rape every woman who –

Mrs Wannop throws her lunch at him. He throws his lunch at her. Valentine shouts into the phone.

VALENTINE

Edith . . .? What . . .?

EXT. KENT COUNTRYSIDE – DAY

High summer. Valentine cycles past the White Horse.

EXT. DUCHEMIN RECTORY – DAY

Mrs Duchemin seems not to have slept for a week.

MRS DUCHEMIN

I thought of you because . . . because you're mixed in
with the kind of women who . . . who . . .

Valentine is listening with anxious eager concern.

VALENTINE

What is it? What can I do?

MRS DUCHEMIN

How do you get rid of a baby?

Valentine is nonplussed.

VALENTINE

But . . . you don't mean you? Mr Duchemin has – hasn't
he? – Mr Duchemin . . .

MRS DUCHEMIN

Duchemin has been in the asylum for months, and I'm
caught – (*viciously*) because that little jumped-up son of
an Edinburgh fishwife didn't know his business better
than to . . .

Mrs Duchemin moans and sobs.

VALENTINE
(*amazed*)

You mean you and Mr Macmaster? I never dreamt . . .

MRS DUCHEMIN
(*enraged*)

What did you think we were doing? – Comparing our
beautiful souls?

VALENTINE

Well . . . yes! That *is* what I thought. And poetry! Oh,
Edith! – your prince, your chevalier!

MRS DUCHEMIN

That guttersnipe, shooting off like a tomcat in heat –

VALENTINE
(*agonised*)

Don't, Edith!

MRS DUCHEMIN

I know when it was.

VALENTINE

I suppose you must. (*But puzzled.*) When what was?

Mrs Duchemin stares at her.

MRS DUCHEMIN

Valentine, do you know how babies are made?

VALENTINE

Of course I do! . . . Only, I thought . . . Do you mean you
can do it without making a baby?

MRS DUCHEMIN

Oh . . . go home, you goose!

She collapses in tears. Valentine starts to cry, too.

VALENTINE

I'm sorry . . . I'm so . . . pointless. Everything is so
horrible, beastliness everywhere, and I live like an ant,
but I thought at least there was you, living for love –
someone rising clear above the muck for me, reaching for
beautiful things, talking about art and poetry with your
brilliant friends . . . and loving . . . being loved . . . and
now there's nowhere left and nothing . . .

EXT. GROBY GREAT TREE – DAY

*Against a threatening sky, the great cedar's branches creak and
stir in the wind. Among the small objects hanging down or*

fixed to the trunk are a few evoking the war – bullet casings, photographs of boys in uniform, a soldier's cap-badge.

INT. SIR REGINALD'S OFFICE (WHITEHALL) – DAY

Sir Reginald smiles encouragingly across his desk at Christopher who is glancing through a file.

> SIR REGINALD
>
> The French are saying we're not pulling our weight. The Prime Minister wishes to show that when measured against the respective populations of single men of fighting age, and suchlike, our contribution compares very favourably with the French.

> CHRISTOPHER
>
> Does it? This document lumps in seventy-two battalions of Kitchener's Volunteers, who aren't on the Western Front because they're still in training without half their kit.

> SIR REGINALD
>
> That's a million men under arms committed to the fight!

> CHRISTOPHER
>
> This is all about who's in charge of strategy, I suppose.

> SIR REGINALD
>
> Our masters take the view that the Western Front must be under dual command, not, repeat not, under a *single* command, which would mean *French* command, obviously.

> CHRISTOPHER
> (*disingenuously*)
> Why would it mean that, sir, obviously?

> SIR REGINALD
>
> Lord, I thought you were supposed to be clever. Because the French army is ten times the size of the British army! Because the war is being fought on *French* soil, not British soil! Because –

He realises what he has got himself into.

Now look here, Tietjens, I took you for a sound man.
The Department exists to show that just as there are
different ways to put things in words, there are different
ways to put things in numbers!

Christopher puts the file on the desk.

CHRISTOPHER
I detest and despise the work I am asked to do in the
Department – whose purpose seems to be to turn
statistics into sophistry, and vice versa. I am resigning.
Good morning.

Sir Reginald, dumbstruck, recovers.

SIR REGINALD
Resigning? Don't you want to be a man of influence?

CHRISTOPHER
No. I'd rather be cannon fodder.

EXT. WHITEHALL/WAR OFFICE – DAY

*Evidence of a state of war: sentries, military traffic, officers in
uniform passing in and out. Christopher, top-hatted in full
office fig, shows a pass to a sentry on his way in.*

INT. CAMPION'S OFFICE – DAY

General Campion is dictating to Perowne who takes notes.

CAMPION
. . . after which, the adjutant will stand the battalion at
ease and the band will play 'Land of Hope and Glory' . . .

*In response to Christopher's knock at the open inner door,
Campion waves Christopher inside.*

CAMPION
Sit down, Chrissie, you damned fool. (*To Perowne.*) And
then the adjutant will call out, 'There will be no more
parades.' Then fall out. And so on. Try that on them.

Perowne nods shiftily at Christopher and scuttles out.

> CAMPION
>
> I'm supposed to invent a ceremonial for disbanding the Kitchener battalions.

> CHRISTOPHER
>
> Disbanding?

> CAMPION
>
> We don't want them clogging up the army once the war is over. So don't hitch your wagon to me if you want to see some fighting – you can see where my opinions have got me.

> CHRISTOPHER
>
> The single-command business? That's what did for me at the office.

> CAMPION
> (*angrily*)
>
> But what the hell has it got to do with you? And now you think you'll be some use as a soldier? Have you told Sylvia?

> CHRISTOPHER
>
> Not yet. She'll say the same as you, I suppose.

INT. SYLVIA'S BEDROOM (GRAY'S INN) – DAY

Sylvia is in bed. Christopher, dressed from the office, sits near the bed. Sylvia is half crying and looks unglamorous for the first time.

> SYLVIA
>
> I think you're a fool.

> CHRISTOPHER
>
> The office is going to get me out anyway. Too many black marks against me.

> SYLVIA
>
> Go, then. Add your little bit to the suffering, even if it's only your own. (*Pause.*) I can't sleep in the night now,

because pain is worse in the dark, it spreads into every corner, black like ink, like printer's ink . . . newspapers dripping hate and lies every day . . .

Christopher reaches for her hand.

Don't touch me *now*! – when it's too late . . .

Christopher turns to leave.

CHRISTOPHER
I'm going across to tell Macmaster . . .

SYLVIA
Yes, do. You're such a paragon of honourable behaviour, Christopher, you're the cruellest man I know.

INT. MACMASTER'S FLAT – DAY

Light fading at teatime. A very large, beautiful room. There are perhaps two dozen men and women scattered about in groups, mostly languid, mostly 'arty', but including a few 'properly dressed' men; and mostly under forty. Tea is the refreshment. Joss-sticks burning. Macmaster entertains a group, Mrs Duchemin swans around, and it is clear that a weight has been lifted from their minds since we saw them three or four months earlier.

Two women come and go, talking of Michelangelo.

MICHELANGELO WOMAN
. . . at times like this, one realises that no one has ever, ever captured grief like Michelangelo in his *Pietà* . . .

Mrs Duchemin perches briefly on the arm of a chair occupied by a Critic.

CRITIC
. . . doggerel, with respect, or rather with no respect at all – it's simply doggerel, canine in the comparative case, with the 'L' tacked on for . . . for luck!

MRS DUCHEMIN
Who are we talking about? Whom.

Elsewhere:

MACMASTER

. . . they go about together looking like Stravinsky and Isadora. Unhappily, *she* looks like Stravinsky and *he* looks like Isadora . . .

There is a tea table where we now see Valentine in charge of the pouring.

Macmaster's servant, Ferens, lets Christopher into the room. Valentine sees him. Christopher sees Valentine. Mrs Duchemin doesn't see him.

CHRISTOPHER

Miss Wannop . . .

VALENTINE

Mr Tietjens.

MACMASTER

Tietjens!

Macmaster has spotted him and now dashes to him.

CHRISTOPHER

Hello, Vinnie. I forgot it was Friday. I had something to tell you . . .

Macmaster seizes him delightedly.

MACMASTER

People will be leaving soon.

CHRISTOPHER

Then I'll talk to Miss Wannop meanwhile . . . (*For Valentine's hearing.*) Though she's not pleased to see me.

MACMASTER
(*laughing*)

The war has turned her against men as a sex. First, you must greet Edith.

Macmaster bears Christopher away.

CHRISTOPHER

Is . . . everything all right now?

MACMASTER

What? Oh – yes. The Bishop turned out to be a Christian –
he knew Duchemin was a dangerous lunatic!

*The Michelangelo Woman has Mrs Duchemin to herself for
a moment.*

MICHELANGELO WOMAN

Is your abortionist here? I'd like to kiss her.

MACMASTER
(*showing up*)

Guggums! – Look who's come!

INT. MACMASTER'S FLAT – NIGHT

Later.

*Dark outside, lights low inside, a glow from the fire in the
grate. Christopher sits alone on the fender seat. Almost all the
guests have left. A young couple are engrossed with each other
on the window seat. Macmaster and Mrs Duchemin and a
remaining guest, a 'properly dressed' man, are at a distance,
turning the pages of a folio on a bookstand. The man's name is
Ruggles.*

Christopher walks towards Valentine, who is at her post.

MACMASTER

Oh – Chrissie – come and be introduced . . . This is
Tietjens, the star of the Department.

RUGGLES

Actually, I share rooms with your brother Mark.

CHRISTOPHER

Really? You must be the new lodger.

*He goes over to Valentine, leaving Ruggles furious and
Macmaster embarrassed.*

CHRISTOPHER

Miss Wannop, come over to the fire and tell me why you won't talk to me.

He goes back to his seat on the fender.

Valentine follows Christopher and takes the other corner seat on the fender. The fire-glow is almost the only light reaching Christopher and Valentine.

CHRISTOPHER

What is that smell, do you know?

VALENTINE

Chinese incense sticks.

CHRISTOPHER

Ah. So those were the geniuses. Well, who am I to judge? That man over there isn't a genius, his name's Ruggles – he's something to do with handing out honours at the Palace. Macmaster has got his ear. It's perfectly proper, the only clean way. The British way. (*Pause.*) Well . . . I came to tell Macmaster I'm joining the army.

Valentine stays quiet.

I hope we respect each other. I, at least, tremendously respect you, and hope you respect me.

He looks at her. She won't meet his eye.

You don't respect me? (*Pause.*) I'd have liked you to have said it.

He shifts on the fender as though he might get up.

VALENTINE
(*cries out*)

Oh, what difference would it make to anything when there is all this pain . . . this torture . . . I haven't slept a whole night since . . . I believe pain and fear must be worse at night . . .

The young couple from the window seat have approached.

YOUNG MAN

We're going to leave you to your war talk. For myself
I believe it is one's sole duty to preserve the beauty of
things, all that's preservable, I can't say otherwise.

*The couple leave, pausing only to say goodbye to the three by
the bookstand.*

CHRISTOPHER

I have to tell Macmaster I'm leaving the office. (*Pause.*)
Dear . . .

The word lands indistinctly on Valentine. She looks up.

. . . So queer . . . my wife used almost the exact words
you used . . . not an hour ago, and she too said she
couldn't respect me.

Valentine springs up.

VALENTINE

She didn't mean it. *I* didn't mean it. We have to do
everything we can not to lose our men, don't you see?
Besides, you know you are more useful here.

CHRISTOPHER

They'll never have me back. The sentimentalist must be
stoned to death. He makes everyone uncomfortable.

VALENTINE

You shouldn't be proud of despising your country.

CHRISTOPHER

Oh, don't believe that! I love every field and hedgerow.
The land *is* England, and – once – it was the foundation
of order, before money took over and handed the country
to swindlers and schemers – the Toryism of the pig's
trough.

VALENTINE

Then what is *your* Toryism?

CHRISTOPHER

Duty. Duty and service to above and below. Frugality.

Keeping your word. Honouring the past. Looking after your people, and beggaring yourself if need be before letting duty go hang. If we could have stayed out, I would have gone to fight for France, for agriculture against industry, for the eighteenth century against the twentieth, if you like. I hoped you'd understand me.

VALENTINE

Oh, I understand you! – You're as innocent about yourself as a child. You would have thought all the same things in the eighteenth century.

CHRISTOPHER

Of course I would, and I would have been right! (*Laughs.*) But you do make one collect one's thoughts. Do you remember our ride in the mist, what you said about me? Three years ago. Well, I'm not that man now.

VALENTINE

What? I can't remember.

CHRISTOPHER

I'm not an English country gentleman who'll let the country go to hell and never stir himself except to say, 'I told you so.'

VALENTINE

Yes. I said that. I said you ought to be in a museum. I was so happy, I think I wanted to provoke you into . . . (*she laughs*) bursting out of your glass cabinet.

CHRISTOPHER

It's a choice now between bad and worse. Well, I have a hulking body to throw into the war and nothing much to live for, because what I want, you know I can't have.

VALENTINE

What is it I know?

Each is on the brink of speaking openly, declaring what is unsaid between them. He draws back from the brink.

141

CHRISTOPHER
(*pause*)
What I stand for is gone.

VALENTINE
But to live for? You have something to live for.

CHRISTOPHER
What is that?

Valentine draws back from the brink.

FLASHBACK: EXT. FOG – NIGHT

Slow motion: Valentine surfaces shining through an ocean of mist almost into Christopher's arms, their faces close enough to kiss.

INT. MACMASTER'S FLAT – BACK TO SCENE

Valentine's eyes are closed and leaking tears. It is almost dark by the dying fire.

VALENTINE
(*cries out softly*)
Why didn't you kiss me then? Oh, why didn't you?

She opens her eyes to look at him, but he has gone. She looks up in time to see him closing the door behind him.

INT. CONVENT – NIGHT

Sylvia kneels by her narrow bed, more in thought than in prayer, her eyes open. After a moment she pulls a pillow off the bed and puts it under her knees, and resumes.

INT. GRAY'S INN (BREAKFAST ROOM) – DAY

The painting by Girtin is on a little stand on a side table. Christopher, breakfasting alone, is in khaki, an army officer's uniform.

INT. OPERA BOX – NIGHT

Sylvia, Mrs Satterthwaite and Brownlie occupy the box. The aria they are listening to continues over all the following scenes which are silent.

EXT. WANNOP'S COTTAGE – DAY

Edward, under arrest, is taken away by two Policemen.

INT. BUCKINGHAM PALACE – DAY

From a regal hand, Macmaster, in formal dress, receives a decoration. (He is being made a Companion of the Order of the Bath.)

INT. WANNOP COTTAGE – NIGHT

Valentine and Mrs Wannop are drawing a home-made poster for PEACE NOT WAR. *A stone thrown from outside breaks the window. Valentine jumps up as another stone breaks a window.*

EXT. TRENCH – DAY

Christopher at war . . . walks crouched along a flooded trench in the rain, past crowded soldiers in capes and tin hats.

INT. OPERA BOX – NIGHT

On Sylvia with her thoughts. The aria continues.

EXT. SKY – DAY

The fish eagle circles, high up.

Fade to black.

End of Episode Two.

Episode Three

CAST OF EPISODE THREE

in order of appearance

CHRISTOPHER TIETJENS	Benedict Cumberbatch
SYLVIA TIETJENS	Rebecca Hall
VALENTINE WANNOP	Adelaide Clemens
FOOD EMPORIUM MANAGER	Dominic Coleman
MARK TIETJENS	Rupert Everett
MACMASTER	Stephen Graham
MRS WANNOP	Miranda Richardson
EDITH DUCHEMIN	Anne-Marie Duff
REVEREND DUCHEMIN	Rufus Sewell
MRS SATTERTHWAITE	Janet McTeer
BROWNLIE	Jamie Parker
FATHER CONSETT	Ned Dennehy
GENERAL CAMPION	Roger Allam
LADY CLAUDINE	Clare Higgins
GLORVINA	Sasha Waddell
GENERAL HAGGARD	Ronald Pickup
TIETJENS SENIOR	Alan Howard
RUGGLES	Sebastian Armesto
MEDICAL OFFICER	Jeroen Lenaerts
GERALD DRAKE	Jack Huston
MARIE LEONIE	Lyne Renée
MICHAEL (8 YEARS OLD)	Rudi Goodman
REVEREND (EFFIE'S HUSBAND)	Christopher Bowen
EFFIE	Candida Benson
CRITIC AT MACMASTER'S FLAT	Jurgen Delnaet
GRAND ACTRESS	Hilde Heijnen
MICHELANGELO WOMAN	Siobhan Hewlett
BANK CLERK	George Potts
SANDBACH	Malcolm Sinclair
EDWARD WANNOP	Freddie Fox

INT. PROVISIONS MERCHANT — DAY

London, 1916.

In a high-class, well-patronised food emporium, Sylvia is shopping in Sylvia style, followed around by the frock-coated and devoted Manager. She is dressed for November.

> MANAGER
>
> I took the liberty of keeping back for you some lamb cutlets. Supplies have been . . .

> SYLVIA
> (*a dazzling smile*)
> You're very good to me, Mr Penny.

> MANAGER
> (*reading his pad*)
> So far we have plover's eggs, orange marmalade, a game pie, a pork pie, the strong Cheddar . . .

> SYLVIA
> And, oh, I don't know, a Dundee cake . . .

> MANAGER
> All to go to Gray's Inn with your regular order, Mrs Tietjens?

> SYLVIA
> No, no, to be delivered to Captain Hans von Grunwald-Merks, Alexandra Palace. (*Laughs.*) Yes, I know! – they've turned it into a prisoner-of-war camp for German and Austrian officers.

> MANAGER
> I remember the Captain. Half Moon Street, I believe.

SYLVIA

Isn't it ridiculous? . . . And a tin of toffees . . .

EXT. PROVISIONS MERCHANT – DAY

Sylvia leaves the shop. The pavement and roadway are busy. A two-seater toots at her, with Sylvia's pal Bobbie at the wheel. Bobbie pulls in and waves. Sylvia waves and goes to the car. Before she can open the passenger door, it is opened for her by a very young Staff Officer, one of a pair and both as pleased as puppies. Sylvia is saluted into the passenger seat.

STAFF OFFICER

I say, you're not going to leave us so soon after we've met?

SECOND OFFICER

Not without a rendezvous?

Sylvia won't play, but Bobbie loves it.

BOBBIE

You look divvy in your new uniforms!

She gives them a smile and takes off into the traffic.

SECOND OFFICER

I say, they're on, you know!

STAFF OFFICER

Tally ho, then!

He shouts for a passing taxi.

EXT. LONDON STREET – DAY

Bobbie drives, laughing and looking over her shoulder.

BOBBIE

They're still there.

SYLVIA

You shouldn't tease, Bobbie.

EXT. GRAY'S INN DAY

Bobbie's car arrives at speed at Sylvia's street door.

BOBBIE
Well, that was fun, nearly.

They get out of the car. Sylvia's attention is on two women, Valentine and Edith Duchemin, alighting from a horse cab. Sylvia pauses thoughtfully. Edith and Valentine enter Macmaster's building. Bobbie hasn't stopped talking.

BOBBIE
Do you know what, though? Johnnie got white-feathered, poor thing, so he's going to chuck in the munitions office. He says now women are doing the men's jobs, they might as well do his.

The Officers' taxi appears round the corner with a head out of the window and a shout of 'Tally ho!' Bobbie squeals happily and darts through the door, following Sylvia.

INT. GRAY'S INN – DAY

The women are halfway up the stairs when the Officers burst through the street door, mimicking a hunting horn.

SECOND OFFICER
View! View halloo!

Sylvia turns to them. Her face is coldly contemptuous.

SYLVIA
You will stop where you are!

The Officers stop, their faces falling.

SYLVIA
Do you think it shows a respect for your brother officers fighting and dying at the Front to chase after their wives?

Bobbie adjusts her expression to the new game.

STAFF OFFICER

I say – look here –

SECOND OFFICER

We thought you and your friend . . .

Sylvia towers over them, staring them down, blazing now.

SYLVIA

We are the women of England, steadfast and true. We
stand by our men so that they can go out with stout
hearts to kill the Hun, while young ticks on the General
Staff are doing their doubtless vital war work in the
comfort and safety of home –

SECOND OFFICER
(*almost in tears*)

Oh, I say – dash it all –

SYLVIA

Yes, you may well blub! By God, if you don't leave this
instant, I will find out your names and write to your
mothers! – I will write to *your house-masters*! – your old
school shall know of this –

*It's the coup de grâce. The Officers retreat stumbling down the
stairs, apologising and abject.*

*The moment the street door bangs shut, Sylvia and Bobbie fall
on one another, spluttering with merriment.*

SYLVIA

Oh, it's all such bosh!

EXT. COUNTRYSIDE, RYE (WINTER) – DAY

In picture-book England, Valentine bicycles towards Rye.

EXT. RYE – DAY

*Valentine arrives outside a butcher's shop and dismounts,
taking a string bag out of her bicycle basket.*

INT. BUTCHER'S SHOP — DAY

There is very little meat on show. Two Women customers fall silent on Valentine's entrance. The Butcher, wrapping meat, avoids her eye.

> VALENTINE

Good morning.

Silence.

> WOMAN

You'll have some German sausage put by, Mr Hedges, for them as have a taste for it . . .?

The other Woman snickers.

> BUTCHER
> (*to Valentine*)

There's no call for you to wait, Miss Wannop. I have nothing for you.

> VALENTINE

None of anything? Not a sheep's heart or a piece of liver?

> BUTCHER

That's right. There's not enough for everybody and anybody now. You'll best find somewhere else to fetch your meat.

> WOMAN

You could try in Lewes when you visit your brother, you could do that.

Valentine half leaves in silence, but turns back.

> VALENTINE

My brother is not in Lewes Gaol now, he's in minesweepers because that's saving lives, not taking them. We're not pro-German. We're against this war, and if you knew anything about it, you'd be against it, too.

She leaves the shop.

EXT. WANNOP COTTAGE – DAY

Valentine bicycles home. Her string bag has some vegetables and small packages.

INT. WANNOP COTTAGE – DAY

Dressed for warmth, Valentine and her mother share a lunch of tinned sardines and vegetables.

MRS WANNOP

We should move to London, Valentine, before the butcher is joined by the baker and the candlestick maker. I'll need to be available for the critics and journalists for my novel . . . and you need a job. I'll write to Mr Tietjens, and ask him if he can do something.

VALENTINE
(*emotionally*)

How can Mr Tietjens do anything? And why should he? Don't you think he's got enough to do, murdering German soldiers for no good reason?

MRS WANNOP

I meant his father, of course. 'Mr Tietjens'! Does Christopher call you 'Miss Wannop'?

VALENTINE

What else would he call me? It's you he's pals with.

MRS WANNOP

Well, don't get upset.

VALENTINE

Why shouldn't I? The war has turned decent people into beasts, ordinary people like Mr Hedges the butcher. And your 'Christopher' – who knows damn well we're being lied to every day – just lets his great lump of a body fall into place in the slaughter, to kill until he's killed. It's . . . just being a man, isn't it?

She pushes her plate aside.

You can have my sardines.

MRS WANNOP

No, thank you. (*Pause.*) The *Daily Mail* has asked me to
write ten ways to spot a German spy for three guineas,
and I can't think of any. This is when I miss Christopher.
He'd rattle them off for me, five minutes on the telephone
and a joke on the end . . . Oh, Mrs Duchemin telephoned!
Her husband is being discharged from the asylum.

VALENTINE
(*shocked*)

He can't be. He's dangerous!

MRS WANNOP

Cured. Sane as sixpence. Naturally she didn't sound too
pleased. I suppose it hasn't occurred to you that she's that
little critic's mistress.

VALENTINE

Why do you think that?

MRS WANNOP

If she were not she wouldn't need you to chaperone her
to his flat. (*Pause.*) Do you think 'no sense of humour'
could count as one?

VALENTINE

What?

MRS WANNOP

No sense of humour and a duelling scar – that's two.
No sense of humour, duelling scar, photographing likely
landing places for a German invasion . . . now I'm getting
the idea.

INT. MACMASTER'S FLAT – DAY

Macmaster is at ease with a drink and the Evening News. *He
has acquired a monocle since we last saw him.*

*His servant Ferens appears at his elbow with an envelope on
a salver. Ferens retires. Macmaster opens the envelope. It
contains nothing except a white feather.*

INT. DUCHEMIN RECTORY – DAY

'Mrs Duchemin' is now 'Edith'.

Edith walks up and down in fury. Valentine sits meekly.

> EDITH
>
> Really, the vanity of those people. Self, self, self!

> VALENTINE
>
> What people?

> EDITH
>
> The doctors, of course! Duchemin was perfectly happy in the asylum. *Beautiful* gardens. He wanted for nothing. Now I don't know how I'm going to . . .

> VALENTINE
>
> Yes . . . I see . . .

> EDITH
> (*crossly*)
>
> No, you do not. You've seen Vincent's rooms. It costs money to make the right impression. How am I to account to my husband upstairs?

> VALENTINE
>
> Oh! And how much did you . . .?

> EDITH
>
> A lot. Vincent has a position to keep up now, since he was honoured by His Majesty.

Valentine notices water dripping down a wall.

> EDITH
>
> As a Companion of the Order of the Bath, he has been raised to –

> VALENTINE
>
> Edith, is he in the bath?

> EDITH
>
> You obviously haven't understood a thing.

Valentine jumps up, pointing at the wall, which is reddening as the water flows down it. Edith screams.

INT. DUCHEMIN BATHROOM – DAY

Duchemin is under water in the overflowing bath, and the water is blood-red.

INT. MACMASTER'S FLAT – DAY

Macmaster in high spirits leads the way into the dining room where a little spread of a feast has been laid out.

> MACMASTER
> Ah – the funeral baked meats!

> EDITH
> *(rebuking him)*
> Guggums! I'm in mourning!

Macmaster pops a champagne cork, pecks Edith on the cheek.

> MACMASTER
> I'm sorry, Guggums.

Macmaster pours champagne into three glasses.

> MACMASTER
> *(earnestly to Valentine)*
> But you do see, don't you, that my work is important. As a single man, my position was becoming . . .

> VALENTINE
> Yes . . .

> EDITH
> *(solemn)*
> To my dear husband.

> MACMASTER
> *(ardent)*
> To my wife.

They toast and kiss. Valentine joins in the toast.

VALENTINE
Your marriage is timely, because mother and I are coming
to live in London. I'm going to be games mistress at a
girls' school in Ealing!

Edith is not pleased, but Macmaster gallantly toasts Valentine.

MACMASTER
To games – and mistresses!

*Edith interprets this as a faux pas about Valentine, but is not
displeased.*

EDITH
Guggums! Tactless!

Valentine is bewildered, unsure of what is meant.

EXT. MACMASTER'S FLAT – DAY

Valentine lets herself out, glad to be outside.

INT. GRAY'S INN FLAT – SAME TIME

*Sylvia is at her 'Swedish exercises'. This involves breathing
deeply at an open window in gym kit. Thus, she sees
Valentine, so young, so clean, so trim and shining.*

*Sylvia is suddenly riveted by her. Her hand goes to her St
Anthony medal on a chain round her neck. At that moment,
Valentine's covert glance meets Sylvia's stare. Valentine looks
away in confusion, and hurries off. Sylvia stares after her, half
amused.*

EXT. WATEMAN'S – DAY

1917.

*Wateman's is Mrs Satterthwaite's house in the West Country,
a Georgian mansion with all the trimmings, including well-
kept garden and stables. On a crisp clear January day, Mrs
Satterthwaite, handy with secateurs, is editing shrubs where*

blackened by frost. Father Consett is in conversational attendance.

A Groom leads a beautifully turned-out hunter to the front of the house and waits with the horse.

INT. WATEMAN'S, BEDROOM — DAY

Sylvia, in an impeccable riding outfit, considers herself in a cheval mirror. Her maid, Hullo Central, gives her a couple of squirts with a scent atomiser.

EXT. WATEMAN'S, GARDEN — DAY

> MRS SATTERTHWAITE
> It seems you'll have to entertain Brownlie this morning.

> FATHER CONSETT
> He must entertain himself. A walk with a packed lunch is my plan.

> MRS SATTERTHWAITE
> It's quite wrong of Sylvia to keep her hunter. Every decent animal in the county was taken by the army, so there's no hunting anyway while the war's on. She's making me look unpatriotic. Which I'm not.

> FATHER CONSETT
> Of course you're not, you're as patriotic as meself.

She gives him a glance for that.

> MRS SATTERTHWAITE
> 'England's difficulty is Ireland's opportunity' is what *you* mean.

> FATHER CONSETT
> Tush! There's two battalions of the Irish Volunteers fighting the Germans.

> MRS SATTERTHWAITE
> Yes, and they would have had the harp on their banner if Kitchener hadn't stopped it. If you think helping to beat

159

Germany will give you the six counties with your Home Rule, you don't know your Ulstermen.

FATHER CONSETT

Home Rule is not independence. There's boyos who are like to see it through to the bitter end, I don't doubt.

MRS SATTERTHWAITE

And they'll sup with the Devil himself for the rifles!

Father Consett laughs.

FATHER CONSETT

Patriots all!

INT. BREAKFAST ROOM – DAY

Lord Brownlie – Brownie – is at breakfast, a self-help meal. Sylvia enters breezily. Brownie is sulky. Sylvia goes to help herself from the sideboard.

SYLVIA

Good morning, Brownie. Did you sleep well?

BROWNLIE

No.

SYLVIA

Oh, dear. Are we in a mood today?

BROWNLIE

Why did you lock your door?

SYLVIA

Oh, was that you?

BROWNLIE

Who did you think it was – that Irish thug?

SYLVIA

Well, it's no good talking to you.

BROWNLIE

What did you ask me down for?

SYLVIA

Not to have my doorknob rattled at two in the morning.

BROWNLIE

Sylvia, you know how I feel about you . . .

She brings her breakfast to the table.

SYLVIA

I asked you down because you boodle petrol for your car.
And to make up a four after dinner, and to be pleasant
company for my mother – who, by the way, is not
running a house of assignation.

BROWNLIE

I swear, if you agreed to marry me –

SYLVIA

And – as you've just reminded me – I already have a
husband.

She butters a slice of toast.

BROWNLIE

I mean it, Sylvia. If you promised to divorce and marry
me, I would wait – gladly. I would be patient. It's all your
fault, you know, for being so sweet to me when you want
to be, for giving me hope. Can I hope, my darling? I love
you like . . . Oh, dash it, I wish I were one of those
poetical types.

SYLVIA

Oh, do try. What do you love me like?

BROWNLIE

Like . . . like anything – I love you like anything, Sylvia!

Sylvia meets that, deadpan. Her irony is lost on him.

SYLVIA

You're irresistible. But it's no good. As a Catholic I can't
divorce, and even if I could, Christopher has never given
me any ground.

161

BROWNLIE

I wouldn't be too sure about that.

SYLVIA

But I *am* sure. Christopher is the straightest man I know.
He makes me want to scream.

*She smashes her spoon into her boiled egg. Father Consett
enters ebulliently, rubbing his hands.*

FATHER CONSETT

Ah – look at herself! Penthesilea to the life! Wouldn't you
say so, Lord Brownlie?

SYLVIA

Good morning, Father.

BROWNLIE

Someone in the Bible, is she?

FATHER CONSETT

Not at all, not at all, that would be Bathsheba you're
thinking of.

SYLVIA

I suppose you think that because you're a priest you can
say things I'd horsewhip any other man for.

FATHER CONSETT

There! – Penthesilea, the Queen of the Amazons! Your
mama says you would know the whereabouts of a good
map I recall, showing footpaths and such . . .? Where
would I find that, now?

SYLVIA

In the window seat.

FATHER CONSETT

I'm thinking to have a nice walk to myself this morning.

Father Consett leaves. Brownlie comes to Sylvia.

BROWNLIE

Well, that's not what they say about your husband at the
club!

Sylvia is unimpressed. She finishes her egg.

SYLVIA

And what do they say?

BROWNLIE

Ask Paul Sandbach for one.

SYLVIA

But I'm asking you.

BROWNLIE

Your husband is debauched.

Sylvia laughs, and gets up, leaving.

BROWNLIE
(*following her*)

His pal Macmaster keeps a woman they share right under your nose, if you want to know.

Sylvia snorts with derision.

INT. WATEMAN'S, HALL – SAME TIME

Sylvia takes up a riding crop from a side table and checks her appearance in the mirror above.

BROWNLIE

They were seen on a train, going at it like monkeys . . .

Sylvia is wrong-footed for a moment.

SYLVIA

Who was?

FLASHBACK: INT. TRAIN COMPARTMENT (1908) – DAY

Sylvia's memory.

Sylvia bucking astride Christopher eight years earlier.

INT. WATEMAN'S – BACK TO SCENE

> BROWNLIE
>
> Tietjens and that woman . . . on a train coming down from Scotland.

> SYLVIA
>
> Oh, for heaven's sake! They were seen by a whole crowd of us who'd been at Westershire's.

FLASHBACK: INT. TRAIN (AUGUST 1914) – DAY

Sylvia's memory:

In the corridor of a racketing train, a compartment door with the blind down is suddenly slid open to reveal Christopher and Edith. She is weeping on his shoulder and his arm is around her. Christopher ignores the interruption.

> SYLVIA
> (*voice-over*)
>
> It was the day war was declared, all the shooting parties were hurrying south. Macmaster and Mrs – I forget her name – had been caught out in a hotel in Scotland, and Christopher was rescuing her.

Reverse: the door has been opened by General Campion, who closes the door after a moment in which other startled faces – Sylvia, Lady Claudine, Paul Sandbach – are glimpsed.

INT. WATEMAN'S – BACK TO SCENE

> SYLVIA
>
> He was being gal-lant! So you'd better stop spreading lies about my husband.

EXT. WATEMAN'S, HOUSE – DAY

Sylvia comes out of the door and takes the horse from the Groom, smiling her thanks. She mounts, at home in the saddle. Brownlie comes out of the house, overtakes the walking horse, and grabs the bridle.

BROWNLIE

Then, ask your husband about the Wannop girl – I dare
you!

SYLVIA

I don't know any Wannop, and you're only making it
worse for yourself. Let go.

Sylvia moves her horse. Brownlie holds on.

BROWNLIE

Twenty-three and fresh as paint. Everyone knows Tietjens
has been besotted with her ever since you went off with
Potty Perowne!

*Sylvia, taut with fury, raises her crop to hit him. The crop
descends on her horse's rump and they take off.*

*At the boundary of the garden, Sylvia takes the horse over a
five-barred gate and rides on like the Queen of the Amazons.*

EXT. COUNTRYSIDE – DAY

*Father Consett, holding a very large map folded down, walks
out of some trees, a haversack on his shoulder. The vista which
opens before him includes the English Channel.*

EXT. CLIFFTOP – DAY

*Father Consett sits at a vantage point above the sea. He
munches a sandwich. He lays it aside and reaches into the
haversack for his camera. He takes a photo of the seashore
below him.*

INSERT: *Father Consett being observed through powerful field
glasses.*

REVERSE: *The watcher with field glasses is a Civilian with a
uniformed Policeman next to him, both lying prone.*

INT. CASUALTY CLEARING STATION — FRANCE — NIGHT

The noise of shelling, distant. There is also the sound of moaning and incoherent shouting from a few of the many beds in the makeshift ward. A team of VADs (nurses) are busy in the ward.

Christopher is lying on his back with his eyes open.

A Wounded Man with blood coming through the bandage on his head is shouting 'Get down, get down!'. He gets out of bed, walks to Christopher and starts to strangle him. Orderlies and nurses rush over and pull the man away. Christopher is left with a VAD tidying him up.

> CHRISTOPHER
> Would you mind telling me where I am? And how long I've been here? And . . . what is my name?

A stretcher party hurries into the ward with a nearly dead nurse horribly mutilated by shrapnel. A bomb falls somewhere nearby. The VAD looks at the label tied to Christopher's collar.

EXT. GROBY ESTATE — YORKSHIRE — DAY

Tietjens Senior and General Haggard, guns broken in the crook of their elbows, walk back to the big house, with the dog, carrying three brace of pheasants.

> HAGGARD
> Do you hear from your boy much?

> TIETJENS
> Which one? No, anyway.

> HAGGARD
> Christopher. He's a bit of a rip, is he?

> TIETJENS
> Not that I know. He's liaison officer with the French artillery.

> HAGGARD
> No, he isn't. He went native and was sent back to the lines.

Tietjens grunts with displeasure.

HAGGARD

The French wanted us to send out more of our
Territorials. Kitchener said he needs them here in case the
Germans invade.

TIETJENS

The Germans can't invade if we keep them busy where
they are.

HAGGARD

That's what your son told Kitchener's man.

TIETJENS

Did he? Damn fool . . .!

HAGGARD

Look here – I wouldn't be much of a friend if I didn't
mention it – there's some talk at the club against
your boy. His wife's pro-German, they say . . . and
he's overstretched himself . . . bought a half-share in
'Breakfast' Duchemin's widow and there's a child
somewhere, hers or somebody's . . . A bit of a rip
altogether. Young Brownlie seems to know a lot about it,
I wouldn't know how. Does your boy bank with them?

TIETJENS

Of course he does. Brownlie's are the family bankers.

HAGGARD

Ah.

TIETJENS

I got Jack Westershire to put Christopher up for the club.
I'd have to think about resigning, if . . .

HAGGARD

Steady on.

TIETJENS

If I'd known my eldest wasn't going to sire, I'd have
looked to the young 'un better. I'll let his brother ask
about, see what's what.

INT. MARK'S BEDROOM, THE ALBANY – DAY

Mark Tietjens is shaving at the washstand. He uses a cut-throat. He is in his nightshirt. His servant scoops Mark's loose change from the valet stand and washes it under a tap.

INT. BREAKFAST ROOM, THE ALBANY – DAY

Ruggles, whom we last saw at 'Macmaster's Friday', is having a post-breakfast cigarette over The Times. *He wears formal office dress. Mark comes in, dressed for work, too. They grunt by way of greeting. The Servant enters with Mark's breakfast of bacon and eggs. There is a second copy of* The Times *warming in front of the fire. The Servant folds it and places it by Mark's plate.*

> MARK

Anything in the paper?

> RUGGLES

No. The interesting news is never in the papers. I heard last week that Algy Hyde has sold his wife to General Cranshaw for a commission in the Blues, but you may look in vain in *The Times* . . .

Reaching for the butter, Mark sees that it has a white feather sticking out of it like a quill.

> RUGGLES

It came in my post. We who are doing work of national importance have to put up with the sex-fury of debutantes whose desires can't be accommodated under war-time conditions. Which reminds me – you're up for a 'K', if you want it. Anyone who can transport fifty-four divisions to France without a hitch while never missing a midweek race meeting *deserves* a knighthood, in my opinion.

> MARK

Southern flummery. I suppose I'll have to take it for the Department.

His indifference is genuine. He eats.

Ruggles, you know my young brother Christopher . . .?

RUGGLES
I met him once before he went out. He was insolent.

MARK
Ah. You might pick up what you can about him and let me know.

Ruggles folds The Times *to take with him, and stands up.*

RUGGLES
Glad to.

Mark opens his Times *and scans the war headlines.*

INT. CASUALTY CLEARING STATION – FRANCE – DAY

Christopher is back in uniform and ready to be discharged from the Casualty Clearing Station. Time has passed. He is marked by the experience, but on his feet and functioning. He is being 'signed out' by a Medical Officer, scribbling at his desk. The MO gives Christopher a docket.

MEDICAL OFFICER
First class, one way single to Waterloo – hand this in to the RAMC Duty Officer, he'll take over.

CHRISTOPHER
(*salutes*)
Sir.

INT. GLORVINA'S – DAY

Glorvina, last seen picnicking in Northumbria, is giving tea to Sylvia. Seen from a distance, she dispenses tea like an empress, enthroned under a lantern-roof of stained glass, in a gloomy salon supported by columns.

GLORVINA
The illustrated papers ignore the adulterers I know, the august class of adulterers, but an attractive young wife, constant to her husband, invites gossip when she is seen

here, there and everywhere with this man or that. I sent for you, Sylvia, because you're Roberta's best friend.

SYLVIA

I'm sure Bobbie doesn't . . . but I'll speak to her, of course, Lady Glorvina.

GLORVINA
(*sharply*)

I can speak to my daughter myself. I'm talking about *you*.

SYLVIA

Oh . . .

GLORVINA

I'm so fond of you and Christopher – who, thank God, is safe, I hear, and soon to be home?

SYLVIA

He was not wounded, luckily, only concussed.

GLORVINA

Well, a fresh start, then. I'll give you an address where you can buy hand-knitted socks and mittens to present as your own work to some charity for distribution to our soldiers.

SYLVIA

I'll do nothing of the sort. What an idea!

GLORVINA

The idea, Sylvia, is for you to engage in an act of public patriotism, to offset your exploits with the Esterhazys and Grunwald-Merkses – which have pretty well done for Christopher!

SYLVIA
(*furiously*)

Do you mean to say those unspeakable swine think I'm pro-German because I sent toffees to –

GLORVINA

It's Christopher that suffers. He hasn't got on the way a man of his brilliance should have got on. A friend of his came to see me – Mr Ruggles, he's something about the court – he came to ask me whether something might be done for Christopher. 'It's almost as if Christopher has a black mark against him,' that's how Mr Ruggles put it.

SYLVIA

And I'm the black mark, I suppose!

GLORVINA

Do you know Major Drake?

SYLVIA

Gerald Drake? I used to.

FLASHBACK: INT. HOTEL ROOM (PARIS, 1908) – NIGHT

Sylvia and Drake embrace violently on the floor among wedding preparations.

INT. GLORVINA'S – BACK TO SCENE

SYLVIA

Before my marriage. Why?

GLORVINA

He's an Intelligence Officer. Major Drake told Ruggles he's marked Christopher's file 'Not to be entrusted with confidential work.'

SYLVIA

Christopher is the last decent man in England. How dare they put their knife into him? He's mine!

INT. TRAIN – NIGHT

Christopher is coming home, in a train compartment full of walking wounded.

INT. ALBANY, BREAKFAST ROOM — DAY

Another breakfast, and Ruggles is reporting from a notebook to Mark, who makes notes in a small notebook.

> RUGGLES
> There's an Irish priest caught spying for the enemy – his trial was kept secret . . . Father Consett . . . almost part of the family . . . Let's see . . .

He turns the page.

INT. THE CLUB — NIGHT

In a secluded corner of the dining room, Tietjens Senior and Mark huddle. Mark is consulting his notebook.

> MARK
> . . . on a train coming down from Scotland. Sandbach saw them, so did General Campion . . . Brownlie painted an unpretty picture.

FLASHBACK: INT. TRAIN — NIGHT

False version: Christopher and Edith, in an empty compartment with the blinds drawn, are in pornographic embraces. The door is jerked open . . .

Reverse: Sylvia, Campion, Sandbach and Lady Claudine looking in, caricaturing shock as in a Bateman cartoon.

INT. THE CLUB — AS BEFORE

> MARK
> The money his mother left him must have gone mostly to set her up with Macmaster. God only knows what arrangement they make over her.

Tietjens looks as if he has suffered several hammer blows.

TIETJENS

What else?

MARK

Sylvia's son is probably the result of an affair before her marriage – a man who's a member here.

TIETJENS

Good God.

MARK

I'm sorry to put all this on you, but you want to know, I suppose?

TIETJENS

Go on.

MARK

And then, of course, Christopher took her back after the Perowne business.

TIETJENS

Broke his mother's heart.

MARK

Ruggles says Christopher's willing to sell his wife for money or favours.

TIETJENS

I kept him short – I let him go to the Devil.

MARK

As for his career, he's written off as more or less a French spy. But at least they're our allies. The worser part is, he got mixed up with a young woman, apparently a pacifist suffragette type, pro-German family, Communist brother in gaol for preaching mutiny to the ranks, that sort of thing. You knew her father, dead now, Professor Wannop . . .

TIETJENS

My God . . . Christopher and . . . ?

MARK

At least five people told Ruggles that he gave the girl a bastard before the war.

Tietjens jolts in his chair.

TIETJENS

That's enough.

Mark closes his notebook. Tietjens sits, condemned, thinking for some moments.

TIETJENS

And Groby will go to a papist's child from the wrong side of the blanket. That's bitter, I don't mind saying. We've held Groby in the English Church through twelve reigns, and I let it slip. (*Pause.*) I'll be in the writing room for an hour or so.

MARK

Have you taken a bedroom?

TIETJENS

The midnight train will do well. London was never any good for me.

EXT. LONDON STREET, CLUB LAND – NIGHT

Christopher, in military cap and greatcoat, approaches the steps of the club. He walks heavily, tired, aged.

INT. CLUB – NIGHT

Among coats and hats, deep in the hall, Tietjens and Mark put on their coats.

Christopher enters by the street door. He sees Tietjens and Mark. For a moment Tietjens is aware of Christopher. He turns away. Christopher hesitates, then walks into a side room, leaving the way clear. Tietjens and Mark leave the club.

In the side room Christopher stands by the window watching his father and brother walk away.

INT. SYLVIA'S BEDROOM — EARLY DAY

Sylvia lights a candle and places it. She kneels and prays, with her St Anthony medal to her lips.

EXT. GRAY'S INN — EARLY DAY

Exterior of Gray's Inn.

INT. GRAY'S INN — EARLY DAY

Christopher, in pyjamas, sits on his bed, sleepless.

EXT. GROBY, FIELD — DAY

Tietjens, with a shotgun, walks along the edge of a field, keeping an eye out. He shoots a rabbit. He picks up the rabbit and walks on. He stops halfway along the long overgrown, brambly hedge. With the gun 'broken', he crawls through the hedge until he is out of view. After a few moments there is another gunshot.

EXT. GROBY, FIELD — DAY

Tietjens is lying dead, shot through the heart, with his feet in the hedge, the shotgun lying across his legs, the dead rabbit a little way beyond his head.

INT. CHEZ MARIE-LEONIE, LONDON — EARLY DAY

Mark wakes in a double bed in a room which is not his Albany bedroom. His mistress, Marie-Leonie, a fortyish Frenchwoman, sleeps on. There are early-morning sounds of carts in the street. Mark gets up in his nightshirt and draws the curtains, looks out at the weather. A telephone in the flat starts to ring. Mark is surprised but not alarmed.

INT. SYLVIA'S BEDROOM/DRESSING ROOM, GRAY'S INN –
DAY

Sylvia puts on a robe over her nakedness. Her St Anthony is round her neck. Sylvia walks through the connecting dressing room.

INT. CHRISTOPHER'S BEDROOM

Christopher is still sitting on the bed. Sylvia comes to sit next to him.

> SYLVIA
> Do you mind telling me what actually happened to you?

> CHRISTOPHER
> Something burst near me in the dark. I don't remember what I did. I remember being in the Casualty Clearing Station not knowing my name. Your friends were dropping bombs on the hospital huts.

> SYLVIA
> You might not call them my friends. I still wear my St Anthony to look after you . . . (*She touches the gold disc.*) See?

> CHRISTOPHER
> I beg your pardon. One gets into a loose way of speaking. Then a lot of people carried pieces of a nurse into the hut.

She takes hold of his hand.

> SYLVIA
> Christopher . . .

> CHRISTOPHER
> You cannot conceive the quantity of explosive the armies throw at each other for each man killed! The shells make a continuous noise sometimes like an enormous machine breaking apart. At other times they come whistling towards you in a thoughtful sort of way and then go

crump and the screw-cap flies off, hurtling through the air, screaming. There's a kind of shell which comes with a crescendo like an express train, only faster. Another kind makes a noise like tearing calico, louder and louder. The largest kind of the ones which burst in the air make a double crack, like a wet canvas being shaken out by a giant. Such immense explosions to kill such small, weak animals. (*Pause.*) I have to report to a tin hut on Ealing Common.

SYLVIA

Lie down.

CHRISTOPHER

No, it's true. The War Office now has an outpost at Ealing!

SYLVIA

I don't care.

CHRISTOPHER

I'm to be sent round camp depots to give lectures to soldiers . . .

She would like to make love to him.

She pushes him back down on the pillow letting her robe fall partly open. The St Anthony swings slightly between her breasts, a golden light. But his eyes are closed. So she corrects the robe as she lies down next to him, thoughtful, eyes open.

A telephone starts to ring distantly in the flat. Christopher opens his eyes.

INT. CHEZ MARIE-LEONIE – EARLY DAY

Mark in his nightshirt, holding the phone, listens to the phone ringing in Gray's Inn.

Marie-Leonie, in a dressing gown, brings him a cup of tea. They have received the news of Tietjens's death.

EXT. WANNNOP HOUSE, EALING — DAY

The Wannops have moved to a London suburb, to a very small house in a leafy street of such houses, each a few paces from the pavement and with a small back garden.

A telephone starts to ring faintly in the house.

INT. WANNOP HOUSE, VALENTINE'S BEDROOM — DAY

Valentine is woken by the telephone. It rings a few times and is then answered. Valentine looks at her bedside clock, and gets out of bed. She hears Mrs Wannop cry out. She puts on her dressing gown hurriedly.

INT. WANNOP HOUSE, PARLOUR — DAY

Valentine comes down the stairs and finds Mrs Wannop shaken, putting down the phone in grief. Valentine runs to her and puts her arms round her.

> VALENTINE
>
> Is it Edward?

Mrs Wannop shakes her head. Valentine has a premonition.

> VALENTINE
>
> Mr Tietjens?

> MRS WANNOP
>
> He's dead . . . shot dead.

Valentine lets go of her mother. Showing nothing of the emotion except for the suppression of it, Valentine goes into the adjoining kitchen.

INT. WANNOP HOUSE — KITCHEN — DAY

Valentine fills a kettle and puts it on the gas. She gathers cup, saucers, teapot. Mrs Wannop follows her in, tearful.

> MRS WANNOP
>
> Shot through the heart.

VALENTINE

They *tell* you these things? Who telephoned?

MRS WANNOP

Christopher. Mr Tietjens . . . had some kind of accident, out shooting. Christopher wasn't at Groby, he's just arrived home from France.

Valentine's brain begins to make sense of the news, it takes her a second or two.

MRS WANNOP

He's been blown up, too.

VALENTINE

Who has?

MRS WANNOP

Christopher. But he's all right. I'll be going up for the funeral, of course. That man saved me, you know, after Daddy died.

Mrs Wannop goes out into the backyard, to the 'privy'. Valentine starts shaking so violently, the china she is holding clatters in her hands. She puts it down, her tears flowing now.

VALENTINE

Oh, thank God, thank God.

INT. THE CLUB – DAY

Tietjens has left a letter for Mark: 'Mark Tietjens, Esq.' on the envelope. A Club Porter gives the letter to Mark. Mark opens it.

EXT. GROBY – DAY

The Gardener, holding an open shoebox, collects a clay pipe from a rose bush. He adds it to others in the box, and moves on towards a further rose bush.

EXT. GROBY, NIGHT NURSERY – TWILIGHT

Christopher and Michael sit together on the window seat, in evening light, shadowed by the fronds of the cedar.

> CHRISTOPHER
> Do you see, Michael? He wasn't the man to leave a wounded rabbit the wrong side of a hedge . . .

EXT. GROBY TREE – NIGHT

Small votive objects hang from the lower branches. The lights are on in the house, here and there.

INT. GROBY, DINING ROOM – NIGHT

Family only, dressed for dinner: Mark at the head of an oversize table, Effie and Christopher to his right, Sylvia and the Reverend to his left. They have finished dinner. The butler, Jenkins, places a decanter of port in front of Mark. Mark pours himself some port and pushes the decanter. Sylvia moves the decanter on towards the Reverend.

> MARK
> Anyone from town staying over tomorrow?

> JENKINS
> Only General Campion, sir.

The Reverend, having poured himself a glass, pushes the decanter for Christopher.

> MARK
> The Riding will turn out for the old boy. I'm not expecting much from town. When Grandfather died, half the club came up.

> CHRISTOPHER
> I'd take it kindly if you would include Mrs Wannop in the lunch party.

Sylvia glints at that. Mark nods. Effie looks to Sylvia and stands up to depart. Sylvia follows Effie. The men stand up

Benedict Cumberbatch (Christopher Tietjens) and Adelaide Clemens (Valentine Wannop)

Rebecca Hall (Sylvia Tietjens)

Misha Handley (Michael at four years old) with director Susanna White

Sheila Collings (Miss Fox), Miranda Richardson (Mrs Wannop)
and Michael Mears (Reverend Horsley)

Tessa Parr (Bridget) and Janet McTeer (Mrs Satterthwaite)

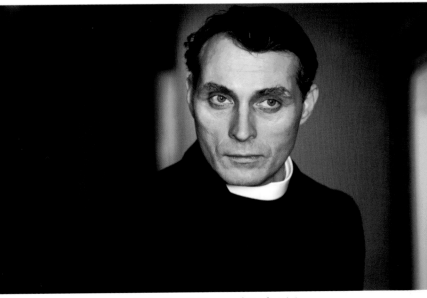

Rufus Sewell (Reverend Duchemin)

Rebecca Hall

Misha Handley and Benedict Cumberbatch

Tom Stoppard and Benedict Cumberbatch

Lucinda Raikes (Hullo Central)

Tom Mison (Potty Perowne)

Tim McMullan (Waterhouse) and Janet McTeer

Stand-off at the golf course

Adelaide Clemens

Sylvestra Le Touzel (Marchant) and Benedict Cumberbatch

Anne-Marie Duff (Edith Duchemin) and Stephen Graham (Macmaster)

Miranda Richardson, Freddie Fox (Edward Wannop) and Adelaide Clemens

Alan Howard (Tietjens Senior) and Rupert Everett (Mark Tietjens)

Rebecca Hall and Benedict Cumberbatch

Ronald Pickup (General Haggard) and Alan Howard

Above: Malcolm Sinclair (Sandbach), Clare Higgins (Lady Claudine), Benedict Cumberbatch and Sasha Waddell (Glorvina). Below: Anna Skellern (Bobbie Pelham)

Steven Robertson (Colonel Bill), Patrick Kennedy (McKechnie), Benedict Cumberbatch, David Dawson (Aranjuez) and William Ellis (Aubrey)

Jack Huston (Gerald Drake)

Roger Allam (General Campion)

Benedict Cumberbatch and Michael Shaeffer (RSM)

Benedict Cumberbatch, Adelaide Clemens and Rebecca Hall

Photographs by Nick Briggs

and sit down again. Mark takes a cigar case from his pocket, lights a cigar.

> MARK
> (*to Jenkins*)

Ashtray.

> REVEREND

Will the inquest be . . . straightforward?

> MARK

Why shouldn't it be? A dozen farmers die the same way every year, dragging a gun through a hedge with the safety off. You'd agree?

Christopher remains eloquently silent. Jenkins returns from the sideboard and places an improvised ashtray.

EXT. EALING STREET – DAY

Springtime.

Christopher, in captain's uniform, comes along the suburban tree-shaded street and approaches the Wannops' door.

INT. WANNOP HOUSE

Mrs Wannop has made a working corner for herself. A small dining table, two chairs, an armchair and an upholstered chaise longue occupy the rest. Christopher is sitting in the armchair.

> CHRISTOPHER

Your new novel is in Hatchard's window. I haven't read it yet. Can't concentrate. I had the stuffing knocked out of me.

> MRS WANNOP

My book won't rescue me from journalism! . . . I have to write an article about war babies and the girls left holding them. 'The shame of our soldiers and sailors.' The trouble is there's no more babies than there were before, so I'm stuck.

CHRISTOPHER

It must be that half the fellows are twice as reckless because they may be killed, and half are twice as conscientious for the same reason.

MRS WANNOP

You've saved me!

CHRISTOPHER
(*laughs*)
My mind must be coming back.

MRS WANNOP

The new book has got me invited to one of Macmaster's tea parties – will you come with me?

CHRISTOPHER

Ah. It is entirely possible that I may not.

The street door bangs and suddenly Valentine in 'school uniform', has joined them, surprised to see Christopher.

VALENTINE

Oh . . . Mr Tietjens.

MRS WANNOP

Valentine, dear –!

VALENTINE

I knew you were back, of course. Mrs Tietjens must be . . . must be so . . .

CHRISTOPHER

Yes. I thought you were at . . .

VALENTINE

Friday is my free afternoon – I'm just home to change for the Macmasters' . . .

CHRISTOPHER

You still pour the tea for Macmaster? I thought that now with your . . .

VALENTINE

Yes, I do. I'm . . . I'm very glad you're . . .

CHRISTOPHER

Yes. Thank you . . . I have to go back to work.

He offers his hand. Valentine shakes hands. With clumsy abruptness, Christopher leaves the house. Mrs Wannop has gone to put a kettle on. Valentine goes past her, through the back door.

EXT. WANNOP BACKYARD – DAY

The backyard is barely big enough to contain the 'privy'. Valentine enters the privy which has a heart-shaped ventilation hole in its wooden door. She closes the door.

INT. WANNOP PRIVY – DAY

Inside, she stands, recovering, doing nothing. In near dark, light from the hole in the door catches her shortness of breath in her features.

The reverse shows a heart-shaped bit of sky.

INT. RESTAURANT – DAY

BROWNLIE

. . . the Groby estate underwrote your husband's private account, you see – if he ever got overdrawn . . .

SYLVIA

What . . .?

Sylvia is being lunched by Brownlie. She waves gaily at Bobbie and Glorvina who are being shown to a table. Glorvina cuts her. Bobbie makes a rueful face.

BROWNLIE

His brother has cancelled the arrangement!

SYLVIA

I don't know what you're . . .

BROWNLIE

It means if your husband goes a shilling into the red, I'll
catch him on the hop.

INT. MACMASTER'S FLAT – DAY

*Valentine is at her post behind silver urns and tea things.
Christopher and Mrs Wannop are among a small group in the
window area. The celebrity of the afternoon, a Grand Actress,
is enthroned near the fire, with Macmaster standing by as chief
courtier. Drawn around them, seated and standing, are
a dozen or more aesthetes, artists, literary types, and a few
society types including a couple of Staff Officers. Edith,
agitated, is trying to be everywhere . . .*

EDITH

Valentine, a cup of tea for Sir Mortimer! . . . Mrs Cumfit,
have you met my little brown bird? . . . Rudi – we're all
so looking forward to your next! . . .

. . . and darting away to break up Mrs Wannop's rival court.

EDITH

. . . Now do come along and hear Miss Delamere telling
us about her triumph as Phèdre in New York . . .

CRITIC

. . . a striking advance, Mrs Wannop, not only on your
last book, but dare I say, on Arnold Bennett's next!

EDITH

You, too, Mr Whipple . . .

*She ignores Mrs Wannop and Christopher. The others trail
after her.*

GRAND ACTRESS

. . . and they kept calling it 'Fedder' – 'I saw your fedder,
Miss Delamere!' It sounded slightly improper.

WOMAN

You were so brave to go!

Edith stops as though electrocuted.

Sylvia has appeared in the doorway, looking about with a noticeable lack of interest. From a bowl near the door, she scoops up a handful of visiting cards, flicks through them looking vaguely puzzled, and lets them fall back into the bowl. The Actress abandons her reply – 'One must for one's art . . .' – alerted by Macmaster's convulsive jump as his eyeglass falls. There is a general turning around. The Staff Officers rise tentatively. A newly married Wife moves to her Husband and holds his hand.

Sylvia's eyes rest a moment on Valentine, who gazes at her in awe. Before Valentine can speak, Christopher has walked straight to Sylvia, and he takes her straight to Edith, expressionless. Valentine watches Sylvia wavering along in a many-pleated skirt which rests smooth on the hips and swings above the ankles. Sylvia greets Edith faintly, offers a languid hand to Macmaster, and ignores the Actress, whom Edith tries to introduce.

Mrs Wannop is alone by the window. Valentine sees Sylvia murmur a question to Christopher, then walk to Mrs Wannop, followed by a wedge of followers, host, hostess and goggling guests. The Grand Actress looks about, bewildered by her isolation.

Sylvia stops a yard from Mrs Wannop and holds out her hand.

SYLVIA

You're Mrs Wannop! The great writer! I'm Christopher Tietjens's wife.

Mrs Wannop puts her hands on Sylvia's shoulders.

MRS WANNOP

You're the most beautiful creature! I'm sure you're good!

Sylvia bends to offer her cheek to be kissed.

Sylvia and Mrs Wannop cause a general movement back towards the fire. The Actress gets up despite herself.

Edith attempts to place Sylvia in the chair of honour. Sylvia guides Mrs Wannop into the chair and another is brought for her, but she ignores it.

Soon Macmaster is leading the conversation and laughing, while Sylvia declines an offer of tea from Edith. Nobody else has sat down.

Valentine, diminished, looks at her fat reflection in a silver urn. Christopher's voice comes from close.

CHRISTOPHER

Your mother is having a regular triumph.

VALENTINE

You're quite gay today. You sound different. I suppose you're better?

CHRISTOPHER

I still forget names, but I'm relatively gay. Some part of my mathematical brain came back to life. I worked out a silly little problem . . .

VALENTINE

What did you work out?

CHRISTOPHER

Oh, I looked over some problem of Macmaster's, really in a spirit of bravado, and the answer just came to me. Do you really want to know? The French were bleating about the devastation in bricks and mortar they've incurred by enemy action. I saw suddenly that it was no more than one year's normal peacetime dilapidation spread out over the whole country.

VALENTINE
(*ironically*)

Really? How wonderful.

CHRISTOPHER

So the argument for French command of the Western Front gets kicked out of court for a season.

VALENTINE
But weren't you arguing against your own convictions?

CHRISTOPHER
Yes, of course. But Macmaster depends on me.

He laughs and she can't help laughing with him. They are for a moment united in a new intimacy.

Sylvia is looking at them with a curl of a smile. She advances, towing the two Staff Officers.

SYLVIA
Oh, Christopher! These boys have a motor – they're going to drive me to the Basils.

CHRISTOPHER
All right. I'll pop Mrs Wannop into the tube as soon as she's had enough and I'll pick you up.

Sylvia drops her eyelashes to Valentine, and walks out, the Staff Officers scampering after her, Edith fluttering.

INT. BROWNLIE'S BANK – DAY

August 1917.

A newspaper, held by soemone reading it, announces RUSSIA WILL NOT MAKE PEACE WITH GERMANY: KERENSKY VOWS TO CONTINUE WAR.

In his office (which befits the scion of Brownlie's Bank) Brownlie is reading the newspaper. A middle-aged Clerk knocks and enters with a leather folder, placing it in front of Brownlie.

BROWNLIE
Thank you.

CLERK
Evidently an oversight, my lord.

BROWNLIE
(opening the folder)
Who? . . . Tietjens!

The folder contains two cheques made out by Christopher.

> BROWNLIE
>
> To his club! . . . And the officers' mess!

> CLERK
>
> Perhaps a letter to Mr Tietjens . . .?

> BROWNLIE
>
> No! Send them back! Bounce them!

> CLERK
>
> My lord . . .?

> BROWNLIE
>
> Send them back *now*. Within the hour.

He closes the folder, hands it to the Clerk, who leaves.

> BROWNLIE
> (*exultant*)
>
> Got you!

INT. MACMASTER'S FLAT – DAY

Edith has the phone to her ear and we catch her just as she emits a scream into it. A beat later we realise it's not bad news, it's a scream of ecstasy. It startles Valentine, who is across the room settling out the tea things for a new Friday.

It is summer. The women are hot in summer dress. Edith, oblivious of Valentine, is having a sort of orgasm into the phone, hardly able to speak or breathe.

> EDITH
>
> Oh God – my God – oh my dearest – I always knew – Oh my genius – my clever little Guggums –

She remembers Valentine, turns her back and whispers into the phone.

> Come home. Now. This instant . . . Because there are certain things I intend to do to you. No. Now. (*She listens and giggles.*) Oh . . . Guggums . . .! Yes!

She puts the phone down and sees Valentine staring at her.
Edith makes a massive recovery into an air of negligence.

> Not that we set much store by these things, but the King
> is seeing fit to confer a knighthood on Vincent.

> VALENTINE
> Oh! Congratulations . . . I'm sure he deserves it.

> EDITH
> It's not for mere plodding. It's for a special piece of
> brilliance that marked him out at the office.

> VALENTINE
> Oh, I know! He worked out some calculation to prove
> that French war damage amounts to no more than a
> normal year's household dilapidation spread over . . .

Edith gives a squeak of horror.

> EDITH
> How did you –? How could you possibly know . . . It's
> a dead secret! . . . Vincent must have told that fellow! –
> your – your . . . No, it wouldn't be Tietjens. He's no
> patriot!

> VALENTINE
> Though he is in uniform, Edith.

> EDITH
> What on earth do you dare mean? You may as well know
> there's not a more discredited man in London. You've got
> personal interests at stake. In our position now, we
> cannot connive at your intrigue.

> VALENTINE
> Intrigue? What can you – ?

> EDITH
> You brazen –! You've had a child by that man! Haven't
> you?

> VALENTINE
> No! I certainly have not! Oh let's not, Edith! For your
> own sake remember you are a woman and not for ever

and always a snob. You were a good woman once, you stuck by your mad husband for quite a long time –

Edith appears to be having a choking fit.

> EDITH

Get out! Get out!

Valentine gets out.

EXT. WANNOP HOUSE – DAY

A Telegram Boy outside the house.

INT. WANNOP HOUSE – DAY

Mrs Wannop is asking the telephone operator for a number. The doorbell rings. She shouts for Valentine, then goes to the front door.

It's a telegram. She's frightened by it. She signs for it. She stands, not daring to open it. The Telegram Boy goes back to his bike.

Valentine, in school clothes, comes from the back of the house, picks the receiver up and listens.

INT. GRAY'S INN – DAY

The phone is ringing in the drawing room.

INT. WANNOP HOUSE – DAY

Mrs Wannop cries out with relief and joy. She enters with the telegram.

> MRS WANNOP

Edward's safe! He's on shore!

She hugs Valentine.

> VALENTINE

Oh – thank God!

MRS WANNOP

I must give the boy a sixpence . . . Ask if Christopher's there.

Mrs Wannop runs out to catch the Telegram Boy.

INT. GRAY'S INN – DAY / INT. WANNOP HOUSE – DAY

Cross-cutting:

Sylvia picks up the phone.

VALENTINE
(*to phone*)
Is Mr Tietjens at home?

SYLVIA
(*to phone*)
Young woman, you'd better keep off the grass. Mrs Duchemin is already my husband's mistress. So keep off!

VALENTINE
(*to phone*)
You have probably mistaken the person you're speaking to. Perhaps you will ask Mr Tietjens to ring up Mrs Wannop when he is at liberty.

SYLVIA
(*to phone*)
My husband is going out to France tomorrow morning. He will be at the War Office at four-fifteen. He will speak to you there. But I'd keep off the grass if I were you.

She hangs up the phone.

INT. WANNOP HOUSE – DAY

Valentine, dazed, hangs up.

INT. GRAY'S INN, DRAWING ROOM – DAY

Sylvia, after putting the phone down, reflects for a moment.

INT. GRAY'S INN, BREAKFAST/DINING ROOM – DAY

Sylvia and Christopher are finishing lunch.

SYLVIA

Is Mrs Duchemin really your mistress? Or only
Macmaster's?

CHRISTOPHER

No, she's Lady Macmaster now. There's a party tonight
to celebrate.

SYLVIA

And what about that girl you were potty about at that
horrible tea party? Has she had a war baby by you?
Everyone says she's your mistress, too.

CHRISTOPHER

No, Miss Wannop is not my mistress.

SYLVIA

It upset Brownie so much, he's going to refuse your
cheques, just to please me.

CHRISTOPHER

Ah! Do bankers do that, just to please their women
friends?

SYLVIA

I told him it wouldn't please me at all. It's all the fault of
this beastly war, isn't it, turning decent people into squits.

CHRISTOPHER

Yes. That's what it is.

SYLVIA

I've no right to put a spoke in that girl's wheel, or yours.
If you love each other, I dare say she will make you
happy. I could wangle you out of going back.

CHRISTOPHER

Thank you, but I prefer to go.

*Christopher takes out his wallet and lays two cheques on the
table.*

SYLVIA

Oh, Christopher! He didn't!

CHRISTOPHER

He did. The club, and my mess bill.

SYLVIA

But – if you needed money . . .

CHRISTOPHER

I didn't. My account was overdrawn for a few hours yesterday because my pay-slip from the army was late.

SYLVIA

Then Brownie will say so! – I'll make sure of that –

CHRISTOPHER

The damage is done, and I don't much care.

SYLVIA

But . . . this means your ruin.

CHRISTOPHER

It certainly means my ruin.

He stands to leave.

SYLVIA

Oh Christopher! – If you had once in our lives said to me, 'You whore! You bitch!' Or about the child. Or Perowne. You might have done something to bring us together. And I daresay if you're shot – oh, Christ! – between the saddle and the ground you'll say that you never did a dishonourable action. In the name of the Almighty, how could any woman live beside you?

CHRISTOPHER

But I have never disapproved of your actions.

SYLVIA

I've done for you. I'm not going to listen to you.

He moves to go.

CHRISTOPHER

You were let down by a brute at the beginning, so you
have the right to let down a man. It's woman against man
now, and ever has been. Mark is going to walk me to the
War Office.

EXT. LONDON STREET — DAY

*Valentine, in her school clothes, jumps off a moving bus as it
turns a corner, going the wrong way for her. She continues on
foot, hurrying.*

EXT. LONDON — DAY

*Christopher's and Mark's route: busy pavements, quiet courts,
public gardens and Victoria Embankment.*

MARK

What have you done with the brass your mother left you?

CHRISTOPHER

I settled half on Michael. The rest I spent on the flat . . .
furniture . . . some notional loans to people.

MARK

Macmaster? I suppose his wife is your mistress?

CHRISTOPHER

No. I backed him just because he asked.

MARK

If a lot of fellows knew that, you wouldn't have much
brass for long.

CHRISTOPHER

I didn't have it for long.

Later:

MARK

Did you settle money on your girl? The girl who had a
child by you. Where do you keep her?

CHRISTOPHER
Hadn't you better mention names?

MARK
No. I never mention names.

CHRISTOPHER
I haven't got a girl. There's no child. I don't want Father's money. I can live on my pay.

MARK
You had a cheque dishonoured at the club this morning.

CHRISTOPHER
You'd better look at my pass-books for the last ten years. This is no good if you don't believe what I say.

MARK
(pause)
I believe you.

Later:

MARK
Then Ruggles is a liar.

CHRISTOPHER
Not really. He picked things up, things said against me – I don't know why.

MARK
Because you treat these south-country swine with the contempt they deserve. I thought you'd been buried so long in their muck . . . Well, you'd better know what our father wanted. His idea was, if you were a pimp, you were to go to hell on clean money, whatever it took, it was no good making a will, I was to see to it.

CHRISTOPHER
Well, you won't be a penny poorer for me! I won't take his money.

MARK
You usually forgive a fellow who shoots himself.

CHRISTOPHER

I don't. I won't forgive him for not making a will, for
calling in Ruggles, for not speaking to me in the club the
night before he died. That was stupidity.

MARK

It was I who called in Ruggles, though.

CHRISTOPHER

I don't forgive you either. The whole damn lot of you.

MARK

Well, don't get shirty about it. You *must* take enough to
be comfortable. Groby will come to you anyway, if you
don't get killed.

CHRISTOPHER

I don't want it. And I loathe your buttered-toast, mutton-
chopped comfort as much as I loathe the chauffeured
fornicators in their town and country palaces.

MARK

My Marie-Leonie makes better buttered toast than you
can get at the Savoy, and keeps herself clean and neat on
five hundred a year. I'd marry the doxy if she wasn't a
papist.

Later:

MARK

So . . . if you haven't got a girl, what do you do for
comforts? Your wife's a regular tart by all accounts.
I suppose you think I've insulted you?

CHRISTOPHER

No. But I'd have thought your faith in 'all accounts' . . .

MARK

Of course, one can see with half an eye she's soppily in
love with you.

Christopher is quietly shocked by that.

CHRISTOPHER

No wonder I make her angry. The sooner I'm in France . . .

Army lorries roar by them, soldiers under tin hats and canvas, not waving, not smiling.

We've seen the last of England. The professional army that saw us through the last hundred years is every man of them dead, and civilisation has gone to war in their place. We're all barbarians now.

EXT. WHITEHALL (WAR OFFICE) – DAY

Christopher and Mark enter under the arch.

MARK

There's one more thing. The boy . . .

CHRISTOPHER

You mean my son.

MARK

Yes . . . You won't mind my keeping an eye on him if you're killed?

CHRISTOPHER

I'll be glad.

EXT. WAR OFFICE ARCH – DAY

Under a cheap shelter against a wall, the lists of war casualties are pinned up for the public, innumerable names. Valentine is looking at them. She sees Christopher and turns on him in extreme distress.

VALENTINE

Look at this horror! And you in that uniform . . .

CHRISTOPHER

This is my brother Mark.

She nods at Mark, undeflected.

I didn't know Mr Tietjens had a brother. How do you do? (*To Christopher.*) I must speak to you, and then I'm going.

Valentine moves away, into the quadrangle, holding Christopher by the sleeve. Mark stands by the shelter, waiting patiently, swinging his umbrella.

VALENTINE
(*intensely*)

Is Edith your mistress?

CHRISTOPHER
(*tired, vague*)

Edith? Who's she?

VALENTINE

Edith Ethel Duchemin! Mrs Macmaster that is!

CHRISTOPHER

Certainly not. How could you ask such a tomfool question? You! The only intelligent woman I know. Don't you *know* me?

VALENTINE

Your wife said, 'Mrs Duchemin is my husband's mistress, so keep off the grass!' Isn't she a truthful person?

CHRISTOPHER

What she says, she believes, but she only believes what she wants to, and only for that moment.

VALENTINE

Oh. It *isn't* true. I knew it wasn't.

He leads her back towards Mark.

CHRISTOPHER

Come along. I've got another tomfool to see inside, then I'm free.

VALENTINE

I can't come with you crying like this.

CHRISTOPHER

Oh, yes, you can. This is the place where women cry.
Besides, there's Mark, he's a comforting ass. (*To Mark.*)
Here, look after Miss Wannop.

*Christopher walks rapidly away. Mark and Valentine follow
more slowly towards the cavernous hall.*

MARK

I say, don't give it to old Christopher too beastly hard
about his uniform . . . He's going out tomorrow and he's
one of the best.

VALENTINE

I'd lay down my life for him!

MARK

I know you would. I know a good woman when I see
one. You're in uniform yourself, so you do war work.

VALENTINE

No. We're hard up, Mother and I, I take gym classes in
a school.

INT. WAR OFFICE, HALL – DAY

*A Commissionaire gives a slip of paper to a Bellboy, who leads
Christopher into the depth of the building.*

Mark leads Valentine to a bench.

MARK

Look here! My father wanted your mother to be
comfortable. I'm here on business!

VALENTINE

Oh! She always said your father would –

MARK

You won't get it quicker by interrupting. You may take
it as if my father left your mother a nice little plum, so
that she can write books. Say, a lump sum giving her an
annuity of £500. Does that sound about right? There'll

be a bit for you and something for your brother. You haven't fainted, have you?

MARK

> VALENTINE

I don't faint. I cry.

MARK

That's all right. I want Christopher to have somewhere to have a mutton chop and an armchair by the fire, and someone who's good for him. You're good for him.

INT. WAR OFFICE – DAY

A general on the Staff sits behind his desk, Christopher opposite.

STAFF OFFICER

What's the matter with the camp depots? What are these mutinies about?

CHRISTOPHER

You get men who think they've deserved well of their country, and you shave their heads –

STAFF OFFICER

Lice . . .

CHRISTOPHER

You allow 'em out for an hour a day when the pubs are closed, you crop them like convicts to stop them appealing to local young women, who don't exist miles from anywhere, you don't let them carry swagger canes, God knows why, and – dammit – if you get two men, chums, from the same regiment, you don't let them sleep in the same hut –

STAFF OFFICER

To stop 'em talking half the night.

CHRISTOPHER

And no cinema in case there's infection! They're first-class fellows! They're in the depots to convalesce and get fit, so they can be sent back. Why in God's name don't you let them have their girls, their pubs and a bit of swank!

Yes. You're the sort of man we want at home. Do you want to go? We can get it stopped.

Christopher hesitates.

CHRISTOPHER

Yes! I want to go.

STAFF OFFICER

Some do, some do not.

INT. WAR OFFICE, HALL – DAY

MARK

. . . I'm going in to see about Christopher – I think I can get him into looking after transport. A safe job. Safeish! No beastly glory about it.

VALENTINE

Do be quick, then! Do get him into transport at once!

Christopher arrives.

CHRISTOPHER

Come on, let's get out of this.

MARK

I'm going in to see old General Hogarth. I suppose you won't shake hands?

CHRISTOPHER

No. Why should I?

VALENTINE

Oh, do!

MARK

You might get killed. You might think, while you're getting killed, 'Oh, I wish I'd –'

CHRISTOPHER

Or I might wish I hadn't, but – Oh, well . . .

They shake hands. Mark raises his hat to Valentine and goes away into the building.

CHRISTOPHER

Will you be my mistress tonight? I'm going out tomorrow at 8.30 from Waterloo.

VALENTINE

Yes! Yes, of course I will!

CHRISTOPHER

Where? I'll give Macmaster's party a miss.

VALENTINE

No. You must go. Come late, after eleven is best. I'll be at home. We'll have to be quiet, though.

CHRISTOPHER

We'll be quiet. I tell you . . . from the first moment . . .

VALENTINE

I know.

People – civilians and military – are passing. Christopher and Valentine stare at each other.

VALENTINE

When did you . . . ?

CHRISTOPHER

My colours are in the mud. It's not a good thing to find oneself living by an outmoded code of honour. People take you to be a fool, and I'm coming round to their opinion.

VALENTINE

Yes. But we were in a carpenter's vice, it was like being pushed together, every minute since the first moment. I've waited. Oh, my dear!

EXT. WHITEHALL – DAY

Christopher watches Valentine cross Whitehall, her skirt whisking the back of a bus going north.

INT. MACMASTER'S FLAT – NIGHT

A large loud party fills the flat . . . among them are Sandbach, Lady Claudine, Westershire, Sylvia, Ingleby . . . and people from Macmaster's tea parties. The men are in evening clothes or uniform.

INT. WANNOP HOUSE – NIGHT

Mrs Wannop and Valentine stand quietly hugging each other.

MRS WANNOP
I never believed Mr Tietjens would forget us. Never. I'll sleep well tonight – first time since war began.

VALENTINE
Yes . . . I will too.

INT. MACMASTER'S FLAT – NIGHT

Macmaster, wearing his decoration round his neck, is in the thick of things, having his hand shaken. Edith is in excelsis, fielding congratulations. Propped up on a table is a photograph of Macmaster being knighted. Ruggles finds Christopher.

RUGGLES
A great thing, his knighthood. Dining at the club tonight?

CHRISTOPHER
No. I've resigned.

RUGGLES
(*embarrassed*)
The membership committee . . . Well, the Duke, actually, well, your wife in fact – anyway your resignation has not been accepted.

Christopher excuses himself to escape. Sylvia intervenes.

CHRISTOPHER
I understand I have to thank you.

SYLVIA

Brownlie begged! – begs to have the honour of your continuing to draw on his bank . . .

CHRISTOPHER

For that, too, then.

SYLVIA

Are you leaving?

CHRISTOPHER

Yes. I have an engagement.

EXT. WANNOP HOUSE – NIGHT

An upstairs light goes out. There is a low light downstairs.

INT. WANNOP HOUSE – NIGHT

Valentine bathes in a tin tub on the kitchen floor.

INT. MACMASTER'S FLAT – NIGHT

Christopher is edging his way out. Macmaster spots him as he edges out of the door to the landing.

INT. MACMASTER'S FLAT, LANDING AND STAIRS – NIGHT

People are still arriving. Christopher moves down the stairs against the current. Macmaster arrives on the landing and sees him, and follows him, almost ignoring the hailing of those coming towards him.

INT. MACMASTER'S FLAT, HALL – NIGHT

Macmaster catches up with Christopher.

MACMASTER

Chrissie . . . wait . . . you're not going? . . . I wanted to explain . . . This miserable knighthood . . .

CHRISTOPHER

It's all right, old man. We've been pals long enough for a
little thing like that not to . . . I'm very glad . . . Truly.

*They shake hands, Macmaster tearful. He adjusts his voice to a
whisper, as guests pass by.*

MACMASTER

And . . . Valentine . . . she's not here. Don't tell me
Guggums – oh, God, if I thought! –

CHRISTOPHER

It's all right. It's all right. She's at another party. I'm going
on . . .

MACMASTER
(*tearfully*)

Tell her . . . You may be killed! I beg you to believe – I'll
never . . . never abandon . . .

CHRISTOPHER

Yes. Well . . .

MACMASTER

Well.

*Tietjens opens the door. When he looks back, the staircase is
empty except for Sylvia watching him go with a curl of a smile.*

INT. WANNOP HOUSE, HALL/PARLOUR – NIGHT

*Valentine is bathed and dressed. She opens the front door by
an inch and leaves it like that.*

*The parlour room is dimly shaded. The furniture has been
slightly rearranged, leaving the chaise longue some space.
Valentine drapes a cloth over the chaise. She retreats and sits
down to consider the effect.*

FANTASY SEQUENCE: INT. WANNOP HOUSE – NIGHT

*Valentine's point of view: she lies naked on the couch,
mimicking the Rokeby Venus.*

She dispels the image, standing up at the sound of the door being pushed open. She darts out of the room.

INT. WANNOP HOUSE, HALL – NIGHT

Edward Wannop is there, in uniform, teetering, drunk.

> EDWARD
> Valentine! Meet my . . .

Two young Sailors roll into view behind him.

INT. WANNOP HOUSE – NIGHT

Later: Edward and his two friends and Mrs Wannop in her dressing gown are sprawled on the furniture having a sing-along party, beer bottles in hand. Valentine drinks from a beer bottle.

EXT. WANNOP STREET – NIGHT

Christopher walks towards the house. As he gets closer, he sees Valentine sitting on the kerb outside.

> CHRISTOPHER
> The trains . . .

Valentine looks at him, smiling, pitifully.

It takes Christopher a moment to understand. The singing from indoors tells him all he needs to know.

> CHRISTOPHER
> Ah. It does make one believe in . . . something. I'm so sorry, Miss Wannop.

> VALENTINE
> Help me up.

EXT. EALING – NIGHT

There is one cab, a horse cab, in the rank outside a station.

The Cabdriver wakes.

Christopher and Valentine stand together.

> CHRISTOPHER
>
> We're the sort that . . . do not.

> VALENTINE
>
> But when you come back.

> CHRISTOPHER
>
> That night we drove through the mist – five years ago! –
> you said I'd never take you to Groby, and I never will.
> I told Mark I didn't want it. I can't live at Groby with
> you. A trollop from the servants' hall to scandalise the
> parson, that would be understood, but not a lady. They
> insist on standards from women of quality, otherwise
> they'll let go their own and the estate would go to ruin.
> Well, leastways in Yorkshire.

> VALENTINE
>
> I'll be ready. I'll be ready for anything you ask. Oh, my
> dear – come back!

Christopher nods, touches his folded gloves to his cap.

> CHRISTOPHER
> (*calls to Cabdriver*)
>
> West End!

He gets into the cab. The cab moves away.

INT. GRAY'S INN, DRAWING ROOM – NIGHT

*Christopher enters. He does not turn on any lights. The room
is darkly moonlit. He pours a whisky and sits down, fatigue
and defeat in his bearing. A small sound makes him aware of a
cloudy patch of white at the far end of the room. He realises
that Sylvia is sitting there.*

> SYLVIA
>
> Oh, don't tell me you didn't . . .? (*Accusingly.*) You
> didn't, did you?

CHRISTOPHER

Let's not quarrel now. There's something I've decided about.

SYLVIA

Don't you dare tell me it was for my sake.

Sylvia gets up and comes to him. She is wearing a nightdress.

She was ready to drop into your mouth like a grape! How could you be such a skunk?

CHRISTOPHER

I have to pack my things for France.

She rips the gold chain from her neck and throws it down with its St Anthony medal.

SYLVIA

You might as well! Couldn't you bring yourself to seduce that little kitchen maid? There'd have been a chance for us.

She stalks away.

CHRISTOPHER

I've decided about Michael.

She turns to stare at him.

INT. GRAY'S INN – DAWN

Christopher packs for France. He tosses a revolver into the suitcase. Sylvia is putting on a robe over her nightdress.

CHRISTOPHER

. . . for I must to the greenwood go . . .

SYLVIA

Do you mean it? I may bring up Michael as a Catholic?

CHRISTOPHER

As a *Roman* Catholic . . . you'll teach him, please, to use that term . . . but I am obviously not the man to have charge of the future master of Groby. I am not a whole man any more.

SYLVIA

When did you . . . ?

CHRISTOPHER

When my cheques were dishonoured –

SYLVIA

No – it was only that squit –

CHRISTOPHER

But I let it happen. My father believed the squits, too, but I let *that* happen. A fellow who can't do better than that had better let the mother bring up the child. I loved the little beggar with all my soul from the moment I saw him. Perhaps that's the secret.

SYLVIA

Oh, I thank God that He has softened your heart.

CHRISTOPHER

You'll have Father . . . Father . . .

He angrily slams the lid of the suitcase.

Not my heart, my brain!

SYLVIA

Father Consett.

CHRISTOPHER

Consett! An intelligent priest – he'll teach as much sense as nonsense.

Sylvia blazes.

SYLVIA

Father Consett was hanged when you were in France. They dared not put it in the papers because he was a priest, and all the witnesses were Ulstermen. And yet I may not say this is an accursed war.

CHRISTOPHER

You may for me.

209

EXT. HOLBORN – DAWN

An army lorry and a horse-drawn goods wagon are the only vehicles abroad at this hour. The lorry stops for Christopher's thumb. He throws his suitcase on board and climbs up. The lorry recedes into the early light.

End of Episode Three.

Episode Four

CAST OF EPISODE FOUR

in order of appearance

BOBBIE PELHAM	Anna Skellern
SYLVIA TIETJENS	Rebecca Hall
GENERAL HAGGARD	Ronald Pickup
LORD BEICHEN	Leslie De Gruyter
LADY CLAUDINE	Clare Higgins
BERTRAM	Jonathan Coy
GLORVINA	Sasha Waddell
SANDBACH	Malcolm Sinclair
VALENTINE WANNOP	Adelaide Clemens
MRS WANNOP	Miranda Richardson
GENERAL CAMPION	Roger Allam
COLONEL LEVIN	Elliot Levey
LATIN TEACHER	Anna Maguire
MRS FERGUSON	Lucy Briers
FIRST TEACHER	Emma Dewhurst
SECOND TEACHER	Tilly Blackwood
MARK TIETJENS	Rupert Everett
CHRISTOPHER TIETJENS	Benedict Cumberbatch
SERGEANT MAJOR COWLEY	Nick Holder
O NINE MORGAN	Kyle Redmond-Jones
CAPITAINE THURSTON	Pierre Van Heddegem
POTTY PEROWNE	Tom Mison
CANADIAN CAPTAIN	Louis Talpe
GIRTIN	Jeroen Batseleer
MCKECHNIE	Patrick Kennedy
O FIVE THOMAS	Tom Rhys Harries
HOTCHKISS	Nicholas Lumley
GUARD SERGEANT	Jonathan Sawdon
ARMY GROOM	Tat Whalley
HOTEL MANAGER	Gert Lahousse
SCHOOLGIRL 1	Bea Wavell Grant
SCHOOLGIRL 2	Harriet Lindsay-Stewart
SCHOOLGIRL 3	Oriane Nell Grant
GENERAL O'HARA	Iain Mitchell
SERGEANT COOK CASE	Jonathan Ryland

EXT. LORD BEICHEN'S HOUSE, LONDON – NIGHT

December 1917.

A grand town house. London is darkened, and the house is lit lit only by a dim portal lamp.

INT. LORD BEICHEN'S HOUSE, DINING ROOM – NIGHT

The Earl of Beichen (Lord Beichen, born Nathan Stavropolides) is a corpulent newspaper lord. He is presiding over a white-tie dinner for eight. The table has plenty of room for them. Clockwise from the host it seats: Lady Claudine, General Haggard, Sylvia, Bertram (a member of the War Cabinet and husband of Lady Glorvina), Bobbie (Sylvia's pal), Paul Sandbach MP (husband of Lady Claudine), and Lady Glorvina, on Beichen's right.

Bobbie is Beichen's new mistress. Beichen is besotted with her.

The dinner is just getting under way, the Butler offering the first of the wines, and the guests in pairs breaking the seal on dinner conversation as we make a tour around the table.

> BEICHEN
> (*to Glorvina*)
> Bertram tells me you lost a window in the last raid.

> LADY CLAUDINE
> (*to General Haggard*)
> Edward's command is at Rouen, or 'somewhere in France', I'm supposed to say . . .

> BERTRAM
> (*to Sylvia*)
> Will you go the the Sackvilles' squash?

SYLVIA

I thought I might.

SANDBACH
(*to Bobbie, flirting*)
No – no vote for you, I'm afraid – it's going to be for
married women over thirty.

EXT. LORD BEICHEN'S HOUSE, LONDON – NIGHT

*A Motorcyclist, the headlight masked, pulls up outside and
goes to deliver a newspaper to the front door. A Footman
answers his ring and takes the newspaper.*

INT. LORD BEICHEN'S HOUSE, LONDON – NIGHT

The dinner is at a late stage.

*Sylvia and Bobbie communicate for an instant by glances –
Sylvia ironically congratulatory, acknowledging Bobbie's
staggering necklace; Bobbie defiant, and yet indicating with a
shrugged shoulder and widened eyes that she is the amazed
object of forces stronger than herself.*

HAGGARD
(*to Beichen*)
. . . horses decimated by pink-eye . . .

BEICHEN
You should put that fellow Hotchkiss in charge of the
horse lines. The war horse needs to be hardened.
Mollycoddling will ruin him. Hotchkiss is the man you
need in France.

HAGGARD

Hotchkiss?

BEICHEN
You'll find him in *Horse World* advertising embrocation.
Get hold of Hotchkiss! The *Comet* will back you.

A Footman places a folded newspaper by Lord Beichen.

The first edition, my lord.

Beichen gives the newspaper his proper attention. The Daily
Comet *is a popular broadsheet. Haggard makes a note in a
dainty leather notebook.*

BERTRAM
(*to Haggard*)
Sylvia wants a pass to IBD Rouen, General, she needs to
talk to her husband.

HAGGARD
Strictly out of bounds to wives, I'm afraid, Mrs Tietjens.

SYLVIA
What about mistresses? I bet there's a few of those
behind the lines. It's jolly unfair.

*Beichen calls cheerfully down the table to Bertram, giving the
fresh* Comet *to the Butler to deliver.*

BEICHEN
Here you are, Bertram – might as well spoil your dinner
as your breakfast! The *Comet* exposes the scandal of
our out-of-touch command in Flanders. In the name of
the British Tommy, the *Comet* demands new blood –
ideas, I should say, not blood, new thinking to end the
stalemate.

BERTRAM
(*wearily*)
I'm sure it does, but it's your own fault for building up
Puffles in the first place.

SANDBACH
Wait till the German spring offensive gives him a bloody
nose, Beichen, and *then* we can bring him home.

HAGGARD
(*drily*)
Is that why you're keeping the C-in-C short of troops,
Bertram?

                    BERTRAM
                   (*brazenly*)
Not entirely; it's also to tell the French, if they want us to
strengthen the line, they'd best shut up about the single
command.

                    HAGGARD
                   (*outplayed*)
Well, you have a point there.

                    BERTRAM
If we gave Puffles the men, he'd lose half of them in a week.

                    GLORVINA
If I had my way, we'd let the French go to blazes.

                 LADY CLAUDINE
Quite. There won't always be a European war but there'll
always be an Empire.

                   SANDBACH
What about Salonika, Bertram?

                    BOBBIE
Salonika! Nathan, isn't that where your people
originally . . .

                   BEICHEN
Not originally, my dear!

The table laughs uncommitedly.

                    SYLVIA
I say, it would be nice if we could forget the war just for
five minutes . . .

The air raid siren starts wailing. Sylvia joins in the laughter.

   I give up!

EXT. NIGHT SKY OVER RIVER THAMES AND LONDON
LANDMARKS

Searchlights probe the sky. The air raid is in progress. CRW

Nevinson's painting of 1916, 'Among London Searchlights', is the model.

Sound: drone of German bombers and anti-aircraft batteries, and some muffled explosions on the ground.

EXT. WANNOP HOUSE, EALING — NIGHT

The same air raid is audible.

In the parlour there is a blanket hanging from the small dining table to make a cave. Valentine is crouched under the table. Mrs Wannop is seated at the table, writing. The windows are blacked out.

VALENTINE

Mother . . .

MRS WANNOP

I'm just finishing . . .

VALENTINE

It'll be the finish of you if you don't . . .

Mrs Wannop joins Valentine under the table.

MRS WANNOP

I'm writing to Christopher. At least he isn't in the casualty lists – I always look.

VALENTINE
(snappish)

Of course he's not. He's not in the fighting – his brother got him into a job looking after horses!

INT. LORD BEICHEN'S HOUSE, GUEST'S CLOAKROOM — NIGHT

Sylvia and Bobbie are making cosmetic repairs in the mirror. The 'all-clear' sounds.

SYLVIA

There it goes . . .

BOBBIE

Sylvia, I need you to rally round. Johnny's behaving appallingly, poor lamb.

SYLVIA

Oh, about your *divertissement*.

BOBBIE

It's not a *divertissement*, Sylvia, I'm bolting!

SYLVIA
(*appalled*)

Oh . . . *Bobbie*! You and . . . ? But he's –

BOBBIE

It's not his fault he's a Jew.

SYLVIA

Fat, I was going to say. It's his fault he's fat.

BOBBIE

I thought you were my pal. What else can I do? He wants me to! (*With a meaningful look, about the sex.*) Anyway, you'd be surprised. He wants to marry me. Actually he's very sweet. So I need you to get Johnny over the hump. (*At Sylvia's raised eyebrow.*) No, just take him out and about. He's a good old sausage, I want to do my best for him.

SYLVIA

That's all very well, but I've a mind to go and see Christopher in France . . . I've written to General Campion . . .

INT. BATHROOM, CAMPION'S QUARTERS, INFANTRY BASE DEPOT, ROUEN, FRANCE – DAY

The HQ is a small chateau on the edge of the town. General Campion is preparing to shave (he does so during the scene). His bathroom is immense but shabby, not grand, with ancient plumbing. His Servant (an army private) is providing the hot water from a large pitcher; which done, he leaves. Campion meanwhile is reading a letter from Sylvia with a jaundiced eye.

220

He puts the letter aside. He is watched by Colonel Levin, a slight, dark, good-looking, sensitive, beautifully tailored and groomed Staff Officer who is Campion's chief assistant.

There is evidently a German reconnaissance plane somewhere above, because a few near and distant guns are banging away at it. The view from the window beyond Campion's shaving mirror offers some indications of military presence and activity.

CAMPION

I wish the fellow would write to his damned wife, or at least stop her writing to me – it's not my job to reassure the wives of officers that their husbands are still alive, dammit, it's quite enough having to write to them when they're not.

LEVIN

There's a movement order come in for Captain Tietjens, sir . . . from the War Office, Room G 14 R. It was misrouted when he had his spell in hospital, and has only now caught up, I'm afraid . . .

CAMPION

Movement? To where?

LEVIN

Divisional horse transport.

CAMPION
(*exploding*)

Well, you can tell Room G 14 R, whoever the hell they are, that I'm not parting with Captain Tietjens! – He's the only officer on the base who can get his draft into marching order on time. Not that he isn't a confounded nuisance. (*A thought.*) I could give them Captain McKechnie when he's back from divorce leave – he's sane enough for horses, isn't he?

LEVIN

Captain McKechnie has returned from leave, sir, but he omitted to get divorced.

CAMPION
(*angrily*)
How dare he not get divorced? He told me his wife was
co-habiting with – an Egyptian, wasn't it? – some sort of
dago anyway.

LEVIN
No, sir, an Egyptologist. They have agreed to . . . to share
her.

CAMPION
(*outraged*)
The dirty dog! I'll strip him of his commission! (*Broods a
moment.*) A damn fine officer when he isn't going mad,
and a Vice Chancellor's Latin prize man, too . . . (*Bitterly.*)
Another brilliant fellow . . . like Tietjens. That's a
thought . . . they can be brilliant together.

INT. SCHOOL STAFF ROOM, LONDON – DAY

*In her gym-mistress uniform, Valentine enters the Staff Room,
carrying a sports ball which she puts away in a cupboard. One
or two members of staff are reading the papers, one or two
others marking exercise books. Valentine turns over the pages
of a magazine.*

LATIN TEACHER
(*to another teacher*)
Does *subter* take the accusative or the ablative?

VALENTINE
Both. Accusative when it's 'under' as a motion, ablative
when it's 'under' as a state.

*The Latin teacher looks at Valentine in surprise. Valentine is
staring at a photograph of Sylvia with a man at a ball.*

INT. ALBANY – DAY

*Valentine has brought the magazine to Mark in his bachelor
flat. She is upset. Mark studies the caption of the photograph.*

MARK

'. . . pictured at Lady Hazlitt's Ball with the Hon. Johnnie Pelham . . .'

VALENTINE

'Mrs Christopher Tietjens, whose husband is in hospital at the Front'!

MARK

Sylvia must have told them that herself. The paper wouldn't put the knife into her – women like Sylvia are the jam on their bread and butter.

VALENTINE

Why would she do that?

MARK

To let him know she's on the warpath. Well, don't worry about Christopher, it was only pneumonia, and not at the Front. He's a hundred miles from the nearest German trench. Nothing to worry about except air raids.

VALENTINE

Are they dropping bombs on him?

MARK

My dear, they're dropping bombs on you, and yet here you are.

VALENTINE

But I thought Christopher was looking after horses somewhere safe.

MARK

That's the War Office for you. But an Infantry Base Depot is a soft posting so long as you're not sent back to your battalion.

VALENTINE

Oh, anything but the trenches!

EXT. THE CAMP, INFANTRY BASE DEPOT (IBD), ROUEN — DAY

A regimental band is having a band practice on the parade ground . . . on which there is plenty of room for others, engaged in bayonet practice and various kinds of training under instructors.

In so far as we can be aware of the scale of the camp, it is vast. The transient thousands of troops sleep in bell tents, and the permanent staff live in 'lines' of canvas 'huts' with celluloid windows. Larger wooden structures are the orderly rooms, kitchens, messes, etc. Whitened stones mark the 'lines': the streets and avenues of the camp. Out of sight for now is the main gate and its guardhouse.

The band is practising a Christmas carol. The strains faintly reach Christopher's orderly room.

INT. CHRISTOPHER'S ORDERLY ROOM, IBD, ROUEN — DAY

This is a wooden hut of decent size. There is a blanket-covered table from which Christopher manages the affairs and the paperwork of the unit. The table is covered with files and neat piles of paper. Bully-beef boxes serve as chairs. There is a coke brazier, and a smaller table nearer the door for the NCOs. Christopher is attended by Sergeant-Major Cowley, a thick-set, walrus-moustached regular of twenty years' service. Cowley's manner is disciplined and respectful but not too formal.

Christopher is reading a note from Campion.

CHRISTOPHER
General Campion is attaching a Captain McKechnie to my unit for rations and discipline. What's that about?

COWLEY
I can't say as I can say, sir.

CHRISTOPHER
'A Vice Chancellor's Latin prize man . . .'! Well, I'm sure that will come in useful.

Christopher turns to his pile of papers, examines the top one.
His tone manages to be correct and subtly satirical.

CHRISTOPHER
Fire extinguishers! We indented the Royal Engineers.

COWLEY
(*agreeing*)
Sir!

CHRISTOPHER
The Royal Engineers said that for fire extinguishers we
had to apply to Ordnance. Ordnance said there was no
provision for fire extinguishers for Dominion units
passing through an Infantry Base Depot . . . and that the
proper course was to obtain them from a civilian firm at
home and charge them against barrack damages.

COWLEY
Yes, sir.

CHRISTOPHER
So I have here a letter from the leading British
manufacturer of fire extinguishers, telling me it has been
forbidden by the War Office to sell fire extinguishers to
anyone but to the War Office direct. Thank God we have
a navy.

COWLEY
Yes, sir.

Christopher picks up the next letter.

CHRISTOPHER
The police office, Cardiff . . .

COWLEY
O Nine Morgan is outside, sir. Application for
compassionate leave – his wife sold their laundry business
to someone, name of Evans, now she can't get the money.

CHRISTOPHER
True as far as it goes. The police say his wife is now
living with Mr Evans, who is a prizefighter, and we

should keep O Nine Morgan here if we know what's good for him. In he comes.

CsongorCOWLEY

Sir!

Cowley effects that with a display of shouting, saluting and foot-stamping. O Nine Morgan faces Christopher.

CHRISTOPHER

Well now, O Nine Morgan . . .

EXT. GROBY – DAY

Exterior of Groby House.

INT. NIGHT NURSERY. GROBY – DAY

Michael is eight. Marchant, Michael's nurse, helps him into very new clothes . . . shirt, tie, shorts . . . with Michael's school trunk open and already packed for boarding school. Neither Marchant nor Michael is happy that he's going.

MARCHANT

You won't be far from Groby. You'll have your holidays here when Father's home from the war.

Michael nods.

INT. MARK'S BREAKFAST ROOM, ALBANY, LONDON – DAY

Mark is eating unattractive bacon and eggs with gusto. Sylvia has accepted a cup of tea, which she ignores. A copy of The Times *is 'airing' on a chair in front of the fire. Mark eats and listens, contributing not a word.*

SYLVIA

. . . because there are things I have to discuss with Christopher, and what is the point of being Permanent Secretary of the Department of Transport if you can't transport me – I put it like that – between London and Rouen? This is family business, Mark. Obviously it makes sense for Michael to live at Groby in the mean time . . . with me, naturally. This would require some of the money which would otherwise be going to Christopher. No doubt he would have enough left to make a home with Miss Wannop and the baby he gave her – well, I won't go into his behaviour as a husband, but he should damn well pay for it.

Mark has finished his breakfast and stood up, listening but unacknowledging. He leaves the room and returns with hat and umbrella. He takes and folds The Times.

MARK

I have to go to the office. As far as I'm concerned Groby is Christopher's to do what he likes with . . . So if you can produce his written authorisation, I have no objection to your living at Groby. But, of course, if what you say is true, he might want to live at Groby with Miss Wannop.

Sylvia sees that he is a match for her. She makes the best of it.

SYLVIA

Well, that's why I'm asking you now to –

MARK

I'm afraid you overestimate my authority, which does not extend to France and in any case does not exceed General Campion's in matters that concern the army. Thank you for coming to see me.

He holds the door open for Sylvia. She stands and leaves with a parting shot.

SYLVIA

Utter nonsense! I'll buy a ticket at the station! See if they can stop me.

INT. CAMPION'S HQ, IBD, ROUEN – DAY

Campion is in conference with Levin and a French army officer, Capitaine Thurston, liaison officer with the British, dealing with the French railways.

*Capitaine Thurston is not new to us. He is the man who
spotted Sylvia and Perowne at the hotel in Rouen in 1912.*

*Campion is reading a letter from Sylvia. Levin and Thurston
wait and watch his scowl. He's rattled.*

CAMPION

Never known a woman like her – she says she's coming
to see for herself! On no account – *on no account* – is
Mrs Tietjens to be allowed within fifty miles of Rouen –
understood? Inform the War Office, the Provost-Marshal,
the port authorities, the railway authorities . . . I will not
have skirts around my HQ!

*Levin murmurs assent. Campion puts Sylvia's letter aside. He
collects himself.*

CAMPION

More importantly, General Perry is now on the telephone
twice a day. He has troops who were due to be relieved
weeks ago, and I have troops waiting for Ordnance to
supply them with eyebrow tweezers while our political
masters have been changing their minds whether to
send them up the line or ship them to Salonika or
Mesopotamia or Timbuktoo. So I have one draft of
Canadian troops ready to go to the Front today, that's
Captain Tietjens's draft. Capitaine Thurston, do I have
the trains or do I not?

THURSTON
(*French accent*)
You have the trains, sir, and the co-operation of the
French railway, going east certainly.

CAMPION
I want these troops on their way to Flanders before
London can blink!

THURSTON
Oui, mon général.

CAMPION
(*to Levin*)
Champagne at two o'clock!

EXT. CAMP GATES, IBD, ROUEN – DAY

The camp is a mile outside Rouen. The first houses – and the end of the tramline – are in view. A Rolls-Royce with a military pennant arrives at the camp gates. The Guard turns out smartly. The arrival of General Campion's car is a regular occurrence.

The Rolls continues up a slope from which the tents and huts of the camp spread out.

EXT. OFFICERS' MESS, IBD, ROUEN – DAY

The Rolls pulls up outside. The Driver lets Campion out. Levin gets out, and follows Campion into the Mess Hut.

INT. OFFICERS' MESS, IBD, ROUEN – DAY

A dozen Canadian Junior Officers are being served champagne by Mess Orderlies. Christopher is among them. Campion's entrance commands everyone's attention.

> CAMPION
> Good day to you, gentlemen. Everyone got a glass?
> Splendid.

A telephone rings somewhere in the mess.

> Well, now – it's been our privilege to fit out you and your men for the task ahead. Somebody deal with that telephone. It is a great task, and thanks to Captain Tietjens and his unit, you go to it in good order.

Christopher's attention drifts to the papers and magazines on the table where he's standing. An Orderly passes the answered phone to Levin.

> CAMPION
> You will be relieving soldiers who have been in the trenches for many weeks.

Levin listens to the phone in consternation. Christopher sees a photograph of Sylvia and Johnny Pelham (a different photo, of Sylvia and Pelham at the theatre). He flinches.

He reads the caption.

CAMPION

Believe me, three thousand fresh troops under keen young officers is just what the Hun doesn't want to face in our part of the line.

Levin has hung up and is feverishly scribbling a note in his notebook.

So remember your training, and keep discipline at all times.

Christopher, his face stone, sees Levin hurrying to interrupt Campion.

Discipline and training will keep you alive – remember it. I'll be at the railhead to see you off. Form-up at twenty-hundred, air raids permitting –

Levin hands him the note. Campion reads it. His expression doesn't change.

CAMPION

That's in the event of there being no further orders. Thank you! Captain Tietjens, come with me!

Campion strides to the door. Christopher wonderingly, falls in with him. Levin follows a few paces behind.

CAMPION
(viciously)

The draft has been countermanded. I'll find out what's going on, but you had better be ready to get the men back under canvas tonight.

CHRISTOPHER

Yes, sir. May I ask what . . .?

CAMPION

No, you may not.

EXT. VICTORIA STATION, LONDON – DAY

Sylvia alights from and pays off a taxi. She has a smallish smart suitcase and a 'vanity' case. A Porter is already coming to take her luggage.

PORTER
Which train, madam?

SYLVIA
I don't know . . . Dover, I suppose . . .

She hears her name called, and sees Perowne, who is also taking leave of a taxi. Perowne is a very smart Major in charge of a dispatch case.

SYLVIA
Potty! What are you . . . ?

PEROWNE
King's Messenger!

SYLVIA
King's Messenger?

PEROWNE
Glorified postman, really, but frightfully important! – Locked carriages, private cabin, saluted through the gates . . . Where are you off to?

SYLVIA
Where are you?

An Assistant Station Master appears at Perowne's elbow, with a 'This way, sir.'

PEROWNE
Gosh, I've missed you, Sylvia.

Sylvia puts her arm through his.

EXT. OFFICERS' MESS, IBD, ROUEN – DAY

A reprise. Campion's Rolls pulls up outside. Campion and Levin alight as before.

INT. OFFICERS' MESS, IBD, ROUEN – DAY

A reprise of General Campion's farewell drink with the Officers of the Canadian draft . . . Levin and Christopher in attendance as before, and also Thurston this time.

> CAMPION
> . . . I can't tell you where your boat will dock but believe me the war where you're going is every bit as important as the war in Flanders, and you will get your chance at the Hun.

A telephone starts ringing.

> I dare say you're disappointed. Stop that telephone. I dare say you will have to learn new tricks for new conditions.

Levin is handed the answered phone. He listens.

> But I know you and your men will enjoy the challenge. You will form your men up at seventeen-hundred hours for the march to the railhead. We'll try to send you off by nineteen-hundred, before the expected air raid. That's all, gentleman – good luck!

Levin hangs up the phone looking concerned. Campion strides to the door. Thurston follows close behind.

At the entrance, Levin falls in with Campion nervously.

> LEVIN
> It was Major Perowne, sir, calling for a driver. He's at the station.

> CAMPION
> Good.

> LEVIN
> And . . . and he's got Mrs Tietjens with him.

Campion stops as though shot.

EXT. GARRISON HQ, IBD, ROUEN – DAY

General Campion stands outside to receive his unexpected guest. The Rolls arrives. Perowne, with his dispatch case chained discreetly to his wrist, gets out of the car and, seeing the General, advances, stops, salutes.

> CAMPION
>
> I will break you for this. I will smash you.

Perowne goggles and moves by as Campion adjusts his expression for Sylvia, who is approaching in all her glory.

> SYLVIA
>
> General! How lovely! – We've all been missing you.

EXT. INFANTRY BASE DEPOT – NIGHT

An air raid in progress. Bombs falling . . . guns responding . . . the depot lit up by the flash of explosions.

INT. CHRISTOPHER'S ORDERLY ROOM – NIGHT

Christopher and McKechnie sit opposite each other, with bully-beef boxes for chairs. Cowley and a Canadian Sergeant-Major, Ledoux, sit at the smaller table near the door. Two 'runners' – Welsh privates – crouch on the clay floor by the glowing brazier which is the hut's only light. A lid like a funnel sits on the brazier, light gleaming from punched holes. There are hooded candlesticks lacking candles.

McKechnie is about thirty, dark, good-looking, and currently reacting badly to the noise of the raid, which is considerable. Christopher has not been told McKechnie is unstable.

The guns of the base boom around them. Bombs explode hugely with a staccato of secondary sounds following. The hut shakes. After one especially loud bomb, McKechnie jumps up violently. Tietjens motions him to sit down.

During all this, the two runners are having a quiet conversation which becomes semi-audible between explosions. One of the runners is O Nine Morgan, in a rage about being refused leave. Cowley is fretting to the other Sergeant about the draft being delayed.

The three couples are not listening to each other. Amid the noise, scraps of talk emerge.

MCKECHNIE

Who the hell are you to tell me to sit down? I'm gazetted senior to you.

He continues in that vein.

O NINE MORGAN

. . . sold it to some bugger, Evans – if I thought it was William Evans of Castell Coch, I'd desert . . .

COWLEY

(*to Ledoux*)

. . . midnight before we can march them off. It's not right to keep men hanging about like that. They don't like it . . .

CHRISTOPHER

Set an example, can't you, McKechnie?

Their voices are obliterated by a short pandemonium, followed by a lull, in which McKechnie talks continuously, under the other voices.

MCKECHNIE

. . . if I screamed louder than the bombs, that would fix it, I'd be all right.

SECOND RUNNER

Lost the fuckers.

COWLEY

Not so much swear words, O Five Thomas.

Cowley comes over to Christopher.

COWLEY

While it's gone quiet, sir, we could send a runner to the sergeant-cook to tell him we're going to indent for the draft's suppers.

MCKECHNIE

. . . the millennial circle will close on itself to a point,

all time and space bound into an atom, all noise, all the
idiot noises of populations and copulations . . .

*Cowley wants the runners out of the way while the Captain is
having a turn.*

COWLEY

And the other one can take the 128s to Quarter . . .

They are all three talking at once.

CHRISTOPHER

Send the runner to Depot and say that if candles are not
provided for my orderly room by return of bearer, I –
Captain Tietjens commanding Number Sixteen Casual
Battalion – will bring the whole matter of supplies before
Base HQ tonight.

MCKECHNIE
(*mutters*)

What's it all about? That's what I want to know!

*Christopher looks to the door to see the runners leaving, the
Canadian Sergeant-Major following, Cowley looking out at
the reflections of flames.*

MCKECHNIE

You're no sort of soldier! They say up at HQ that your
wife has got hold of your friend the General – I know all
about you . . .

CHRISTOPHER

I assure you, you are mistaken if you call the General a
friend of mine. I haven't a friend in the world. (*Calls.*)
Sergeant-Major! – Don't let the Dominion troops leave
their dug-outs till the all-clear! (*To McKechnie.*) Look
here, are you mad? Stark staring? If you let yourself go,
you'll go further than you wish.

An anti-aircraft battery comes back to life.

CHRISTOPHER

They imagine they've found the Hun again . . .

INT. CAMPION'S HQ, IBD, ROUEN – NIGHT

At the same moment, Campion is giving dinner to Sylvia, Levin and Capitaine Thurston, in surprisingly civilised style. Bombs are falling but not close.

Thurston knows that Sylvia knows that Thurston remembers seeing her with Perowne in the Rouen hotel in 1912.

Thurston is unfazed because he's French. Sylvia is unfazed because she's Sylvia.

> SYLVIA
> *(to Thurston)*
> I must say you look divine in your uniform.

> THURSTON
> *Enchanté, madame.*

> SYLVIA
> *(to Campion)*
> I knew *le brave Capitaine* and his wife in London before the war . . . and didn't we see each other somewhere in France in 1912?

> THURSTON
> In Rouen, madame. *Extraordinaire!*

> SYLVIA
> Does Christopher know I'm here?

> CAMPION
> No. As soon as his draft leaves for the station, he'll have a few hours to come to the hotel. Failing that, my officers are under orders to attend my regular entente cordiale party tomorrow.

> SYLVIA
> Why can't I see him now?

> CAMPION
> You may have noticed there's an air raid . . .

> SYLVIA
> Isn't that normal? This is where the war is.

LEVIN

The Captain's on duty and can't leave the camp. I've booked you the room next to his. There is a connecting door.

SYLVIA

If Christopher is billeted at the hotel, why doesn't he sleep there?

LEVIN

He bunks down in the hut lines . . . We're all working under difficult circumstances.

Levin sips his wine. Sylvia gives him an expressive look.

SYLVIA

Are we?

EXT. CHRISTOPHER'S ORDERLY ROOM, IBD, ROUEN – NIGHT

An explosion close to Christopher's orderly room – a hut or similar blows up.

INT. CHRISTOPHER'S ORDERLY ROOM – NIGHT

In the echo of an explosion, loud drops of iron rain spatter all around the hut, and a tearing sound, and then the sharp knock of a small piece of shrapnel on the table between Christopher and McKechnie. McKechnie picks it up.

MCKECHNIE

Don't think I'm afraid of a bit of shrapnel.

CHRISTOPHER

They ought to let my orderly room have tin hats.

MCKECHNIE

Our headquarters are full of Huns doing the Huns' work.

CHRISTOPHER

Do you believe that tripe? It's the English doing it.

There is another explosion, muffled, as through deep in the earth . . . causing somehow the subsequent noise of many

237

*doors slamming, then a heavy silence . . . in which Thomas
skips into the hut snorting and carrying two fat candles.*

THOMAS

Nearly got me, surely to goodness, I did run, oh I did
run!

CHRISTOPHER

You can go into shelter with the Dominion troops, if you
like.

THOMAS

No, I'll wait for my mate, Cahpt'n sir.

*Christopher shoves the candles into the spring that holds them
in the hooded lamps and lights them. They make small pools
of light on the table.*

MCKECHNIE

I was in for the Foreign Office before all this began.

CHRISTOPHER

I suppose you speak seven languages.

MCKECHNIE

Five. And Latin and Greek of course. Here it comes.

It does. Iron rain after the bang.

*A figure – O Nine Morgan – bursts through the door and
stands, already dead, like a scarlet spectre, divided up the
middle between khaki and blood.*

O NINE MORGAN

'Ere's another bloomin' casualty.

*He pitches over on the brazier and then the ground, falling
across Thomas's legs.*

Cowley and Christopher try to lift Morgan off Thomas's legs.

THOMAS

Pore fucking O Nine Morgan, surely to goodness I did
not recognise the pore –

CHRISTOPHER
Get out from under him, damn you!

COWLEY
This ain't your job, sir.

Thomas gets out from under.

MCKECHNIE
(*to Christopher*)
You'll get all sticky.

Cowley goes to the door and bellows for a bugler. Christopher holds the dead man in his arms. Thomas pours water from a jug into a basin.

Christopher looks down at the half-face of Morgan grinning up at him in his arms.

COWLEY
(*outside*)
Bugler, call two sanitary lance-corporals and four men. Two sanitary lance-corporals and four men with an ambulance stretcher.

EXT. CHRISTOPHER'S ORDERLY ROOM – NIGHT

Cowley goes back into the hut as the Bugler calls as requested: prolonged, mournful separated sounds on the booming flashing night.

INT. CHRISTOPHER'S ORDERLY ROOM – NIGHT

O Nine Morgan is on the floor. McKechnie replaces the lid on the brazier. Christopher sits down at the table, his boots in a rivulet of Morgan's blood.

Christopher puts his hands into the basin of water, which accepts the blood.

The second runner, Thomas, crouches down and starts rubbing Christopher's boots with a rag.

CHRISTOPHER

Thomas . . . O Nine Morgan was your mate?

THOMAS

He was a good pal, poor old bugger. You would not like, surely to goodness, to go to mess with your shoes all bloody.

CHRISTOPHER

If I'd given him leave, he would not be dead now.

THOMAS

No, surely he would not. But it is all one, Cahpt'n. Your honour is a good cahpt'n.

INT. CAMPION'S HQ, IBD, ROUEN – NIGHT

Sylvia is on her fourth glass of wine, and tending towards surliness.

SYLVIA

I know why Christopher doesn't sleep at the hotel. He's got his mistress in Rouen, with the child. How old is that child now? Five?

Capitaine Thurston looks on, bemused.

CAMPION

No. Of course not. I know nothing about – if you're talking about Miss Wannop – I'm not prepared to . . . Even if his treatment of you has been . . . which I'm not defending –

SYLVIA

Yes, Miss Wannop, Christopher's little suffragette. I've got nothing against them being pro-German – I have German friends myself –

LEVIN

Oh, I say, steady on –

CAMPION

Yes, stop doing . . . what does your mother call it? – shower baths . . .

SYLVIA

Oh, you think minding about Miss Wannop and her baby
in Rouen –

CAMPION

I expressly denied –

SYLVIA

– is Sylvia pulling the strings of the shower bath?

LEVIN
(*desperate*)

I say, they've got the vote, though – I saw it in the *Sketch*.
Will you vote, Mrs Tietjens?

Sylvia stares at him uncomprehendingly.

SYLVIA

I am not going to the hotel until I have seen Christopher
with my own eyes.

The all-clear sounds.

EXT. THE CAMP, IBD, ROUEN – NIGHT

*The all-clear is being sounded. Then silence. A bit of moon in
the January sky.*

*Christopher, wearing his 'British warm' with the sheepskin
collar, stands near his orderly room hut. Some way off, two or
three fires are burning. Christopher is trembling with shock.
He recovers slowly, and goes back into the hut.*

INT. CHRISTOPHER'S ORDERLY ROOM – NIGHT

*Christopher walks in to find McKechnie at work on papers
under the bright light of a hurricane lamp. McKechnie is
having a sane phase, in his own manner.*

*The hut has been put to rights, the blood reduced to a stain on
the clay floor.*

MCKECHNIE

There's a note from your foul General.

CHRISTOPHER

What does it say?

McKechnie tears open a small buff envelope. Before Christopher has realised the note is for himself only, McKechnie reads it out.

MCKECHNIE

'For God's sake. Can't you control your woman?' Well, it didn't say it was private. 'You are more trouble to me than all the rest of my command put together.'

Christopher starts shaking. He needs to steady himself. He seizes a piece of paper and writes a vertical line of alphabet letters on it.

CHRISTOPHER

Give me the rhyme-words for a sonnet. That's the scheme of it.

MCKECHNIE

I know what a damn sonnet is – what's your game?

CHRISTOPHER

Give me fourteen end-rhymes of a sonnet and I'll write a sonnet. In two and a half minutes.

MCKECHNIE

If you do, I'll translate it into Latin hexameters in three – *under* three minutes.

They speak as though uttering deadly insults.

CHRISTOPHER

Get on with it then. A, B, B, A – A, B . . .

A figure looms by him.

(*Angrily.*) Yes – what is it?

He sees a white-whiskered RASC Second Lieutenant of about sixty.

Good God. Who are you?

HOTCHKISS

Hotchkiss. They said to find you. Are you Captain Tietjens?

CHRISTOPHER
(*angrily*)
Don't you know how to address an officer?

HOTCHKISS
Oh, yes, sorry – sir!

CHRISTOPHER
How long have you been in the army?

HOTCHKISS
Two weeks.

McKechnie throws his piece of paper across the table.

MCKECHNIE
There you are. Two and a half minutes from now.

Christopher proceeds to ignore Hotchkiss, and starts writing.

HOTCHKISS
I have to go to Division horse lines, and I seem to have been put in charge of taking your soldiers to some place called Bailleul . . . er, sir.

EXT. GUARD POST, THE CAMP, IBD, ROUEN – NIGHT

Campion's Rolls drives up to the camp gate and stops. The Driver opens the rear door for Levin. Sylvia is in the Rolls but remains inside. Levin speaks to her, and is saluted through the gate.

INT. CHRISTOPHER'S ORDERLY ROOM – NIGHT

Christopher is writing.

HOTCHKISS
(*to McKechnie*)
There's pink-eye running rife in all the service horses. I've made a study of it. I was sent for by the War Office. I suppose Lord Beichen knew about me from my publications. I'm a Professor of Equine Studies.

MCKECHNIE
Well, you're a stout fellow. Who bamboozled you into taking the draft to Bailleul?

CHRISTOPHER
(*writing*)
You could speak to Colonel Johnson – you'll find him in Sixteen IBD Mess, he'll be interested to meet you – he's got a Hun horse captured on the Marne, I ride him myself.

He throws his completed sonnet at McKechnie.

HOTCHKISS
Well . . . if you say so. Many thanks.

Hotchkiss leaves the hut.

MCKECHNIE
Two minutes and eleven seconds. I'm not starting till I've checked it's a sonnet.

COWLEY
(*entering*)

GSO 2, sir.

He means that Colonel Levin is coming. McKechnie folds the sonnet.

MCKECHNIE
You understand I have not read it. I'll turn it into Latin in the time stipulated when I'm free.

Cowley comes to attention as Levin enters. Christopher and McKechnie stand up. Levin, with no top coat, his tailored uniform glittering with silver, brass and red bits of identification and his knee-boots shiny, seems to have strayed in from a musical comedy.

LEVIN
Number Sixteen Draft not left yet! Oh, deah, deah! We shall be strafed to hell.

Cowley considers it his responsibility to protect his officers from the Staff.

COWLEY

We had to wangle everything, sir – desert boots, malaria powders . . .

LEVIN

Oh, deah, oh deah . . . but Sergeant-Major! –

COWLEY

And then unwangle everything for normal in a hurry when it was changed back to Bailleul . . .

MCKECHNIE

It makes you wonder who's in charge, sir.

LEVIN

Oh, deah me! Ah, I see you're there, McKechnie. Feeling well? Feeling fit?

Levin dusts his knees with a handkerchief.

CHRISTOPHER

I've just had a man killed on my hands because we have to draw tin hats for my orderly room on an AFB from Aldershot.

LEVIN

Oh, good gracious me! Killed! Here! You certainly *have* been unfortunate. Why wasn't your man in the dug-out? There'll have to be a court of inquiry. We can't have casualties among Colonial troops.

CHRISTOPHER

He was one of my orderly room, sir, not a Dominion man.

LEVIN

Only a Glamorganshire? It makes, of course, a difference. Oh well . . . but always something, Captain Tietjens, always unfortunate . . . something mysterious about it. Well – look here – can you spare me ten or twenty minutes? It's not exactly a service matter.

EXT. CHRISTOPHER'S ORDERLY ROOM – NIGHT

Christopher and Levin come out. Levin drops his rank and becomes abject.

LEVIN

You have to come down to the gate. I hate to keep a woman waiting.

CHRISTOPHER

You mean, your . . . ?

LEVIN

As it happens, I was spotted at the station and now my French lady friend thinks I've got an English mistress. Come on!

CHRISTOPHER

Are you dragging me down there to deal with your absurd love life?

LEVIN

Mine? It's yours!

Christopher, misunderstanding, is physically rocked.

LEVIN

The poor woman is in a dreadful state of anxiety about you. You haven't written to her once, she says.

CHRISTOPHER

You can't mean Miss . . . ?

He stumbles into a half-run, Levin trying to keep up.

EXT. GUARD ROOM, CAMP GATE, IBD, ROUEN – NIGHT

Sylvia has got out of the Rolls. The Guard Sergeant has turned out the guard for Sylvia – half a dozen Soldiers at attention. Sylvia, in her travelling coat, has captivated the Sergeant, the Guard and two goggling Sentries.

SYLVIA

Do you swear it?

SERGEANT

Cross my heart, miss. I saw the Captain with my own
eyes this very morning, miss!

SYLVIA

I've been dreadfully worried about him.

The Guard and Sentries cannot contain their smirking delight.

SERGEANT

You're welcome to wait in the guardroom, miss . . .

SYLVIA

No, it's perfectly all right now. I don't need to disturb
Captain Tietjens when he's on duty, so long as he's all
right. You've all been absolutely sweet . . .

EXT. THE CAMP, IBD, ROUEN – NIGHT

*Christopher is hurrying downhill. As he comes into sight of
the guardroom and gate, he sees the Rolls leaving. The car's
interior light is on. Sylvia, like a mermaid in an aquarium, is
borne away into the night. Christopher goes out of shock into
shock.*

CHRISTOPHER

Oh, God . . . Sylvia . . .

LEVIN
(*catching up*)
Dammit! – She's taken the car!

INT. CHRISTOPHER'S QUARTERS, IBD, ROUEN – NIGHT

*Christopher sleeps over in a borrowed 'hut' made of sailcloth,
with celluloid windows. A cupboard, a bed, a table, a chair,
a washstand, a paraffin stove, an oil lamp.*

*Christopher, demented, shivering, sits on the bed. His lips
move. His mind escapes into audibility. 'What is she up to?'
A voice asks for him outside. Christopher lifts the flap of the
hut, and sees Sergeant-Major Ledoux.*

LEDOUX

Beg your pardon, sir. This man, sir, of the Canadian
Railway lot, 'is mother's just turned up, come all the way
from Toronto.

CHRISTOPHER

What's his name? Get in here.

*The three of them crowd into the hut, Girtin and Ledoux
standing stiffly, Christopher relapsing to sit on the bed.*

LEDOUX

Girtin, sir. His mother's in a decent estaminet at the end
of the tramline, just a step from the camp.

Christopher looks at the boy.

CHRISTOPHER

If you're asking to leave the camp to see your mother, it's
impossible. Absolutely impossible. You must know that.
The draft is about to leave. You can see for yourself it's
impossible, can't you?

GIRTIN

I can't say, sir, not knowing the regulations. But my
mother has lost two sons already and she wants to say
goodbye to me. I didn't know my brothers were dead till
I got to Aldershot.

CHRISTOPHER

What sort of fellow is this?

LEDOUX

Very good man, sir, one of the best, clean conduct sheet,
no trouble.

CHRISTOPHER

Do you understand what will happen to you if you miss
the draft?

GIRTIN

Yes, sir.

CHRISTOPHER

You will be shot.

248

GIRTIN

Yes, sir.

CHRISTOPHER

Literally. Shot at dawn.

GIRTIN

Yes, sir.

CHRISTOPHER

And I will lose my commission, forgive my mentioning it.

Girtin makes to say something.

LEDOUX
(*sharply*)

Don't you hear the officer is speaking? Never interrupt an officer!

CHRISTOPHER

Give this man a two-hours' pass. The draft won't leave for two hours, will it?

LEDOUX

Yes, sir. No, sir. Thank you, sir. 'Bout turn!

Girtin about-turns.

Abruptly left on his own again, Christopher lies down on the bed. A photo frame is next to the bed, a photograph of Michael. He closes his eyes.

Later:

Christopher comes out of his half-sleep. A sound has done it: the rhythmic, brushing sound of the draft marching away, passing not far from the canvas wall by his head, and receding. He closes his eyes again.

INT. SYLVIA'S ROOM, HOTEL, ROUEN – NIGHT

The sound of marching men . . . waking Sylvia.

An interior door is open to the connecting room, also a bedroom, empty now, Christopher's room.

249

Sylvia gets out of bed and goes to her window in her nightdress to watch the draft going by. She becomes aware of a nearer sound, which she identifies as a tapping at her door. She turns and sees the door handle moving.

INT. BEDROOM CORRIDOR, HOTEL, ROUEN – NIGHT

Perowne, at Sylvia's door, taps and tries the handle, calling softly ('Sylvia, dash it!') before giving up and retreating.

INT. SYLVIA'S ROOM, HOTEL, ROUEN – NIGHT

Sylvia turns back to the window, where the sound of the march is fading. More distantly a train whistle is heard.

INT. CHRISTOPHER'S QUARTERS, IBD, ROUEN – NIGHT

Christopher, lying awake, hears the draft coming back.

McKechnie puts his head in Christopher's door.

> MCKECHNIE
> The draft's come back!

McKechnie's head disappears. Christopher pulls on his trousers, cursing, despairing.

McKechnie's head returns.

> MCKECHNIE
> By the way did you give a pass to one of the Canadians?

> CHRISTOPHER
> Why?

> MCKECHNIE
> Hasn't been seen since.

McKechnie disappears.

> CHRISTOPHER
> (*bitterly*)
> Naturally.

INT. SCHOOL CHANGING ROOM – DAY

Now in the role of 'changing-room monitor', Valentine is among a crowd of 'hockey girls' in a space of washbasins, lockers and clothes pegs, where Valentine's girls are washing and combing, etc.

There is a row of shower stalls, each with a sunflower shower-head and two hanging chains with ring-pulls, controlling 'hot' and 'cold'. Sounds of girls in the showers.

> SCHOOLGIRL 1
>
> So does that mean you will vote in the next election, miss?

> VALENTINE
>
> If I'm old enough. I won't be thirty for . . . oh, years!

> SCHOOLGIRL 2
>
> Do you know Mrs Pankhurst, miss?

> SCHOOLGIRL 3
>
> She's your heroine, isn't she, miss?

> VALENTINE
>
> Well . . . I don't know, Annie, I'm certainly not hers. She said the other day that pacificism was a disease.

> SCHOOLGIRL 2
>
> You wouldn't be a pacifist if you had a sweetheart in the war, would you, miss?

> VALENTINE
>
> More than ever, of course. Hurry up, the bell will go in a minute.

> SCHOOLGIRL 1
>
> Have you got a sweetheart in the war, miss?

Valentine is caught in the headlights.

Before she can answer, one of the Schoolgirls, standing on a chair, reaches over the partition of the nearest shower and pulls the 'string' which turns the water cold. There is a shriek

from the occupant of the shower, and collusive laughter, and
Valentine is glad of the distraction.

INT. CHRISTOPHER'S ORDERLY ROOM, IBD, ROUEN – DAY

*Christopher, behind his table, is presiding over his 'courtroom'
with Cowley in faithful attendance, and two large Military
Policemen and Girtin standing to attention in front of him.*

CHRISTOPHER

. . . so at a few minutes before eleven p.m. when the
prisoner was putting his mother on the tram, the prisoner
called you a damn brute for no reason, least of all
because you made a discourteous comment about the
lady, is that right?

MILITARY POLICEMAN

Yes, sir!

CHRISTOPHER

And then, having engaged the prisoner in conversation,
by no means calling him 'a blankety-blank colonial
conscript', you discovered that it was two minutes past
eleven, so very properly you charged him with being off-
base and 'conduct prejudicial'.

MILITARY POLICEMAN

Sah!

CHRISTOPHER
(*to Cowley*)

Mark the charge sheet 'case explained'. (*To Girtin.*)
Dismiss!

GIRTIN

Sir!

*Girtin salutes, stamps, about-turns and goes. Cowley sucks his
lip in appreciation. Christopher turns to the Policemen in cold
fury.*

CHRISTOPHER

I am a hair's breadth from recommending a court of

inquiry into your conduct. If there is any – *any* repetition, by God you will regret it.

He nods to Cowley and busies himself with his paper.

COWLEY
(*shouts*)
Witnesses, dismiss!

The Military Policemen perform the necessary manoeuvre and leave, Cowley following them out. A moment later, Cowley returns making astonished sounds through his moustache.

COWLEY
Provost-Marshal won't like it, sir. General O'Hara loves his police like his own ewe lambs.

CHRISTOPHER
The French railwaymen going on strike was a bit of luck for that Canadian lad, though.

COWLEY
They heard rumours the draft was for overseas.

CHRISTOPHER
If I'm needed I'm going to ride Schomburg over to the Hotel de la Poste and take my wife to the General's tea party for the locals.

EXT. COUNTRYSIDE ABOVE ROUEN – DAY

Christopher is riding Schomburg, the German charger, a chestnut, accompanied by a Groom on a roan. A fair frosty January day. Christopher rides comfortably among woods and empty fields. The war seems far away. The groom is watching Schomburg, knowing that Christopher is unhappy with the horse's gait.

CHRISTOPHER
What the hell is the matter with this horse? Have you been keeping him warm?

PRIVATE
(*outraged*)

No, sir. The 'oss 'as been put in 'oss-standings of G Depot.
By orders of Lieutentant 'Otchkiss.

CHRISTOPHER

Did you tell him that it was my orders that Schomburg
was to be kept warm? – in the stables of the farm behind
Number Sixteen IBD?

PRIVATE

The Lieutenant says 'osses 'ave to be 'ardened, sir. 'E said
as 'ow henny departure from 'is orders'd be visited by the
hextreme displeasure of Lord Beecham, KCVO et cetera.

CHRISTOPHER

Well, listen carefully. When you fall out at the Hotel de la
Poste, take both horses back to the farm stables. Make
sure the windows are closed and stop up any chinks. Give
the horses oatmeal and water as hot as they will take it.
Finally, if Lieutenant Hotchkiss makes any comments,
refer him to me.

INT. RECEPTION AND LOUNGE, HOTEL, ROUEN – DAY

*We were here five years ago with Sylvia and Perowne . . . who
are among the people making use of the conservatory/lounge
now.*

*Walking in from outside, Christopher sees them – Sylvia's
unmistakable head of hair, her face turned away, and Perowne
in profile. Christopher stops. He moves to go to her, then
checks. He turns away and, now calm, he takes out his pocket
book. Then Sylvia sees Christopher in the reflection of a
glassed painting.*

PEROWNE
(*bleating*)

How can you forget? – it's the very place where you left
me and ruined my life! So fair's fair. Will you leave your
door unlocked tonight?

SYLVIA

That's Christopher!

Perowne jerks in his chair, losing his hold on his hat, stick and gloves, then shrinks back into the wickerwork.

SYLVIA

I can see him in the glass. He's seen me, too.

PEROWNE

Good God . . . what are we going to do? What will *he* do? He'll smash me to pieces!

SYLVIA

He wouldn't do anything to a girl like you. A decent man doesn't hit girls.

Christopher has given his card to the Hotel Manager, affecting not to have seen Sylvia and therefore not directing him to her.

SYLVIA

Oh, damn his chivalry! So as not to embarrass me. He'll leave it to me.

The Hotel Manager comes into the lounge, looks around and comes to Sylvia with the card on a salver.

HOTEL MANAGER

Pardon . . . I did not see madame . . .

SYLVIA

(*without looking at the card*)

Dites à ce monsieur que je suis occupée.

The Hotel Manager bows and retreats.

SYLVIA

He looks ill.

PEROWNE

What's he doing?

SYLVIA

Giving me the social backing he thinks it's his duty as my husband to give. He's Jesus Christ calling on the woman taken in adultery.

Christopher retrieves his card from the salver with no change of expression and replaces it in his pocket book.

SYLVIA

By all the saints, I'll make that wooden face wince yet. I'll bring him to heel . . . He's going upstairs.

PEROWNE

He's probably gone to wreck your bedroom.

SYLVIA

It's no good trying to awaken sentimental memories in me. Has Christopher got a girl in this town?

PEROWNE

No, he's too much of a stick. He never even goes to Suzette's. Look here, will you let me come to your room tonight or not?

Sylvia bursts into laughter.

PEROWNE

What's your game? Hell and hounds, you can't have come here for *him*! What's your game?

INT. CHRISTOPHER'S ROOM, HOTEL – DAY

Christopher has changed into a fresh uniform. He is ready to leave. He opens the connecting door and pauses, looking into Sylvia's room . . . her intimate things on the dressing table, her silks hanging up or thrown over the back of a chair. He picks up a silk slip and buries his face in it.

INT. LOUNGE, HOTEL, ROUEN – DAY

Sylvia sees Christopher in the glass . . . leaving the hotel without a glance.

SYLVIA

I'm going to my room to tidy up for the General's tea party. Wait for me. I'm not going to look as if I couldn't find a man to escort me.

PEROWNE

Campion will send me to the trenches if it looks like that.

SYLVIA

Do you mean you wouldn't die for me, Potty?

PEROWNE

Hang it all, what a cruel fiend you are.

SYLVIA

I'm a woman desperately trying to get her husband back.
If Christopher would throw his handkerchief to me I
would follow him round the world in my shift.

PEROWNE

No, you wouldn't. You're just wanting to make him
squeal.

SYLVIA
(quietly)

For that I'll leave my door unlocked, and be damned to
you! I don't say you'll get anything, or like what you get,
but it's up to you.

INT. CAMPION'S HQ, IBD, ROUEN – DAY

*Campion is the host. Levin, Thurston, McKechnie, Christopher
and other Officers mingle with the guests, who are local
dignitaries and some wives. British Army Orderlies in white
waiter's jackets circulate with trays of drinks. Languages are
bad French and bad English. The local Mayor wears his chain
of office.*

*Capitaine Thurston introduces Levin to a senior Railway
Official.*

THURSTON

. . . Regional manager of the railway . . .

LEVIN
(shaking hands)

Railways? Oh deah, oh deah . . . what is going on with
you chaps? Hating the Hun has to come first, otherwise –

THURSTON
(*translating falsely, in French*)
Colonel Levin congratulates you on the superhuman
efforts of the *chemin de fer* . . .

Campion has cornered Christopher.

CAMPION
(*to Christopher*)
. . . Well, why do you treat her so damnably?

CHRISTOPHER
Sir, I don't have to discuss my . . .

CAMPION
I mean for heaven's sake – Sylvia is the finest, the cleanest
–

*There is a climate and gravity change. Sylvia has entered with
Perowne, her shrinking escort. Perowne meets Campion's glare
and sidles into hiding. McKechnie skulks darkly, drinking.*

*Sylvia comes to Campion and Christopher. Christopher tilts
his face in impassive greeting. They have not spoken for
months.*

CAMPION
My dear . . . you've come to do your bit for the Grand
Alliance. You have already seen each other. Good!

CHRISTOPHER
Yes . . . I made time to call at the hotel, sir.

*Campion is already on a different trajectory, moving off to
shake some more hands.*

SYLVIA
I suppose I should thank you for making things clear.

CHRISTOPHER
I don't understand you.

SYLVIA
You didn't come back to the hotel to sleep. You prefer all
the fun of camping out with your Boy Scouts, do you? Or

did you spend the night with your mistress in her little nest in this frightful town?

CHRISTOPHER

I hardly got any sleep anywhere. There was a railway strike which landed me with three thousand men I'd dispatched to the front lines three hours earlier. The French way of telling us that . . .

SYLVIA

I'll scream if you don't stop.

CHRISTOPHER

I'm sorry. I have forgotten how to be . . . how to be at peace, I suppose. How is Michael? He hasn't written to me.

SYLVIA

He hardly knows you. I came to settle things between us. Will you come to the hotel tonight?

McKechnie butts in without ceremony, taking a buff envelope from his wallet.

MCKECHNIE

See? Still sealed.

Campion rejoins them. McKechnie turns away rudely, unnoticed.

CAMPION
(*to Sylvia*)

I'll send a driver for you in the morning, o-eight-hundred.

SYLVIA

Where am I going?

CAMPION

You're going to the station and think yourself lucky.

SYLVIA

I will. You've been sweet.

EXT. HOTEL DE LA POSTE, ROUEN – NIGHT

An air raid is in progress – not a full-scale raid, but an enemy plane overhead, with a few rounds of anti-aircraft fire. One of the guns is in the hotel garden.

INT. SYLVIA'S ROOM, HOTEL, ROUEN – NIGHT

Sylvia, dressed for dinner, is in her room, waiting, walking restlessly.

INT. RECEPTION LOBBY, HOTEL – NIGHT

Christopher is dog tired. He pauses in the dark lobby, aware of the dancing and romancing going on in the lounge. There is no one behind the reception desk. He goes behind for his key and realises that a couple are making love on the floor. He can't see anything.

Christopher takes his key. The lovers remain unaware of him. A Provost-Marshal, General O'Hara (the most senior rank of Military Police, a tall, purple-faced white-moustached veteran) shows up with a torch.

> O'HARA
> (*angrily*)
> Captain Tietjens. I got your chit of this morning . . .
> I must say . . .

Christopher comes to attention for him.

> O'HARA
> Marking 'case explained' on a charge sheet I signed
> myself is pretty strong.

> CHRISTOPHER
> If you would see fit, sir, to instruct your men not to call
> Colonial troops damned conscripts –

> O'HARA
> They are damned conscripts!

CHRISTOPHER
No, sir, not one of them. Voluntarily enlisted.

O'HARA
(*explodes*)
You damned insolent – You haven't heard the last of it!

CHRISTOPHER
Sir!

INT. BEDROOM CORRIDOR, HOTEL – NIGHT

Christopher arrives in the dimly lit corridor and opens his door with a key.

INT. CHRISTOPHER'S BEDROOM, HOTEL – NIGHT

Christopher enters. The room is softly lit. More light flows from the connecting door. Sylvia comes from her room.

SYLVIA
Christopher . . . you look half dead.

CHRISTOPHER
Not far off it. Have you had dinner?

SYLVIA
I vamped an old fool of a general over a cutlet. Then the air raid started and he went off to order everybody about.

CHRISTOPHER
General O'Hara.

SYLVIA
What have you been doing?

CHRISTOPHER
Since I saw you? Let me think.

He has to sit down. He sits on the bed.

Well, I inspected two thousand nine hundred and thirty-four toothbrushes. Most of them were clean, because the troops use their button-brushes for their teeth, to keep their toothbrushes clean for inspections.

SYLVIA

So you betrayed me with a battalion! You need a brandy. I'll call down.

CHRISTOPHER

Rum and hot water, if you would.

SYLVIA

Of course. Would you like to bathe?

CHRISTOPHER

I think I would, you know.

The AA gun in the garden flashes and bangs. A maroon makes a loud bang some distance away.

SYLVIA

It's sheer cheek putting a gun where people of quality might be sleeping or wishing to converse.

Sylvia goes into her room, to the telephone. Christopher takes off his tunic and unbuttons his shirt. Sylvia returns with a few letters.

SYLVIA

They're not answering. I'll try again. I've brought a few letters which came for you, two from Mrs Wannop, who doesn't seem to know that her daughter is your mistress, and one from your brother Mark which begins, 'Your bitch of a wife came to see me.' You should read that first, it's what I came to see you about.

CHRISTOPHER

Thank you.

He takes the letters and sits on the bed.

SYLVIA

The War Office brilliantly sent it on to the flat. I've always understood that your idea of marriage is that a husband and wife should be able to read each other's letters.

Of course.

Christopher glances through Mark's letter.

Sylvia goes back into her room. She uses the telephone. No one answers downstairs. She goes back to Christopher's bedroom.

SYLVIA

I'll go –

She sees that Christopher is asleep on his back with the letter in his hands. She hesitates and returns to her room, not quite closing the door.

Sylvia's room:

She starts to undress.

Christopher's room:

The gun bangs outside. He doesn't stir. Someone knocks on his door, not specially loudly. He jerks to his feet and goes to open the door.

A Night Porter is at the door with an envelope. Christopher thanks him and closes the door. He reads the short note in the envelope. He is incredulous and furious.

SYLVIA
(*out of shot*)

What is it?

He looks to the connecting door.

CHRISTOPHER

The draft has been brought forward. I have to be at the camp by 4.30 . . .

Christopher walks into:

INT. SYLVIA'S BEDROOM – SAME TIME

Sylvia, a robe over her nightdress, sits at her dressing table like a bride preparing for the night . . . dabbing a large powder puff into the recesses of her robe.

Christopher pauses, Sylvia calmly finishes powdering and returns the puff to the box.

SYLVIA

It's ridiculous that a man of your abilities should be at the beck and call of a lot of gaga old fools like the one downstairs. You shouldn't be here at all. You're not fit.

CHRISTOPHER

Nobody posted to a Base Depot is fit. That's why we're here.

Christopher sits on a bench seat at the foot of the bed.

I'm sorry that you felt you had to come all this way to settle something I would have been perfectly happy for you to settle for yourself. Groby is at your disposal if you want to live there with Michael . . . and of course with sufficient income to keep it up.

SYLVIA

That means you don't intend to live there yourself. Or you intend to get killed. I should warn you that if you do get killed, I shall cut down the cedar. It darkens the drawing room and the rooms above. (*Pause.*) At last I changed the expression on your face.

CHRISTOPHER

I haven't the slightest intention of getting killed. But it's not really up to me. If I were to be sent back to my battalion . . .

Sylvia stands to take off her robe. Without it she is next to nude.

SYLVIA

Your brother refers to me as 'that whore'. I haven't had a man, Christopher, for five years and more. Not one. I haven't let myself be kissed, or touched. Not once, not since Perowne. Potty Perowne! Can you see how I must

264

have been feeling, to go away with a fool like Potty? I was not in my senses. I broke under your forbearance, your permanent well-mannered forgivingness for my doing the dirty on you when I married you not knowing – still don't know! – whether my child was yours or Gerald Drake's. You forgave without mercy. To scream blue murder and throw me out would have been a kindness compared to five years under your roof banished from your comfort – oh, look what you brought me to! Throwing myself at you in my whore's trousseau! My heat must have put a spell on all the sentries and ticket-inspectors, the musk of five years wanting a man, they must have smelled it – well, don't bother now, I've changed my mind –

But Christopher, with a moan wrenched from him, has already grasped her. She lets him hold her. Over his shoulder she sees –

The door handle of her bedroom door turning.

Sylvia sees it and ignores it. Christopher, kissing her hair, holds her. They wheel and stagger in their embrace. Over her shoulder, Christopher sees her door slowly opening, a face peering in. He lets go of Sylvia and, roaring with rage, he hurls himself at the door, pulling it open and bodily throwing Perowne across the corridor. He does not know it is Perowne, who is in a dressing gown.

Corridor:

Perowne lands heavily and yells out. Christopher slams shut the bedroom door.

Along the corridor, another door is flung open, and General O'Hara, also in a dressing gown, sees Perowne on the floor.

O'HARA

What's going on?

INT. SYLVIA'S ROOM – BACK TO SCENE

Christopher turns off the light.

CHRISTOPHER

Get into bed.

Sylvia's spirits are transformed, lightened. She jumps on the bed with a laugh. Christopher turns off the only lamp lit.

CHRISTOPHER

I didn't see who it was.

SYLVIA

Potty, I expect. I'd forgotten about him!

The door bursts open, breaking the catch.

O'HARA

Where is the hussy?

CHRISTOPHER

This is my wife's room. I ask you to leave this instant.

O'HARA

We'll see whether she's your wife or not – she didn't mind making eyes at *me*!

Corridor:

A uniformed Subaltern – one of O'Hara's Redcaps – comes from the stairs.

Sylvia's room:

CHRISTOPHER

Leave this room!

O'HARA

You assaulted an officer. What's the game here?

O'Hara staggers against the door jamb.

CHRISTOPHER

Look, are you drunk?

O'HARA
(*enraged*)

By God, I'll have you for that!

Christopher sees the Redcap behind O'Hara.

CHRISTOPHER

If you do not take General O'Hara away, I shall order you to arrest him for drunkenness.

O'HARA

Consider yourself under arrest! Return to your quarters.

Christopher pushes O'Hara out of the door and closes it.

Corridor:

The Redcap respectfully strong-arms his drunken superior away. Perowne watches from his cracked-open doorway, looking apprehensive, then closes his door.

Sylvia's room:

She turns on the lamp.

SYLVIA

Well! What a lark!

CHRISTOPHER

I'm under arrest. (*Pause.*) Why must you . . . everywhere you go . . .

SYLVIA

Well, Potty asked for it.

CHRISTOPHER

I'm sure he did. I asked for it, too. Sylvia . . . I'm so sorry.

The all-clear sounds.

EXT. THE CAMP — DAY

A regimental band is having band practice on the parade ground. Bright and shining, Campion and Levin walk at a smart pace between tents and huts.

INT. CHRISTOPHER'S ORDERLY ROOM — DAY

Christopher is sitting upright behind his table. He is properly dressed but for his shoulder-strapped belt. He is asleep. Voices outside wake him. General Campion enters, followed by Levin. They look as if they have emerged from a Turkish bath, a barber, a tailor and a boot-smith. Christopher comes to attention as Campion enters. Behind him, Levin slowly bats his eyes at Christopher to convey a meaning which is mysterious to him.

> CAMPION
> I notice, Captain Tietjens, that you have no fire extinguishers on your unit. You are aware of the disastrous consequences that would follow a conflagration . . .

> CHRISTOPHER
> Yes, sir. I was informed by Ordnance that there is no provision for fire extinguishers for Dominion troops under an Imperial officer. I applied, as advised, to civilian –

> CAMPION
> I didn't ask for your memoirs. Make a note, Levin. Go and get your belt. You will go round your cook-houses with me in a quarter of an hour. You can tell your Sergeant-Cook.

> CHRISTOPHER
> You are aware, sir, that I am under arrest.

> CAMPION
> I gave you an order! To perform a duty!

> CHRISTOPHER
> Sir!

Christopher dismisses himself from the General's presence and from the hut. Levin, on Campion's nod, goes with him.

EXT. CHRISTOPHER'S ORDERLY ROOM – DAY

Christopher, from sheer fatigue, needs Levin's steadying hand. They walk-march.

LEVIN

You're doing splendidly. You understand, you're released
from arrest – if you're given an order to perform a
duty . . .

CHRISTOPHER

Of course I understand. It's the last thing I want!

LEVIN
(*anguished*)
You can't refuse! A court martial would be . . . He'd
be . . . He thinks the world of . . .

CHRISTOPHER

What did Perowne say?

LEVIN
(*almost in tears*)
Perowne told General O'Hara – oh, I couldn't possibly!

CHRISTOPHER

He told O'Hara he went to Mrs Tietjens's room at her
invitation?

LEVIN

It's impossible to believe anything against . . .

CHRISTOPHER

It's true. He did. But my wife was after fun, not adultery.
What has she told the General?

LEVIN

The General has not seen Mrs Tietjens. He could not
trust himself. He said she would twist him round her
little finger.

CHRISTOPHER
(*laughs*)

He's learning.

LEVIN

He refused to let Perowne speak. He said Perowne could
choose between going up the line and being broken by his
regiment.

CHRISTOPHER

My God . . .

LEVIN

He believes so absolutely in Mrs Tietjens. It's broken the
General's heart. Something he heard from the Capitaine,
the liaison officer . . .

*A soldier – a Batman – comes towards them carrying a mug of
tea on a tray.*

CHRISTOPHER
(*to the Batman*)

Put that down and tell Sergeant Case to come to my
quarters at the double.

The Batman changes course, at the double.

INT. CHRISTOPHER'S HUT, IBD – DAY

*Christopher takes his belt (waist and shoulder strap) from a
hook. He is clumsy with fatigue. Levin helps him to put it on.*

LEVIN

I'm supposed to ask you: was O'Hara drunk? The General
is anxious for your opinion. He and O'Hara graduated
together from Sandhurst.

CHRISTOPHER

Then . . . O'Hara was not drunk.

LEVIN

Campion will be immensely . . . gratified.

CHRISTOPHER

As Provost-Marshal, he had the right to enter my room. I
pushed him out, which is an assault on a senior officer.
I'd be happy to plead guilty to that. And to being drunk,
of course. An officer does not strike generals sober.

LEVIN

Your mania for taking the blows –

CHRISTOPHER

I'd rather be broken than have this hell raked up.

Sergeant-Cook Case comes panting to the open doorway.

CHRISTOPHER

Case! General Campion is going round the cook-houses, in fifteen minutes.

CASE

Right, sir!

CHRISTOPHER

Don't serve out white clothing.

CASE

The General likes to see them in white. He won't know white clothing has been countermanded, sir.

CHRISTOPHER

If you do that, one of your cooks will tuck some piece of dirty clothing into a locker where the General will find it.

CASE

Yes, sir, there's always one piece of clothing in a locker for GOCIC's inspection and General Campion will always find it. I've seen him do it three times.

CHRISTOPHER

This time, the man it belongs to goes for a court martial.

Case salutes and hurries off.

EXT. PARADE GROUND, IBD – DAY

The band practice plays a slow march.

EXT. CHRISTOPHER'S ORDERLY ROOM, IBD – DAY

Campion sits on a bully-beef case, writing at the table. Christopher stands waiting. Campion finishes writing.

CAMPION

Sit down.

Christopher sits down.

CAMPION

Captain Tietjens, I would be glad of your careful attention. This afternoon, you will receive a movement order. You are not to regard it as a disgrace. It is a promotion. I am requesting General Perry to give you the appointment of second-in-command of the Sixth Battalion of his regiment. What's your medical category?

CHRISTOPHER

Permanent base, sir. My chest is rotten.

Campion puts the cap on his pen and folds the paper he has been writing. He continues to speak as he makes for the door.

CAMPION

I should forget that if I were you. The second-in-command of a battalion has nothing to do but sit about in armchairs waiting for the Colonel to be killed.

CHRISTOPHER

If you say so, sir.

CAMPION
(*leaving the hut*)

Who is your sergeant cook?

CHRISTOPHER
(*following*)

Sergeant Case, sir.

EXT. CHRISTOPHER'S ORDERLY ROOM, IBD — DAY

Campion and Christopher step out of the hut.

CAMPION

Sergeant Case . . . He was in the Drums when we were in Delhi. He ought to be at least Quartermaster now . . . but he had a woman he called his sister . . .

CHRISTOPHER

He still sends money to his sister.

CAMPION

He went absent over her when he was a Colour-Sergeant.
Reduced to the ranks. Twenty years ago, that must be.

*The band is still playing. Campion sighs and faces Christopher
with fresh emotion.*

CAMPION

God help you, Chrissie, there's nothing else I can do.
I can't put you on my staff. You crossed General O'Hara
in some row over his Redcaps, never mind threatening
him with arrest, so now you've got a black spot against
your name as regards access to Intelligence. Next –
dammit – the commander of the Ninth French Army is an
intimate friend of mine but in the face of your confidential
report from your time in French liaison, that's blocked.

CHRISTOPHER

If you examine the report, sir, you will find that the
unfavourable insertions are initialled by an Intelligence
Officer, Major Drake, who doesn't like me.

CAMPION

What difference does that make? Not many officers do
like you. Are you aware that there's a hell of a strafe put
in against you by an RASC Second Lieutenant called
Hotchkiss?

CHRISTOPHER

That was about Schomburg, sir. I'd rather die than subject
any horse for which I'm responsible to the damnable
theories of Lieutenant Hotchkiss!

CAMPION

It looks as if you *will* die on that account! There was a
request from your brother Mark through Room G 14 R
in the War Office that you be given command of the
horse lines of Nineteenth Division . . . but Nineteenth
Division is attached to Fourth Army now, and it is Fourth
Army horses that Hotchkiss is to play with. How can
I send you there to be under his orders?

CHRISTOPHER

Yes, sir. You cannot.

CAMPION

I can send you home – in disgrace – or I can send you to your battalion. You're finished here. I cannot have men commanded by an officer with a private life as incomprehensible and embarrassing as yours.

CHRISTOPHER

Yes, sir.

CAMPION
(*bursts out*)

I had taken that woman to be a saint . . . I swear she *is* a saint . . .

CHRISTOPHER

There is no accusation against Mrs Tietjens, sir!

CAMPION

By God, there is! . . . Sylvia and Perowne were seen by Capitaine Thurston together in the Hotel de la Poste in 1912! Can you beat it?

CHRISTOPHER

Were they? Well, what is one to do if a woman is unfaithful?

CAMPION

Divorce the harlot or live with her like a man! What sort of fellow wouldn't see that?

CHRISTOPHER

Yes . . . but still, there is . . . or used to be . . . among families of position . . . a certain . . .

CAMPION
(*stops*)

Well?

CHRISTOPHER

On the part of the man . . . a certain, call it, parade!

CAMPION

Was there! Well, there'll be no more parades for *that* regiment. It held out to the last man, but you were him.

He walks on, Christopher with him. They continue to walk towards the cook-house, where Levin has stationed himself, waiting.

INT. THE COOK-HOUSE, IBD — DAY

The cooks, in white, stand to attention, holding ladles. Everything is gleaming. Campion enters with Levin and Christopher behind. Case salutes. Campion taps him on the chest with the heel of his hunting crop.

CAMPION

How's your sister, Case?

CASE

I'm thinking of making her Mrs Case, sir.

CAMPION

I'll recommend you for a Quartermaster's commission any day you wish.

CASE

My sister would not like it, sir. I'm better off as a first-class warrant officer!

With a light step, Campion goes swiftly to the cupboard panels marked TEA, SUGAR, SALT, FLOUR, CURRY PWDR, PEPPER ... *Campion taps the heel of his crop on* PEPPER. *He speaks to the breath-held Cook standing beside it.*

CAMPION

Open that, will you, my man?

Case stares. Levin fears the worst. Christopher looks on and smiles for the first time.

COOK

Yes, sir.

EXT. PARADE GROUND, IBD – DAY

The band breaks into a jaunty quick-step, Christopher's smile by other means.

INT. CAMPION'S ROLLS-ROYCE, ROUEN – DAY

The Rolls is moving.

> DRIVER
> I hope you had a good visit, miss.

> SYLVIA
> Very good, thank you. Did the draft get off, do you know?

> DRIVER
> It did, miss. Captain Tietjens' draft, at five o'clock. You know the army, then, miss, the lingo!

Sylvia takes out the powder box given to her by Drake.

> SYLVIA
> I should say so! – I'm the Captain's lady.

She checks her face in the powder box. Its mirror is still broken.

EXT. ROUEN – DAY

The Rolls approaches the railway station.

End of Episode Four.

Episode Five

CAST OF EPISODE FIVE

in order of appearance

GENERAL CAMPION	Roger Allam
COLONEL LEVIN	Elliot Levey
CHRISTOPHER TIETJENS	Benedict Cumberbatch
MCKECHNIE	Patrick Kennedy
POTTY PEROWNE	Tom Mison
VALENTINE WANNOP	Adelaide Clemens
MRS WANNOP	Miranda Richardson
CAPTAIN NOTTING	Henry Lloyd-Hughes
AUBREY	William Ellis
RSM	Michael Shaeffer
2ND LIEUTENANT BENNETT	Hugh Mitchell
COLONEL BILL	Steven Robertson
DUCKETT	Frederik Lebeer
GERMAN BATMAN	Mathias Vergels
SCHOOLGIRL	Antonia Clarke
FIRST TEACHER	Emma Dewhurst
SECOND TEACHER	Tilly Blackwood
MRS FERGUSON	Lucy Briers
LATIN TEACHER	Anna Maguire
ARANJUEZ	David Dawson
MICHAEL (8 YEARS OLD)	Rudi Goodman
MARCHANT	Sylvestra Le Touzel
HULLO CENTRAL (EVIE)	Lucinda Raikes
MRS SATTERTHWAITE	Janet McTeer
SYLVIA TIETJENS	Rebecca Hall
GLORVINA	Sasha Waddell
BERTRAM	Jonathan Coy
GRIFFITHS	Ken Verdoodt
CORPORAL SUTCLIFFE	Alexander Cobb
GERALD DRAKE	Jack Huston
EDITH DUCHEMIN	Anne-Marie Duff
MACMASTER	Stephen Graham
MARK TIETJENS	Rupert Everett
MARIE-LEONIE	Lyne Renée

INT. CAMPION'S HQ, INFANTRY BASE DEPOT, ROUEN – DAY

February 1918.

General Campion is at his desk with Colonel Levin in attendance, examining a 'movement order' with sardonic resignation.

CAMPION

So . . . we have Captain Tietjens, whom the War Office wanted transferred to the command of Nineteenth Division's horse-lines . . .

INT. RAILWAY WAGON, FRANCE – NIGHT

CAMPION
(*voice-over*)

. . . going instead to the trenches to take over as second-in-command of the Sixth Battalion, Glamorganshires . . . and we have Captain McKechnie – who detests Tietjens because he considers second-in-command of the Sixth Glamorganshires to be his by right – going instead to take charge of Nineteenth Division's horse-lines, which he sees, correctly, as a humiliation . . . And finally we have Major Perowne, last heard of attempting to enter the bedroom of Mrs Tietjens, allegedly at her invitation, being sent back to his battalion as a punishment . . .

In a slow-moving baggage car, among boxes of supplies and equipment, Christopher, McKechnie and Perowne are huddled under blankets, resting against their kit-bags. Christopher is insecurely asleep. McKechnie's eyes are open, staring, angry. Perowne's eyes are closed but he is awake and frightened.

INT. CAMPION'S HQ, INFANTRY BASE DEPOT, ROUEN — DAY

CAMPION

. . . and all I can say is that it takes a movement order of some genius to send these three officers up the line sharing transport.

INT. RAILWAY WAGON, FRANCE — EARLY DAY

The three officers are sitting where they can. A near-miss shakes the wagon, which is now stationary.

PEROWNE

Shouldn't we get out of the train while it's stopped?

MCKECHNIE

Why?

PEROWNE

The Huns are *aiming* at the train.

MCKECHNIE

They never hit what they're aiming at. Think of those two pretty sisters who had the tea shop in Poperinghe.

PEROWNE

What about them?

MCKECHNIE

Blown to bits. The Huns couldn't have been aiming at a tea shop.

Another explosion shakes the wagon. McKechnie takes an envelope from his wallet.

MCKECHNIE
(*to Christopher*)

Please note that the seal is unbroken. As soon as the raid stops, I'll translate your sonnet into Latin in under three minutes. I suppose you believe that I have not read your sonnet? You don't perhaps imagine that I opened this and made a copy?

CHRISTOPHER
Yes! No! I don't care!

MCKECHNIE
(*to Perowne*)
You can be witness. Latin hexameters, in under three
minutes . . . Teach him to come the sonneteer with me!
He sells his wife to generals for promotion.

Perowne becomes enraged.

PEROWNE
Take that back, you swine! You're speaking of a lady
you're not fit to – to – not that, not that – not that it's for
me to defend her.

MCKECHNIE
(*to Christopher*)
What's this, what's this?

CHRISTOPHER
(*sharply*)
McKechnie, get yourself under control, or the first thing
I'll do is report you to the MO, and you'll find yourself
under the care of the mad-doctors.

MCKECHNIE
Report me to Terence? Terence is my pal. We're all pals in
the battalion. Best battalion in the line. How we worked
at it! Now I'm banished to a horse-coper's job in
Transport. (*He becomes maudlin.*) And poor old Bill the
CO has got *you*. Poor old Bill. You're no soldier. Do you
think you're an infantry man? You're a bolster, a big
baggy bolster.

*Artillery fires at a plane overhead. Small bits of the wagon are
ripped away by aerial machine-gun fire. Perowne cries out,
then starts whimpering.*

MCKECHNIE
(*undeflected*)
Poor battalion, poor bloody old pals . . .

PEROWNE

Oh God . . . are we going to die?

MCKECHNIE

Poor old Bill who sweated for the battalion . . .

PEROWNE

What do you think it's like, Tietjens, when you stop one?
When you know this is it! Death!

CHRISTOPHER

Your faculties are numbed. You feel no pain, no
apprehension.

PEROWNE

Thank you, Tietjens. Thank you.

MCKECHNIE

Poor old Bill!

The train jolts forward.

CHRISTOPHER

Thank God, we're moving.

EXT. WANNOP HOUSE — DAY

Exterior of Wannop house.

INT. WANNOP HOUSE, VALENTINE'S BEDROOM — DAY

Valentine wakes.

INT. VALENTINE'S BEDROOM, AS BEFORE — DAY

Valentine in her nightdress opens the curtains.

INT. VALENTINE'S BEDROOM, AS BEFORE — DAY

Valentine washes at the washstand.

INT. WANNOP HOUSE, STAIRS — DAY

Valentine coming down, dressed for school.

VALENTINE

I can smell bacon!

INT. WANNOP HOUSE, PARLOUR — DAY

The small dining table is set for breakfast. There is a tiny vase with a few snowdrops.

VALENTINE

And snowdrops!

A posted Valentine card is by her place. Mrs Wannop calls from the adjoining kitchen.

MRS WANNOP

Happy birthday, darling!

Valentine reads her unsigned Valentine card, with a smile.

Mrs Wannop comes from the kitchen with plates of bacon, scrambled powdered egg, toast.

VALENTINE

Where did you find snowdrops?

MRS WANNOP

I didn't pick them, I'm afraid . . . well, I picked them in Shepherd's Market.

They exchange a kiss. Mrs Wannop sets down the tray. The sideboard is stacked with paper and books.

VALENTINE

Thank you for my Valentine card.

MRS WANNOP

Me?

Mrs Wannop brings a small wrapped present from the sideboard, and a telegram.

MRS WANNOP

Open your present, so I can change it straight away if it's wrong.

VALENTINE

I'm sure it won't be wrong.

MRS WANNOP

And there's a telegram for you!

Valentine's interest is pricked.

She opens the telegram. She slows herself down.

MRS WANNOP

Someone's remembered your birthday.

VALENTINE

It's in Latin . . .

MRS WANNOP

From Christopher!

Valentine had that thought.

VALENTINE
(*reading the telegram*)
'IUCUNDA NATALIA SODALIS VIVAT COMMUTATIO
OCTOBRIS.'

Valentine is concealing a severe disappointment.

It's from Edward . . . Glasgow postmark.

She gives Mrs Wannop the telegram.

VALENTINE

He must be on shore. That's good, anyway.

MRS WANNOP

'Happy birthday, comrade . . . Let live . . . the
commutatio of October . . .'

VALENTINE

'Long live the October Revolution.' I suppose he thought
it might not get through, now the Bolsheviks have made
peace with Germany.

MRS WANNOP

Is my son a Bolshevik now!

286

VALENTINE

Well, it's enough to make anyone Bolshevik! – sending men and boys to murder each other in millions!

Valentine pushes aside her parcel.

I don't want a birthday if he's lying dead . . .

MRS WANNOP

He's not dead, he's in Glasgow.

Valentine meant Christopher. She gets up abruptly and hurries to the stairs. Mrs Wannop catches on, catches up.

INT. WANNOP HOUSE, VALENTINE'S BEDROOM – DAY

Mrs Wannop comes in hesitantly. Valentine is drying her face on a towel.

MRS WANNOP

You are surely not in love wi:h Christopher Tietjens? You mustn't be. He's a married man.

VALENTINE

But when he comes home he'll make me his mistress. Or he won't.

MRS WANNOP

But you wouldn't! And *he* wouldn't!

VALENTINE

Oh, you've always thought he's infallible! He'll keep *some* of his principles. He won't divorce his wife. I don't care. I used to think love was a kind of literature. But every word Christopher Tietjens and I ever said to each other was a declaration of love.

EXT. COMMUNICATION TRENCH, FLANDERS – DAY

With a Subaltern to guide him and carry his kit-bag, Christopher is making his way along an unpopulated trench. This is not the trench facing the enemy. It is at right angles, a communications trench. Christopher is walking from 'behind the lines' towards the Front.

INT./EXT. BATTALION HQ DUG-OUT, FLANDERS – DAY

There is a Sentry at the entrance, who salutes Christopher smartly as the Subaltern takes him through.

This dug-out is the cellarage of an obliterated farmhouse. It has a number of 'rooms', for 'runners', NCOs, stores, sleeping spaces for the Commanding Officer (currently absent) and a handful of immediate colleagues. Among them are Aubrey, a languid toff, Terence, the Medical Officer, and Dunne, the Intelligence Officer. There is some furniture. In the orderly room, the Subaltern hands Christopher over to the adjutant, Captain Notting.

> CHRISTOPHER
> (*saluting*)
> Captain Tietjens reporting for duty.

> NOTTING
> (*shakes hands*)
> Notting. I'm the Adjutant. The CO is inspecting our trench.

This makes one of the officers, Dunne, give out a snort-laugh. Christopher notes it.

INT. DUG-OUT – DAY

Notting shows Christopher to a bunk.

> NOTTING
> . . . the battalion is down to a third of its full strength, 328 at last count, call it seventy-five per company. There's nothing for you to do except wait for the German push. Till then, they send over a few shells before breakfast and after lunch, and there's always a chance they'll rush a trench for the fun of it, so we have to keep a sharp look-out. The RSM will take you round while it's quiet.

EXT. THE TRENCH — DAY

The RSM conducts Christopher along a trench, which is under repair by Infantry with shovels. The company commander is a mere boy, Second Lieutenant Bennett, who salutes Christopher.

BENNETT
Bennett, sir.

Every few yards, the trench is partly obstructed by a block of earth protruding inwards from the parapet, to prevent a burst of shrapnel spreading laterally down the whole length.

CHRISTOPHER
Carry on . . . carry on . . .

An officer appears around the next abutment. He is almost as young as Christopher, early thirties. Christopher realises that he is drunk. Holding a hip flask, using the firing-step, the officer climbs up over the parapet and disappears. Christopher is dumbfounded. So are the RSM and Bennett.

RSM
Colonel Williams, sir, the Commanding Officer.

EXT. NO-MAN'S-LAND, FLANDERS — DAY

The CO, 'Colonel Bill', picks his way carefully through an apron of barbed wire and strolls towards the enemy trench three hundred yards away. He takes a swig of whisky.

EXT. THE TRENCH, AS BEFORE — DAY

There is now a group of soldiers with Tietjens and the RSM, clustered around. A Lance-Corporal (Duckett) has his eye to a spy-hole at the top of the parapet.

DUCKETT
Can't see him, sir.

EXT. NO-MAN'S-LAND – DAY

Colonel Bill, humming to himself, strolls to the parapet of the German trench.

The German trench is deserted apart from a soldier, a batman, sitting on a step, wearing an apron, cleaning an officer's boot. The German looks up and sees Bill. He jumps up in alarm and throws his shoe brush at Bill. Bill, startled, throws his flask at the German.

EXT. NO-MAN'S-LAND – DAY

Bill is picking his way carefully back through the barbed wire.

EXT. THE TRENCH, AS BEFORE – DAY

Duckett has his eye to the spy-hole. Christopher steps up on the fire-step to peer over the parapet.

> RSM
> Have a care, sir, for snipers.

> CHRISTOPHER
> They'd be shooting at the CO.

A thump and rattling of gravel announce Bill's return to the trench. His jump down makes him totter.

> CHRISTOPHER
> (*saluting*)
> I'm Captain Tietjens, sir.

Bill ignores Christopher.

> BILL
> Nobody home, Regimental Sergeant-Major!

A German machine gun, too late, opens up, scattering earth from the parapet.

Bill departs along the trench, Christopher watching him go. A barrage of shells explodes elsewhere along the line and behind the lines, then a mile away.

That's the Worcesters getting it.

INT. SCHOOL CORRIDOR, LONDON – DAY

A hand bell is being rung. Valentine, in her 'physical instructor' uniform walks along.

INT. GAMES CHANGING ROOM – DAY

A place of benches, coat-hooks, lockers. A loose scrum of older Schoolgirls is gathered around something furtive and excited going on in a corner. A sixteen-year-old is reading to a group of her peers.

SCHOOLGIRL
'. . . The case of Mrs G is not exceptional. Her husband was accustomed to pet her and have relations with her frequently, but yet he never took any trouble to rouse in her the necessary preliminary feeling for mutual union . . .'

Corridor:

Valentine is approaching the changing-room door, against the current of Schoolgirls answering the summons of the bell, which now ceases.

Changing room:

SCHOOLGIRL
'Because she shyly asked him, Mrs G's husband gave her one swift unrepeated kiss upon her bosom.'

Her audience gasps.

The sound of the door opening puts a flurried halt to the reading.

Valentine pauses in the doorway, aware of something. The group of girls emerge.

VALENTINE
Come along! Didn't you hear the bell?

She lets the girls come past her, holding the door. When they have gone out, Valentine goes further into the room, her curiosity aroused. She goes behind a row of lockers. She knows roughly where the group had been up to something. A stray shoe on the floor makes her bend to put it back into its space, and she discovers a small, slim book, brand new, in a locker.

Valentine reads the title on the spine and then finds the title page, which is headed by the words MARRIED LOVE. *There is a sub-title: 'A New Contribution to the Solution of Sex Difficulties'. The author's name comes next:*

BY MARIE CARMICHAEL STOPES

Valentine sits down on the locker bench and starts to read.

INT. STAFF ROOM, SCHOOL – DAY

Valentine is with a group of women teachers. One of them (Mrs Ferguson) is reading the copy of Married Love.

FIRST TEACHER

You have to report it to the Head, there's no question about that.

SECOND TEACHER

Is it really so terrible?

FIRST TEACHER

Yes, it is, it's the vilest . . . Exposing young women's minds to . . . How much of it did you . . . ?

VALENTINE

Quite a lot of it.

SECOND TEACHER

Read out some more, Mrs Ferguson.

MRS FERGUSON
(*engrossed*)

Buy your own.

SECOND TEACHER

Would it be too wicked if Miss Wannop told the Head she just . . . found it somewhere, in the pavilion or something . . .?

VALENTINE

I've decided. I'm going to put it back.

FIRST TEACHER

You will not!

VALENTINE
(*forcefully*)

Why not? It's a proper book, it's not trash.

FIRST TEACHER

But it's not for children.

VALENTINE

I was a suffragist when I was at the age of our senior girls. I thought getting the vote for women was the only thing that would make me happy. And now we've just got the vote – some of it – some of us – and about time, too! – but it's got nothing to do with happiness. I've found *that* much out.

FIRST TEACHER

It's a book for married women.

VALENTINE

No, it isn't.

MRS FERGUSON
(*engrossed*)

Yes, it is, by George!

VALENTINE

It's a book about 'married love'. Girls want to be married. Some of them will be, and soon. So it's for them, too, and according to Dr Stopes most of them will be unhappy out of sheer ignorance – and their husbands' ignorance. We want them to be happy, don't we?

Mrs Ferguson slaps the book shut, and gives it to Valentine.

We do! Put it back. I'll answer for it to the Head . . . (*She looks at First Teacher.*) If any of you care to sneak. (*To Valentine.*) Good for you, Miss Wannop.

A hand bell is heard.

MRS FERGUSON

You've just got time.

EXT. THE FRONT – NIGHT

Wide: pandemonium – heavy rain, shells exploding, flares bursting over No-Man's-Land . . . Broken trees, barbed wire, mud, flooded craters.

Christopher's eyes: he is somewhere in the 'pandemonium'. His eyes shift wildly.

A German soldier comes over the British parapet as if hurled, and hits the parados (the back wall of the trench). The German, however, has already been shot, in the face, his eyes a mask of blood. A Very flare shows the state of the German, and also a dead infantryman. A stretcher party comes along the trench. Christopher kneels by the German, feeling his neck artery.

CHRISTOPHER

Take the Hun first. He's alive. Our man is dead.

ARANJUEZ

Damn cool, you were, sir! Damn cool!

Christopher twists to look up at the parapet where Aubrey is suicidally standing up, throwing grenades, then picking up a dead man's Lewis gun and firing towards the enemy.

INT. BATTALION HQ, DUG-OUT – NIGHT

The calm after the pandemonium. Bill the CO drinks, reading reports. Aubrey reads a society magazine.

BILL

Do we have a Private Smith? Division says he's a Bolshevik.

AUBREY
(*to no one*)
Do you think Rupert was the handsomest man in England? I don't. I think Pamela Cheyne's chauffeur was.

Christopher is lying on his cot, in a bad state, his eyes closed. There is the sound of miners' picks quietly chip-chipping underground. Asleep or awake, it's a nightmare. Christopher jolts upright. Aubrey catches his eye.

CHRISTOPHER
Can you hear them? The miners.

McKechnie enters the cellar with a flourish.

BILL

McKechnie!

MCKECHNIE
How are the Pals?

AUBREY
Did you get home? How is dear old Piccadilly?

McKechnie shakes hands with the officers, who surround him joyfully. He is given a whisky.

BILL
What are you doing here? Haven't you been cashiered yet?

MCKECHNIE
Not yet, sir! Had to pay you a visit, sir!

He sees Christopher.

Tietjens!

He takes the 'sonnet envelope' from his pocket.

Latin hexameters in under three minutes – when you can give me your attention.

But Christopher is in no state.

EXT. BEHIND THE LINES – NIGHT

Teams of stretcher-bearers trot along a communications trench towards the Front. Where the trench is half-destroyed, there is a body half covered by earth. It is Perowne, lying on his back, grinning in death.

EXT. GROBY – NIGHT

The long grey house, seen entire on a black storm-tossed night.

The giant cedar, crowding one wing of the many-windowed house, creaks and stirs. Nearly all the windows are dark.

Closer – Groby Tree:

We see again the variety of small objects attached to the tree.

INT. NIGHT NURSERY, GROBY – NIGHT

Michael, aged eight, kneels by his bed to say his prayers, as glibly as multiplication tables, Marchant in attendance.

MICHAEL
. . . and God bless Mummy and Daddy and Granny and Granny-and-Grandpa-in-heaven, and Aunt Effie and Uncle Arthur and Marchie and everybody, and God bless me!

MARCHANT
Hop in, and stay in. Mummy will be up to see you.

Hullo Central comes in.

HULLO CENTRAL
She says to bring him down.

MARCHANT
Who's she? The cat's mother? Slippers and dressing gown!

Michael complies.

MICHAEL

Did you hang something from the tree, Evie, so the wood sprites don't get you?

HULLO CENTRAL

The wood sprites won't catch me. Give me bombs any day, bombs are natural.

INT. DRAWING ROOM, GROBY — NIGHT

Mrs Satterthwaite plays patience while Sylvia takes her wine glass to the hearth to molest the coals with the poker.

MRS SATTERTHWAITE

It's stood for two hundred years, it will stay standing until Michael is master of Groby. He can decide to cut it down or not.

SYLVIA

You miss the point exactly. I want that tree gone before Michael has any say in the matter. He'll grow up a Tietjens, backward-looking and sentimental . . . It's paganism, hanging up their bits-and-bobs like savages . . . Why can't we have wood fires at Groby?

MRS SATTERTHWAITE

Because you own coal mines. Or rather, your brother-in-law owns them. The land steward will certainly inform Mark if you order the cedar cut down.

SYLVIA

Let him. Brother Mark has abdicated from Groby. He has chosen the life of a London clubman with an actress in the Gray's Inn Road. And Christopher has decided to live in sin after the war with his little games mistress.

MRS SATTERTHWAITE

That's all it is. You want to make Christopher suffer. Poor boy! Between you and the Germans . . .

SYLVIA

Anyone would think you were *his* mother, not mine.

MRS SATTERTHWAITE

I pray even more fervently for you – as we are taught to
do for all sinners.

SYLVIA

That's what I get for keeping myself chaste all these years!

MRS SATTERTHWAITE
(*scathing*)

You mean since you bolted.

SYLVIA

Potty Perowne deserved me. I chose the path of charity,
as Jesus would have done . . . They say he died with a
smile on his face. Potty, I mean. Well, I'll spare the Groby
Tree for the duration. But if my husband thinks he can
throw me over for that scrub-faced ladies' champion of
the regular-bowel movement . . .

MRS SATTERTHWAITE

He's the only man who perhaps wouldn't, and he'll go
to heaven for it.

SYLVIA

You say that because you think of God as an English
landowner on a colossal scale who never leaves his study,
so is invisible. Well, if Christopher's not in heaven when
the war's over, he won't be in Gray's Inn, not with little
Miss Hockeysticks on my furniture. I'll strip the place!

*Sylvia has reached one of her sudden peaks of demented rage,
just as the door opens to let in Michael, with Marchant behind
him.*

SYLVIA
(*crossly*)

What is it? I said I'll come up!

MARCHANT

I'm sorry, madam.

Marchant takes Michael smoothly out and closes the door.

MRS SATTERTHWAITE

For the sake of your soul, will you go into retreat for a
week or two? You need to reflect on what to ask of God.

SYLVIA

I thought perhaps – India.

MRS SATTERTHWAITE
(*bewildered*)

India?!

INT. NIGHT NURSERY, GROBY – NIGHT

*Michael in his pyjamas sits alone on the window seat, watching
the cedar fronds brushing against the window.*

INT. GLORVINA'S SANCTUM, LONDON – DAY

Sylvia is taking tea with Glorvina.

SYLVIA

And Bobbie . . . ?

GLORVINA

She married quietly abroad.

SYLVIA

Oh . . . so congratulations are due? When?

GLORVINA

September.

SYLVIA

But how lovely for Bobbie . . .

GLORVINA

The only person who comes well out of this is Johnny
Pelham for letting Bobbie divorce him.

SYLVIA

I hope you know, Lady Glorvina, that Bobbie asked me
to get Johnny out of the house when he was being
miserable, and that's all there was to that.

299

GLORVINA

(*drily*)

I suppose you told Christopher.

SYLVIA

I went to see Christopher in France, you know, two months ago. They were working him dreadfully hard, in an enormous camp commanded by General Campion.

GLORVINA

If you've come to ask me to do something for Christopher, I should tell you that Bertram is simply overwhelmed in the War Cabinet . . .

SYLVIA

No, it's the General. He's like a war horse in a paddock. He simply can't be allowed to end his career like that.

GLORVINA

He can, and probably will. That's pillow talk, mind you.

The last comment is a warning, because Bertram, Glorvina's husband, comes in. He is tired out.

BERTRAM

Sylvia . . . excuse me.

SYLVIA

No, please stay if you can, Bertram.

GLORVINA

Stay at your peril. Sylvia has a bit between her teeth.

BERTRAM

(*laughs*)

Well, if I can have a drink – for a few minutes.

He goes to help himself from a decanter.

SYLVIA

I'm concerned for Edward.

Bertram joins them with his drink.

BERTRAM

Campion?

SYLVIA

Why has he got a glorified Quartermaster's job fitting out troops for General Perry's command?

BERTRAM

Because it's a vital job and Campion does it superbly. But General Perry's command is the only fighting command that might become free. He's taken to getting his friends to write to *The Times* about being starved of troops . . .

SYLVIA

Edward Campion should have the sort of job which brings a hero's welcome and a peerage at the end of it . . . and from that, who knows? Perhaps India.

GLORVINA
(*startled, sceptical*)
India? Viceroy of India?

SYLVIA

Why not? The General served with great distinction in India.

BERTRAM

Actually, that's well said.

SYLVIA

And I must leave you. I'm so glad things are settled with Bobbie.

BERTRAM

Thank you, my dear. A carpet seller's son from Turkey or somewhere with the beastliest newspapers in London as a son-in-law is a turn of events.

SYLVIA
(*brightly*)
Just the man to put the public behind General Campion!

INT. GRAY'S INN, DRAWING ROOM – NIGHT

Campion is Sylvia's visitor, for a drink. She has dressed for his benefit.

SYLVIA

How long is your leave?

CAMPION

It isn't leave. I ordered myself home to be at the War Office first thing in the morning to ask whether anyone there understands that if they don't do something about it there'll be nothing behind us except the sea. I'll probably be relieved of my command, but there's not much of a career left for a man of sixty unless he's given a fighting army.

SYLVIA

We'll see. Can you come to Groby for the weekend? It will be very quiet, just Bobbie and her new husband.

CAMPION

I might do that. I'd love to see Groby. How is Christopher?

SYLVIA

Don't you see him?

CAMPION

Ah . . . no. He's at the Front now. I had no choice, after . . .

SYLVIA

Of course you didn't. A chance of glory, then.

CAMPION

Absolutely. A chance of glory. Lucky begger . . .

EXT. TRENCH — DAY

The British line is being shelled in preparation for a German attack. Christopher is crouched in the trench with the RSM yelling at him.

RSM

Commanding Officer in 'B' Company trench, sir!

EXT. ADJOINING TRENCH — DAY

Christopher comes round the traverse and sees Bill there, in the act of throwing empty whisky bottles at the enemy. The CO is drunk. Bennett is out of his depth.

> BENNETT
> Sir, would you please . . . sir . . .

Bill brushes past Christopher unseeingly, falls over, gets up, staggers.

> CHRISTOPHER
> I'll get the Colonel to the MO. Report to me first sign of gas. Two observers in each company, everyone else in platoon dug-outs. I'm taking over temporary command.

> RSM
> (*pleased*)
> Sir!

EXT. TRENCH — DAY (DAWN)

Dawn on the battlefield. All quiet. Heavy hoar frost and mist.

Christopher mounts the firing-step and looks out carefully over the top of the parapet. The ground by his face seems to explode with a whirring movement and sound. Christopher falls back as the lark he disturbed ascends into the sky. Christopher manages a scared laugh.

The RSM is watching over Infantrymen repairing the trench.

> RSM
> There ain't no beastly snipers is there, sir?

> CHRISTOPHER
> A skylark nearly walked into my mouth . . .

> RSM
> There's been a skylark singin' on the morning of every strafe I've ever been in. Wunnerful trust in yumanity, sir, wunnerful hinstinct in the feathered breast by the

303

Halmighty, for 'oo was going to 'it a skylark on a
battlefield?

CHRISTOPHER

I don't know about the Almighty. It's all one to a skylark
whether it's high explosive or a plough.

Christopher climbs back up on the fire-step.

RSM
(*chiding*)
You're a law hunto yourself, sir.

*Christopher looks through a spy-hole, then steps down, looks
at his watch, pleased.*

CHRISTOPHER

Thank you, Sergeant-Major! Thirty-two minutes if the
barrage is punctual.

*Not far away, a cornet is heard, negotiating the notes of a
seventeenth-century air.*

*Christopher and the RSM walk through a section of trench
where half a dozen men under a corporal are busy with
trenching tools.*

CHRISTOPHER

Those men are going to look damn silly without their
bayonets fixed if the Germans storm this trench. Let's
have them fell in, Sergeant-Major.

RSM

Yes, sir. All right you lot, fall in, the Commanding Officer
is looking at you!

*The men 'fall in', a muddy and assorted ragtag army of
Londoners turned into 'Glamorganshires', rifles poking out
of line, packs hunched up.*

RSM

Fix . . . bay'nets!

*Like an inept variety turn, the men fix bayonets and resume a
wavering line, tin hats at all angles, gas-mask boxes dangling.*

CHRISTOPHER

Stand at ease, stand easy.

He is suddenly irritated by the unsmartness, the ineptness.

For God's sake, put your beastly hats straight! All at sixes and sevens . . . it gives me the pip!

The men glance at each other's hats, murmuring amongst themselves.

CORPORAL

You 'ear the orfcer . . . Gives 'im the pip, we do . . . Shove 'im a shade forward, 'Orace . . . You tighten your martingale, 'Erbert . . .

They are gay and rueful, meaning well. One short man sings almost under his breath.

SINGER

'Ez I walk along the Bon di Berlong wiv an' independent air . . .'

CHRISTOPHER

Did you ever hear Coborn sing that, Private?

SINGER

Yes, sir. I was the back legs of the elephant when he sung it in the Old Drury panto.

That causes more muttering – ''Ind legs of the elephink! . . . Good ol' Helephink . . .'

CHRISTOPHER

I'll give every man of you a ticket for Drury Lane next Christmas. We'll all be in London by Boxing Day – or Berlin! Thank you, Sergeant-Major.

RSM

Carry on, Corporal!

Christopher and the RSM move on along the trench.

RSM

A good lot of chaps, sir. The best. Give them the right sort of officers and they'll beat the world.

CHRISTOPHER

If they know what they're doing I don't think it matters too much who gives the order.

RSM

No, sir. They've been frightened these last few days. They're better now.

Christopher understands that he is being complimented. The cornet continues to play, a little uncertainly, some distance away.

CHRISTOPHER

Whistle for the wind to keep up. The Germans are spending themselves until they'll have nothing to meet the counter-attack.

RSM

Tell the men, sir. That's what they need to be told, not the stuff in Divisional Comic Cuts.

CHRISTOPHER

What the devil is that row?

RSM

O Nine Griffiths, sir. Major McKechnie promised to hear him after breakfast, and recommend him to play in the Divisional Follies.

CHRISTOPHER

Captain McKechnie is with us again?

He looks at his watch and keeps walking.

EXT. COMMUNICATIONS TRENCH AND FRONT TRENCH –
EARLY DAY

McKechnie, wearing his parade hat, hurries into the front trench, looking for Christopher. He sees him coming towards him past soldiers repairing the trench, and approaches him in an emotional state.

MCKECHNIE

Come past the next traverse. I want to speak with you.

CHRISTOPHER

The strafe is due in seven minutes . . .

The sun is about to come over an unseen horizon. Christopher follows McKechnie around the traverse, past two observers, one with his eye to a spy-hole. Now they are in an empty stretch of trench.

CHRISTOPHER

You will have to put a tin hat on if you're staying here.

McKechnie looks at him mad-eyed.

MCKECHNIE

How dare you give me orders!

CHRISTOPHER

It wouldn't look well with the Divisional Transport Officer dead in my lines in a parade hat.

MCKECHNIE

The Transport Officer has the right to consult the CO of a battalion he's supplying.

CHRISTOPHER
(*sharply*)

I'm commanding here. You've not consulted me.

McKechnie responds to the tone by almost becoming tearful.

MCKECHNIE

This is what it has come to with the old battalion, the bloody, bloody old Battalion of Pals! What are you going to do about Bill?

CHRISTOPHER

The MO has authority to send the Colonel on sick leave for a couple of months.

MCKECHNIE

You can't be thinking of doing the dirty on Bill! No man could be such a swine!

CHRISTOPHER

Don't be such an ass. Nobody's going to get any glory today. The Germans will be having lunch in this trench.

MCKECHNIE

I know what you're up to. If you got poor Bill cashiered, they'd put in another pukka colonel, but if you send him sick you're pretty certain to get the command as a stop-gap.

CHRISTOPHER
(*angrily*)
Captain McKechnie, you can fall out. Return to duty. Your own duty. In a proper head dress.

MCKECHNIE
(*dropping into a conversational tone*)
Oh well, I suppose if you're in command.

CHRISTOPHER
It's usual to say 'sir' when addressing a senior officer on parade. You're attached to Divisional Headquarters. Get back there. Now! At once!

McKechnie comes to attention and salutes.

MCKECHNIE

Sir!

He remembers something. He takes out his wallet.

Aranjuez comes round the traverse.

MCKECHNIE
I haven't forgotten about your sonnet, sir.

He takes a crumpled envelope from his wallet. Aranjuez, standing by, looks on, interested.

A lone salvo of German shells finds the battalion trench a hundred yards farther down. Christopher and Aranjuez crouch almost to the duckboards. McKechnie appears not to have noticed.

MCKECHNIE
(*shouts*)
Please note the seal is unbroken.

EXT. TRENCH – DAY

Duckett comes holding a sheaf of papers. The Cornet Player can be heard again, picking his way note by note through the same air.

Christopher is approaching. Behind him, McKechnie and Aranjuez follow, conversing amiably.

DUCKETT
(*to Christopher*)
Orderly Room says would you look through these, sir.

Christopher takes the papers and stops to look through them. He takes out a pencil and looks at his watch.

ARANJUEZ
. . . the Petrarchan sonnet is different from the Shakespearean sonnet, sir . . . ?

MCKECHNIE
Of course. A final couplet after three quatrains would be an abomination in the Italian sonnet . . .

CHRISTOPHER
Captain McKechnie, are you still here? I'll tell the cornet to report to you tomorrow for the entertainment. His name is Griffiths. (*To Duckett.*) Find him for me, Corporal.

DUCKETT
Yes, sir.

CHRISTOPHER
And there's a Private Smith, report to Battalion dug-out.

MCKECHNIE
(*to Christopher*)
By the way, General Campion is to take over this Army the day after tomorrow. We got the word at Division HQ.

Christopher stops.

CHRISTOPHER
So Campion's back. It means the French have got the single command.

He's pleased. He'd been on the wrong side of this argument when he resigned his job. So had Campion.

It means we'll be getting reinforcements.

Christopher stuffs the rest of the papers into his tunic pocket and walks on. Aranjuez, with his note-pad ready, following him like an excited puppy.

ARANJUEZ

You wrote a sonnet in two and a half minutes, sir!

CHRISTOPHER

It's a trick.

Christopher knows the air the cornet is playing. He follows it note by note.

CHRISTOPHER

'I know a la-dy fair and kind,
Was never face so pleased my-y mind . . .'

The cornet stops playing.

How is your flame in the linen shop, Lieutenant Aranjuez?
Nanette . . . ?

ARANJUEZ

Minette, sir. If I stop one, sir, you'll tell Minette that . . .

CHRISTOPHER

Little nippers like you don't stop things. Besides, the wind's on our backs. They won't come on without gas.

ARANJUEZ

I remember that Hun in our trench who got shot in both eyes. Your girl naturally won't look at you if you let her down, sir, by losing your beauty.

CHRISTOPHER
(*the song still in his head*)

'. . . her passing by . . .
I did but view . . .
And now I love her till I die . . .'

Christopher looks up and literally sees Valentine as a private in front of him like a Shakespearean cross-dressed twin of herself. Christopher is lost for a moment.

DUCKETT

Griffiths, sir.

Christopher sees that 'Valentine' is a young, fair private with a cornet case of dirty yellow leather.

CHRISTOPHER

Yes, Griffiths. Well, you and your cornet, report to Divisional HQ tomorrow night . . .

He scribbles a note.

Think you can hold a tune by then?

GRIFFITHS
(pleased)

Yes, sir.

CHRISTOPHER
(giving him the note)

All right. Fall out.

A big gun makes a distant 'Crump!' Then many shells.

CHRISTOPHER
(checks his watch)

Right on time.

INT. BATTALION HQ DUG-OUT, ORDERLY ROOM – DAY

Up above, the barrage has started in earnest.

Christopher is at a table with the Battalion papers. There are other officers in the Orderly Room, a Subaltern manning the field telephone, a couple of Runners waiting for errands.

Duckett has delivered 'Private Smith' to Christopher's desk. He is older than Christopher, a Jew and an intellectual. Christopher scans a paper.

CHRISTOPHER

Now look here, Smith, I don't mean to insult you, but
what is your agreeable name?

SMITH

Eisenstein, sir.

CHRISTOPHER

Intelligence thinks you're a Bolshevik.

SMITH

Extreme left, sir!

CHRISTOPHER

I sympathise. Among the people I'd send to prison
immediately are stockbrokers, Whitehall schemers,
landowners who don't look after their tenants, most
Members of Parliament, urban developers . . .

SMITH

We're going to shoot them, sir. What do you call your
system, may I ask?

CHRISTOPHER

Feudalism.

SMITH

I'm an egalitarian, sir.

CHRISTOPHER

The superstition of intellectuals. It wouldn't work in the
army. I shall apply to have you transferred to the Jewish
regiment. I think they're in Mesopotamia.

SMITH

It's a disappointment, sir.

CHRISTOPHER

Nothing I can do. Fall out.

Smith 'falls out'.

NOTTING

The Colonel asks to see you, sir.

INT. BATTALION HQ DUG-OUT, BILL'S SANCTUM – DAY

The Colonel, in open shirt and shorts, is sitting on the edge of his camp bed. Christoper stands 'at ease'. Bill gives him a dark, bloodshot look.

BILL

I don't want to leave my battalion to a man that would knock it about while I'm on sick leave.

CHRISTOPHER

I won't let discipline go to pieces, if that's what you mean, sir.

An immense explosion not far away shakes the cellar.

I ought to go and . . .

BILL

Notting will tell us if anything's wanted. (*Resuming.*) I suppose I could get rid of you . . . with a bad report. Or perhaps I couldn't. They say you're Campion's bastard.

CHRISTOPHER

I'm his godson.

BILL

I'm not going to bring a General on my back – they say you're the devil of a paper soldier.

Another explosion, among the now continuous explosions near and far, knocks bricks from the ceiling.

No, stop where you are. This isn't the strafe. This is only a little extra Morning Hate. You can tell by the noise: that's four-point-twos. The really heavies don't come so fast. They'll be turning on the Worcesters now, and only giving us one every half-minute. That's their game. If you don't know that, what are you doing here? (*He points his finger up.*) You hear?

The noise shifts away.

So you think you can command this battalion? I'm not in a condition to do it myself. The men appear to like you.

They're tired of me. Well – take the Battalion with my blessing.

Notting looks in.

> NOTTING
> Brigade want to know if we're suffering any.

> BILL
> Well, we aren't suffering any, are we?

> NOTTING
> No, not in particular. A shell in the entrance of 'C' Company dug-out, one man dead.

> BILL
> This officer is taking over from me. Oh, tell Brigade we're all as happy as sandboys – with Major Tietjens's compliments. He's in command.

Notting remains expressionless.

> BILL
> (*to Christopher*)
> You may as well make a cheerful impression to begin with.

EXT. THE TRENCH – DAY

The barrage has ceased. The trench is in a number of places reduced to mounds of mud and rubble. The men of the Company in this section are busy with shovels. Christopher is making an inspection, attended by the RSM.

> RSM
> They knocked, sir, but they didn't come in!

> CHRISTOPHER
> They may oblige us tomorrow. You'll have to get your trench restored by morning. Just make sure the men keep their heads down.

A soldier with a trenching tool uncovers part of Griffiths's cornet case. Christopher goes forward and pulls it free. It has been buried open-wide and apparently empty. Christopher lays down the cornet case carefully, in grief.

EXT. NO-MAN'S-LAND – DAY

A mist obscures most of No-Man's-Land.

EXT. TRENCH – DAY

Christopher looks into the mist through a spy-hole.

EXT. NO-MAN'S-LAND / MARSH CHURCH, RYE (IMAGINARY) – DAY

What Christopher is 'seeing': a pony trap with a horse too big for it, moving soundlessly through the mist – an image from 1912 near Rye.

EXT. TRENCH – SAME TIME

Christopher makes a mental effort to shake off the image. He lowers himself into the trench. Aranjuez and Duckett are standing by.

>   CHRISTOPHER
>   (*to Duckett*)
> Tell them in 'B' Company I'm coming round to take a look at them, say ten minutes. Keep blind-side of that mound as you go.

This is where a 'mine shell' has created a miniature mountain between 'B' Company and where they are standing.

>   CHRISTOPHER
>   (*to Aranjuez*)
> Would you ask 'A' Company dug-out for the favour of a sandwich and some coffee with some rum in it.

EXT. THE MOUND — DAY

Negotiating the safe side of the mound, Christopher sits down in sunshine, alone in the world for a moment. He closes his eyes.

FLASHBACK: EXT. NEAR RYE, 1912 — EARLY DAY

Christopher and Valentine sit side by side on the grass slope above the pony trap, in sunlight.

Over: the cornet, as before, is heard picking out the notes of the air.

EXT. THE MOUND — DAY

The sound of the cornet continues from some distance away.

Christopher opens his eyes, realising that Griffiths is not dead after all. He jerks up, brought almost to tears. He sees a figure approaching . . . a Corporal with a makeshift tray. The Corporal is new to us.

EXT. THE MOUND — DAY

Christopher wolfs a nicely cut sandwich, and drinks from a cup. On a flat stone jutting out from the mound, the Corporal, Sutcliffe, has placed a dainty repast on a white towel: a tin pot of coffee, a bowl of lump sugar, a plate of neatly cut sandwiches.

> CHRISTOPHER
> Did you get a bit to eat, Corporal?

> SUTCLIFFE
> Yes, sir. Half a tin of warm mutton and haricot beans while I was cutting the sandwiches.

Sutcliffe has a strong Yorkshire accent.

> CHRISTOPHER
> Middlesbrough?

SUTCLIFFE

Nearly right, sir. My mother is Middlesbrough. I'm from Batley.

CHRISTOPHER

Good God!

SUTCLIFFE

That's right, sir. I've walked to Groby of a Sunday afternoon many a time. My father goes down Batley pit.

CHRISTOPHER

I'd hear the picks sometimes at night, in my father's time and grandfather's . . . Chip, chip . . . It came back to me the other night. I thought it was the Germans mining.

SUTCLIFFE

My sister had a comb hanging from the Groby Tree. They say the old cedar will have to come down one of these days soon.

CHRISTOPHER
(roused)
Do they, by God. I'll prop up the house if I have to!

SUTCLIFFE

I'll help you, sir! It wouldn't be Groby . . .

Christopher finishes the last sandwich, pours the rest of the coffee.

CHRISTOPHER

I'll remember your sandwiches so long as I live. Thank you. Those German shells seem to be coming back. Give the RSM my compliments and would he get his fatigue party under cover as soon as they get close.

SUTCLIFFE

Right, sir.

Sutcliffe goes with the tray, passing Aranjuez. Christopher drains the cup and throws it downhill at a rock, where it smashes.

317

CHRISTOPHER

'So that no toast less noble may be drunk out of it.'

ARANJUEZ

Then there must be someone you love, sir! Is she like Minette?

CHRISTOPHER

Not exactly like her, but, I'm sure, with Minette's best qualities.

ARANJUEZ

Then you'll get her, sir! You'll certainly get her!

CHRISTOPHER

Yes, I probably shall get her . . . Well, that's enough time for 'B' Company to get themselves tidied up. The Germans have done over their trench like a dog we once had would do over a drawing room.

EXT. B COMPANY TRENCH – DAY

The mound allows Christopher and Aranjuez slide down into the 'B' Company trench. Duckett is looking through a spy-hole. The trench has water in it. The men are bailing with shovels. A couple of shovels are leaning against the traverse. Shells have started falling in the vicinity. This is Second Lieutenant Bennett's company.

CHRISTOPHER
(*sharply to Bennett*)
Don't leave your shovels about to get in the way when the attack comes.

Bennett takes it hard.

BENNETT

Yes, sir. Sorry, sir! Sergeant!

The Company Sergeant takes the shovels, shouting in his turn to the nearest soldier.

The noise of shelling becomes overwhelming.

CHRISTOPHER'S POINT OF VIEW

The noise seems to make everything go dark. Then he is watching the trench from above and the world seems to be turning in slow motion as great dollops of liquid mud float around.

Ten feet below him, Christopher's point of view shows:

Aranjuez – his mouth open, screaming soundlessly. One of his eyes is a patch of blood.

Duckett – almost buried by mud, alive.

Bennett – definitely dead, with his torso ripped open by shrapnel.

Christopher hits the earth next to Bennett. Now he can hear Aranjuez screaming. Christopher kneels by Aranjuez and starts to lift him. Christopher is bleeding near the collar. Bullets are going snap-snap into the mound behind them.
Christopher shouts to Bennett's Sergeant.

CHRISTOPHER
Stretcher-bearers, Sergeant!

Christopher, on his hands and knees, tries to stand up. He slides down towards Aranjuez, gets up, plants his feet.

CHRISTOPHER
Are you wounded?

ARANJUEZ
No, sir.

Christopher with all his strength pulls Aranjuez out of the mud by his armpits. The Company Sergeant and a Soldier with shovels are digging out Duckett, who may or may not be dead.

CHRISTOPHER
Get behind the mound!

Aranjuez can't function. Christopher picks him up like a roll of blanket under the arm and staggers upwards and diagonally,

partly protected by the mound, more and more so as he
continues, His strength has almost gone. Round the other side
of the mound, two Stretcher Bearers are struggling towards him.

EXT. TRENCH – DAY

The shelling hasn't let up, but the apex has moved on.

Christopher, mud-caked from head to foot, has got safely
into the next stretch of trench. He is bleeding from a wound
near his collar. He finds the RSM there with an Observer at
a spy-hole, and infantrymen firing and reloading.

> RSM
> You've got a wound, sir. Can you make it to the First Aid
> post?

> CHRISTOPHER
> A wound? Where?

EXT. TRENCH – DAY

Christopher moves along the trench, meeting Stretcher-
Bearers. He is searching his pockets for a field dressing. Just
as he finds one, he sees a vision of an immaculate, elegant,
furious General Campion, who immediately turns out to be
real. Behind him is Notting.

> CAMPION
> Who are you? Where the devil is the Commanding
> Officer of this battalion? Why can't he be found? You're
> disgustingly filthy! You look like a blackamoor! I suppose
> you have an explanation?

Christopher comes to attention.

> CHRISTOPHER
> I am in command of this battalion, sir.

> NOTTING
> (*helpfully*)
> Major Tietjens, sir, second-in-command, temporarily in
> command.

CAMPION

You! Strolling about with your hands in your pockets.
I was mad when I sent you here. I shall send you back.
You can fall out.

He goes by Christopher.

NOTTING

You've been in a bad place, sir. When they said you
stopped one, I thought I should go mad. We *can't* get
through the paperwork!

Notting goes by Christopher.

EXT. TRENCH – DAY

*Silent, slow-motion, and after some beats, Griffiths's cornet
over.*

*Campion, a vision of smartness, pink of face, white of hair,
beribboned and bemedalled, his boots shined, walks towards
an inferno of smoke and blinding explosions of light.*

INT. – NIGHT (SILENT DREAM)

Sound over: Griffiths's cornet.

*Christopher kisses Valentine's naked bosom – briefly, for two
or three seconds, she clasping his head to her.*

INT. WANNOP HOUSE, VALENTINE'S BEDROOM – DAY

*Valentine opens her eyes, instantly awake, catching her breath,
then calm, lying still and thoughtful.*

INT. DIVISIONAL FOLLIES – NIGHT

*Close: Griffiths brings the melody to its close, and lowers his
cornet.*

There is applause.

Griffiths smiles slightly, pleased, shy.

INT. LOUCHE CLUB – NIGHT

A jazz trumpet plays Dixieland rousingly – an anticipation of the Original Dixieland Jazz Band's British tour to come in 1919 – to a packed basement club. Sylvia is one of a posh group 'slumming' at a table, the men and women in evening dress, all in high spirits. The small band, like the Original Dixieland Jazz Band, is white. Couples, including officers in uniform, are dancing energetically.

Sylvia sees someone she knows – Gerald Drake in the uniform of a full Colonel on the Staff. She says something to her companions and goes over to Drake, who is drinking alone.

SYLVIA

Gerald . . . don't pretend you hadn't seen me.

DRAKE

Sylvia. No, I . . .

SYLVIA

I've quite got over you, you know.

DRAKE

Well, that's love, I suppose.

SYLVIA
(cheerfully)

I mean hating you. I got over loving you years ago.

DRAKE
(ruefully)

You haven't changed at all.

SYLVIA
(laughs)

I'm here with a ghastly set. Would you like to take me on somewhere?

INT. GRAY'S INN, BATHROOM / SYLVIA'S BEDROOM – NIGHT

Bathroom: Sylvia is in a robe, filling a rubber implement, a douche, with soapy water.

SYLVIA

You always were such a brute . . . Don't think I'm complaining. If I told you how long since, you wouldn't believe me . . .

Bedroom: Drake is in her bed. Sylvia speaks from the bathroom, out of shot.

SYLVIA

I'm sure I'm safe, but . . .

DRAKE

So why . . .?

SYLVIA

Don't come in . . . Because I'm released. My husband wants a legal separation. Anyway, I don't see why I shouldn't get something out of people taking me for a whore.

DRAKE

I didn't know you hated me.

SYLVIA
(*entering*)

Why ever not? Funking a divorce and leaving me to hold the baby.

She sits down at the dressing table and interrogates her eyebrows with tweezers, using the powder box with the cracked mirror given to her by Drake.

SYLVIA

But Michael's growing up into a Tietjens, so it may have been a panic over nothing. How does one know?

DRAKE

Tietjens turned out all right. He was up for a decoration but General Campion told him there were only a certain number of medals to be given out and no doubt Tietjens would prefer it to be given to someone who'd get more advantage from it. (*Laughs.*) The old boy must have it in for your husband. (*Realising.*) Good Lord, you didn't know? Wounded saving life under fire, months ago!

SYLVIA

How typical. He never tells me anything. Why aren't *you* in France, by the way?

DRAKE

Too valuable. I've been in Washington. American troops are coming over in force now, which means the war is over.

SYLVIA

Really over?

DRAKE

By Guy Fawkes Day, I'd say.

Sylvia is made thoughtful.

SYLVIA

Really? So Christopher will be coming home.

DRAKE

Will you come back to bed?

SYLVIA

No. I can't go through all that again.

She snaps the powder box shut.

EXT. EALING STREET — DAY

Valentine, in school uniform, comes round a corner by a station sign — EALING. A Ragamuffin with a Guy Fawkes on a home-made cart is soliciting her for 'a penny for the guy'. Valentine good humouredly digs for a penny.

EXT. GRAY'S INN — DAY

A taxi arrives, delivering Christopher in uniform with a kit-bag and a suitcase.

INT. MACMASTER'S FLAT — DAY

Christopher's arrival is noticed by Edith at her window. It gives her no pleasure.

INT. GRAY'S INN, DRAWING ROOM — DAY

Christopher stands looking into the room, which has been stripped bare. On the floor are a few books and framed pictures and a telephone. Prominent on the mantel is an envelope with his name on it. He opens it and reads the single sheet inside.

INT. DRESSING ROOM — DAY

Christopher opens a wardrobe. His clothes have been left.

INT. MOVING TRAIN — DAY

Christopher, in civilian clothes, is travelling north, rural England going by.

EXT. GROBY DRIVE — DAY

A country taxi is approaching from a distance.

INT. TAXI — DAY

Christopher, looking out of the taxi, stares.

> CHRISTOPHER
> Stop here.

EXT. GROBY DRIVE — DAY

Christopher gets out of the taxi, and walks towards the house, which we have not seen.

The reverse shows us that the Groby Tree has gone, the great stump remains, obscured by the wreckage of branches and foliage.

INT. SYLVIA'S BEDROOM — DAY

Sylvia, in a composition of white linen, white hangings, white

flowers, is the centrepiece of a glamorous deathbed tableau.
Christopher is controlling his grief and anger.

CHRISTOPHER

I saw your note too late.

SYLVIA
(*faintly*)

But you came in time! Hold my hand, darling, I think I'm
going.

CHRISTOPHER

Your note about the tree.

SYLVIA
(*stronger*)

Oh, the tree! Well, I tried to warn you. Where were you
all this time? Your brother fixed your release from the
army weeks ago.

This is news to Christopher. Sylvia becomes spirited.

SYLVIA

You should have been here to take charge of the estate. If
you won't, needs must, and – (*pleased with her joke*) –
and let the chips fall where they may!

His silence rouses her.

SYLVIA

Couldn't you tear yourself away from your mistress?

CHRISTOPHER

I was in hospital.

He moves to leave.

Goodbye, Sylvia.

Sylvia relapses into theatrical faintness.

SYLVIA

Christopher . . .

*Christopher goes out, closing the door. Sylvia sits up mutinously.
She's not dead yet!*

EXT. GROBY TREE — DAY

Christopher stands amid the wreckage of the tree. A Woodman with an axe is stripping one of the giant fallen branches. Christopher stoops to pick up a soiled ribbon from which hangs a rag doll. He hears a petrol engine, and looks to the field beyond where a new 'motor plough' is at work. He picks up a chunk of cedar.

EXT. BIG BEN — DAY

The minute hand goes to eleven o'clock but Big Ben stays silent.

EXT. WAR OFFICE — DAY

Where we were before, now oddly deserted and silent.

EXT. CHRISTOPHER'S OFFICE, WHITEHALL — DAY

Where we were before, now oddly deserted and silent.

INT. STAIRCASE, WHITEHALL — DAY

Where we were before, oddly deserted and silent.

INT. SIR REGINALD'S OFFICE, WHITEHALL — DAY

Sir Reginald's empty office. Beyond the window is St James's Park, or Whitehall or Parade Ground . . . deserted, silent.

An office clock is striking melodiously.

INT. SCHOOL STAFF ROOM — DAY

The Teachers, including Valentine, stand silently while the Head, a middle-aged bluestocking, addresses them.

                              HEAD
We are told it may be this morning. It may not be. If it is,

three rousing cheers by our girls, followed by an orderly
return to the classrooms would be appropriate –

A quite distant but very large explosion interrupts her,
followed by more maroons going off, then factory hooters, car
horns, church bells, etc. And close at hand the shrill joyful
screams of schoolgirls, the banging of desk lids . . . The
Teachers cry out, embracing, weeping . . .

EXT. GRAY'S INN – DAY

A London backwater . . . but there is a semi-distant sound of
jubilation . . . church bells, ship sirens and hooters, fireworks.

INT. GRAY'S INN, DRAWING ROM – DAY

Christopher carefully places a loaf-sized chunk of cedar next
to a similar one on the mantel.

The room is now 'furnished' with folding canvas camp
furniture, including a camp bed.

INT. MACMASTER'S FLAT – DAY

Macmaster runs up the stairs and enters the drawing room.
With a cry of 'Guggums!' he goes to embrace Edith, but gets
the backlash of her fury.

> EDITH
> When I think of the millions who died, and that imbecile
> Tietjens strolling home without a scratch!

> MACMASTER
> Guggums!

> EDITH
> I was absolutely counting on the Germans –

> MACMASTER
> (*horrified*)
> Guggums!

328

                              EDITH
Suppose he calls in his loans. It would be our ruination.

                           MACMASTER
Tietjens, impossible as it may be for you to understand –

                              EDITH
Then don't try to make me! You sponged off him for
thousands, and now he's got you by – by what you
singularly lack. Since the wife has chosen to reject the
hand of friendship I extended to that harlot, it's time to
bring the mistress back into the fold.

EXT. EALING, STREET – DAY

*There are sounds of music, bells, car horns from all around.
Valentine runs full tilt into her house.*

INT. WANNOP HOUSE – DAY

Valentine and Mrs Wannop are embracing joyfully.

                         MRS WANNOP
Safe! Safe for ever! No more torpedos!

The phone rings.

                           VALENTINE
Edward!

She snatches up the phone.

INT. MACMASTER'S FLAT – DAY

*Edith is on the phone. Many church bells are ringing far and
near. She has to shout.*

                              EDITH
Is that you, Valentine? It's Lady Macmaster here . . .
Edith!

INT. WANNOP HOUSE – DAY

After the phone call, Valentine sits soberly at the dining table.

VALENTINE
Edith said he has no furniture. He appeared to be a bit
mad. He's alone. He asked about me.

MRS WANNOP
But he didn't ask *for* you. Christopher wouldn't ruin you
among your own people, not if you begged to be ruined,
Valentine!

VALENTINE
I'd ruin myself gladly to make him happy for an hour.
I've waited and waited. Don't cry, Mother.

MRS WANNOP
I cannot – I will not – renounce the schooling of my
whole life.

VALENTINE
But this is mine.

EXT. LONDON STREETS – DAY

Valentine runs through the streets.

INT./EXT. TUBE STATION STEPS – DAY

*Valentine leaps up the last steps of a spiral staircase out of the
tube, two at a time.*

EXT. GRAY'S INN – DAY

*Valentine hurries towards Christopher's door – which opens
in her face. Christopher is carrying a chunk of cedarwood.
He is a somewhat changed man since she saw him – a 'walking
wounded' without evident physical injury, not someone
capable of just picking up where they left off.*

CHRISTOPHER
Miss Wannop . . .

                    VALENTINE
                     (*blurts*)
Did you send for me?

                    CHRISTOPHER
No. But I'm glad you came.

                    VALENTINE
I . . . I heard you were ill.

                    CHRISTOPHER
I'm not too bad, all things considered.

                    VALENTINE
What's that . . . ?

                    CHRISTOPHER
I'm taking it to Mark. You can come with me.

INT. CHEZ MARIE-LEONIE – DAY

The flat is furnished in an 'artistic bourgeois' style. Framed 'professional' photographs show Marie-Leonie as a corps de ballet dancer in the 1890s.

The chunk of cedar is on the table. Marie-Leonie regards it with hostility. Valentine is alone with her. Men's voices are heard behind doors.

INT. MARIE-LEONIE'S BEDROOM – DAY

Mark is in a nightshirt, in bed, Christopher standing.

                    MARK
Pneumonia.

INT. CHEZ MARIE-LEONIE – DAY

                    MARIE-LEONIE
                     (*in French*)
Les anglais. First the doctor opens the windows. He wishes to kill my man. And now the brother.

                       331

CHRISTOPHER

Look, did you get me demobbed early? You've done me out of a couple of hundred pounds and I need fifty of it now. I've spent every penny I had, going up to Groby. Did you know about the tree?

MARK

One thing at a time. What do you want fifty pounds for?

CHRISTOPHER

I have some army chums coming by.

MARK

By heaven, if I were myself I'd throw you out. How dare you ask for fifty pounds? I will write you a cheque for a thousand, or ten thousand, if you agree that the money belongs to you, and our father intended you to have it. It's yours. Groby is yours if you want it.

CHRISTOPHER

I don't want it. I don't want father's money either. I want fifty pounds right now! I have Miss Wannop waiting for me, and I expect we'll all be going out to celebrate the Armistice.

MARK

You have Miss . . . ?

CHRISTOPHER

I'm going to ask Miss Wannop to live with me.

MARK

Where? In Australia? Have you thought of shooting yourself?

Christopher violently throws open the bedroom door and goes into the adjoining room.

INT. CHEZ MARIE-LEONIE — DAY

> CHRISTOPHER
> (*entering, in French*)
> Madame, for the love of God, lend me fifty pounds!

Marie-Leonie considers Christopher, and then lifts her skirts and produces a bundle of banknotes. She gives fifty pounds to Christopher.

> MARIE-LEONIE
> *Pas pour le bon Dieu. Pour l'amour.*

> CHRISTOPHER
> *Merci.*

Mark enters with a shawl over his nightshirt.

> MARK
> How dare you bring Miss Wannop here? Are you and Sylvia divorcing?

> CHRISTOPHER
> No.

Mark picks up the cedarwood.

> MARK
> And what the hell is this?

> CHRISTOPHER
> Sylvia had the tree felled.

> MARK
> I know. She asked me. I don't give a damn about the tree.

He throws the wood into the hearth.

> Now perhaps God will change sides.

EXT. GRAY'S INN — DAY

Christopher strides towards his door, Valentine scampering to keep up.

CHRISTOPHER

I will not divorce the mother of my child, and Sylvia will
not divorce me.

VALENTINE

I don't care.

Christopher opens his door with a latchkey.

CHRISTOPHER

I have to bathe and change into my uniform. If my
friends arrive, you might entertain them.

He lets her into the door.

INT. GRAY'S INN, HALL — DAY

*Christopher closes the door. Sylvia is at the top of the stairs in
a white fur coat, looking down at them like an elegant avenging
angel.*

SYLVIA

Darling . . . I'm awfully sorry, rotten timing for you . . .
both. I came to tell you, they're going to operate on me
tomorrow for a cancer, and . . .

Valentine, howling with rage, almost flies up the stairs.

VALENTINE

Liar! You haven't got cancer! You're lying!

*She grasps for Sylvia, who eludes her, stumbling down several
steps.*

SYLVIA

Well, really!

VALENTINE

This is what you do, isn't it?

SYLVIA

What can you mean? Do you know what she means?

CHRISTOPHER

Miss Wannop means, pulling the strings of the shower
bath.

Husband and wife look each other in the eye for a long moment. Valentine waits in suspense. Sylvia cracks – with a laugh.

> SYLVIA
> Christopher, you can't mean it. Look at her! Is she a Girl Guide or something?

She comes down the stairs and studies him.

> Perhaps you do mean it. Well, I wish you both nothing but happiness.

She turns to Valentine.

> Please remember me to your charming mother.

Sylvia lets herself out. Christopher and Valentine stare at each other, astonished by each other.

INT. GRAY'S INN, BATHROOM – DAY

Christopher in the bath.

INT. GRAY'S INN, DRAWING ROOM – DAY

Valentine looks around at the camp furniture. She considers the camp bed and kisses it.

INT. GRAY'S INN. DRESSING ROOM – DAY

Christopher, bathed, in underclothes, puts on a uniform shirt. He hears the doorbell and loud hammering at the distant door.

INT. GRAY'S INN, HALL – DAY

Valentine opens the door to McKechnie, who is in uniform and slightly demented.

> MCKECHNIE
> I must see that fellow Tietjens. It's an urgent matter, about a sonnet.

335

VALENTINE

It's not necessary to shout. Please come in.

Valentine lets McKechnie come in, and closes the door.

MCKECHNIE

I'm Captain McKechnie, formerly second-in-command of
the Sixth Glamorganshires. The Pals!

*The doorbell rings. Valentine opens the door to Bill, the
Colonel, who is carrying two bottles of whisky.*

MCKECHNIE

It's my CO! Good old Colonel Bill, you brought the
hooch!

BILL

McKechnie! Thought I'd got rid of you!

*Aranjuez appears on the step. His face is disfigured, and he has
only one eye. He is accompanied by his Minette, who is thin
and a foot taller than him.*

INT. GRAY'S INN, DRESSING ROOM – DAY

*Tietjens, fully dressed, checks himself in the mirror. Sounds of
a drinking party.*

*Christopher looks out of an upper window at the Macmaster
flat. He sees Macmaster at an upper window looking back.
Macmaster raises a hand, smiling weakly. Christopher raises
a hand.*

INT. GRAY'S INN, DRAWING ROOM – DAY

*The drinking party is well under way. The men are McKechnie,
Bill, Aranjuez and Aubrey. The women are Valentine, Minette,
and two Girls picked up by the officers. Aubrey has the VC
among his service ribbons.*

MCKECHNIE
(*tearful*)

The Pals! The Pals!

SHOUTS

Good old McKechnie!

Minette scowls at Valentine because she doesn't like the way Aranjuez is frisking around her like a puppy.

ARANJUEZ

You are the Captain's dear friend. He saved my life. Wasn't it splendid of Minette to marry me like this? We shall all be such friends. (*About Aubrey approaching.*) Our only VC . . .

AUBREY

(*to Valentine*)

They say you're receiving for Tietjens. He seems to have been sold up! He's a good fat old beggar, old Tietjens, a good officer, one of the best.

VALENTINE

He's quite a good sort, really!

She sees Christopher enter. He is greeted rowdily.

OFFICERS

He's here! Good old Tietjens! Good old Fat Man! Hooch!

A blow on the back sends Christopher smiling into the centre of the group.

CHRISTOPHER

Miss Wannop looking after you? It's chilly in here. Want a fire?

There is a chunk of cedar on the mantel. Christopher takes it and throws it into the grate. He pours some whisky over it and throws a match. The whisky burns blue. Aranjuez pushes Valentine gently into the centre of the circle. There are smashed glasses underfoot. The officers yell and prance around in a circle, picking up a song.

OFFICERS

(*sing*)

Over here! Pom Pom over here!
Pom Pom!
That's the word, that's the word over here . . .

Christopher holds out his arms, inviting Valentine to dance.
She comes forward into his arms.

From here to the end, the continuation of the scene is intercut
with three scenes from the near future:

(1) *Int. Drawing Room, Gray's Inn – Night. Christopher and*
Valentine on the camp bed.

(2) *Ext. Rotten Row, Hyde Park – Day. Sylvia and Campion*
(in uniform) out riding.

(3) *Ext. Parade Ground – Day. A 'Kitchener Battalion' is*
being ceremonially disbanded.

INT. DRAWING ROOM – NIGHT

Valentine kisses Christopher's naked breast.

BACK TO SCENE: INT. DRAWING ROOM – NIGHT

Christopher and Valentine are dancing.

> OFFICERS
> (*sing*)
> Mademoiselle from Armenteers
> Parley-vous!
> Mademoiselle from Armenteers
> Parley-vous!
> Mademoiselle from Armenteers
> She hasn't been – (*beat*) – for forty years,
> Inky-pinky parley-vous.

EXT. ROTTEN ROW, HYDE PARK – DAY

> SYLVIA
> If I divorce Christopher, will you marry me?

> CAMPION
> Good God, no!

His vehemence and a touch on the rein makes his horse recoil,
startling Sylvia's horse into a dance step.

BACK TO SCENE: INT. DRAWING ROOM, GRAY'S INN – NIGHT

Christopher and Valentine dance more closely, eyes closed.

> OFFICERS
> (*sing*)
> She hasn't been – (*beat*) – for forty years,
> Inky-pinky parley-vous.

EXT. PARADE GROUND – DAY

The Battalion on parade, at attention.

> ADJUTANT
> (*shouts*)
> Stand at ease!

The Battalion does so. The band starts to play 'Land of Hope and Glory'.

EXT. ROTTEN ROW, HYDE PARK – DAY

> SYLVIA
> (*laughs*)
> You can't, you know, expect to put an idea out of my
> head just by flurrying the horses . . .

INT. DRAWING ROOM – NIGHT

On the camp bed in the dark, Christopher and Valentine are ravenously covering each other with kisses.

EXT. PARADE GROUND – DAY

The band falls silent. There is a moment of silence.

> ADJUTANT
> (*shouts*)
> There will be no more parades! Atten–shun!

The Battalion comes to attention.

ADJUTANT

Dis–miss!

The Battalion stamps to order and 'dismisses'.

BACK TO SCENE: INT. DRAWING ROOM – NIGHT

Aranjuez dances with Minette. Christopher dances with Valentine.

OFFICERS
(*sing*)

The bells of hell go ting-a-ling-a-ling
For you but not for me.
And the little devils how they sing-a-ling-ling
For you but not for me.
O Death, where is thy sting-a-ling-a-ling
O Grave, thy victoree . . .
The bells of hell go ting-a-ling-ling
For you but not for me!

The cedar log burns brightly in the grate.

The End.